# DO-IT-YOURSELF
# DEMOCRACY

# DO-IT-YOURSELF DEMOCRACY

## THE RISE OF THE PUBLIC ENGAGEMENT INDUSTRY

Caroline W. Lee

OXFORD
UNIVERSITY PRESS

# OXFORD

UNIVERSITY PRESS

Oxford University Press is a department of the University of
Oxford. It furthers the University's objective of excellence in research,
scholarship, and education by publishing worldwide.

Oxford   New York

Auckland   Cape Town   Dar es Salaam   Hong Kong   Karachi
Kuala Lumpur   Madrid   Melbourne   Mexico City   Nairobi
New Delhi   Shanghai   Taipei   Toronto

With offices in
Argentina   Austria   Brazil   Chile   Czech Republic   France   Greece
Guatemala   Hungary   Italy   Japan   Poland   Portugal   Singapore
South Korea   Switzerland   Thailand   Turkey   Ukraine   Vietnam

Oxford is a registered trademark of Oxford University Press
in the UK and certain other countries.

Published in the United States of America by
Oxford University Press
198 Madison Avenue, New York, NY 10016

© Oxford University Press 2015

Library of Congress Cataloging-in-Publication Data
Lee, Caroline W.
Do-it-yourself democracy : the rise of the public engagement industry / Caroline W. Lee.
pages cm
Includes bibliographical references and index.
ISBN 978–0–19–998726–9 (hardback)
1. Political participation—United States.   2. Social action—United States.
3. Democracy—United States. I. Title.
JK1764.L425 2015
323'.0420973—dc23
2014017049

1 3 5 7 9 8 6 4 2
Printed in the United States of America
on acid-free paper

# CONTENTS

Acknowledgments   vii

Introduction: Democracy 2.0?   1

## PART I: THE PUBLIC ENGAGEMENT RENAISSANCE

1. Democracy in Miniature   11

2. The Idealists behind the Curtain   31

## PART II: PROCESS EVANGELISTS: SPREADING THE GOSPEL OF DELIBERATION

3. Challenging Enemy Institutions   63

4. Walking Our Talk   96

## PART III: CIVIC ENGAGEMENT AS A MANAGEMENT TOOL

5. The Arts and Crafts of Real Engagement   123

6. Activating Empathetic Citizens   150

## PART IV: THE SPIRIT OF
## DELIBERATIVE CAPITALISM

7.  Sharing the Pain: The Lessons Deliberation Teaches    189

Conclusion: Down Market Democracy and the Politics of Hope    223

Postscript: Notes on Data and Methods    232

Notes    241

References    257

Index    279

# ACKNOWLEDGMENTS

THIS PROJECT HAS BEEN MANY years in the making, and was less DIY than all hands on deck! First, my greatest debt is to the members of the public engagement community who generously shared their time, humor, passions, and frustrations with me. I hope this book will promote the deep discussions they value.

I am thrilled to have worked with collaborators Elizabeth Long Lingo, Michael McQuarrie, Francesca Polletta, and Edward Walker on projects related to this book, and with my EXCEL Scholars Kelly McNulty, Zachary Romano, and Sarah Shaffer. My wonderful colleagues in Lafayette College's Department contributed in a number of ways.

This research was supported by grants from the Academic Research Committee and the EXCEL Scholars Program of Lafayette College. Brian Balogh and the Miller Center's Democracy and Governance Studies Program at UVA have provided ongoing support and connections to the American political development community. I was also the recipient of generous writer-in-residence grants from Bing Guckenberger and Sasha Lehman. I feel very lucky to have so many places to call home.

Portions of this research are published in *Poetics*, the *Journal of Public Deliberation, Socio-Economic Review, Organization Studies*, and *The Sociological Quarterly*. The editors of those journals, anonymous reviewers, discussants and conference goers shared insights and criticisms that have made this a much better project.

Bill Hoynes got me started on this path. David Meyer and Robert Fishman shaped this project from the very beginning. Too many dear friends, colleagues and mentors to list here have taught and supported me all along the way. I am so grateful to all of them and hope to reciprocate as best I can. Jean Okie and the Cobble Hill People's Party helped me to the finish line.

Many thanks to James Cook and the team at Oxford University Press.

Finally, big hugs to my family, my friends, and to Mike and Molly Nees, with love and affection.

# DO-IT-YOURSELF
# DEMOCRACY

# INTRODUCTION

## Democracy 2.0?

Government should be transparent. ... Government should be participatory. ... Government should be collaborative.

Barack Obama, January 21, 2009[1]

Not only is the Obama White House willing, but they are *wanting* to listen to ideas about how they can be BETTER listeners! (OMG!)

Open government activist and former federal employee, National Coalition for Dialogue and Deliberation listserv posting, January 22, 2009

JANUARY 21, 2009, WAS BARACK Obama's first full day in office as president of the United States. Among the work on his desk that morning was a Memorandum on Transparency and Open Government, which directed heads of executive departments and agencies to start a participatory process to develop rules on open government. All over the country, democracy reformers, still hung-over from Tuesday's inauguration festivities, logged on to their laptops and experienced OMG moments like the activist cited. The executive director of the National Coalition for Dialogue and Deliberation (NCDD) alerted listserv members about "this incredible window of opportunity." A democracy activist from Austin reported "a sense of going outside after a storm, and looking up just in time to see the clouds begin to part, and the sunlight begin to peek through. Federal agencies engaging the public in seeking better

I

ways to engage the public?... Do we dare to hope that this is real?" A staffer at an organization called Information Renaissance responded, "Yes, let's dare to hope!"[2] To those in the public engagement community, Obama's priorities on his first day in office represented a new dawn for democracy in America.

Fast-forward seventeen months to a balmy Saturday morning in early summer. On June 26, 2010, 3,500 Americans of all stripes ignored the beckoning summer sun and engaged in six-hour "Our Budget, Our Economy" round-table discussions on the nation's fiscal priorities across the country—exactly the sort of event intended to get Americans really talking to each other about the common good. The reaction from the left? "A vast right-wing conspiracy" designed to terrorize Americans into cutting Social Security and Medicare. The reaction from the right? A biased civic pageant designed to scare the public into raising taxes.

What of the democracy reformers so eager to get their processes onto the public stage? The preemptive rejection of the "Our Budget, Our Economy" discussions across the blogosphere precipitated distress from public deliberation advocates and leaders. President Sandy Heierbacher again weighed in on the NCDD listserv—fearing that antiengagement rhetoric would manipulate the public not to endorse a particular outcome, but to avoid public engagement altogether:

> I find this situation so alarming and fascinating (and important for us in the D&D community to be aware of) because in the internet age it's incredibly easy for partisan groups and interest groups to spin public engagement efforts in ways that manipulate citizens and threaten our ability to recruit a balance of perspectives and our perceived legitimacy (and therefore our potential impact on decisions). ... Regardless of the process that was used or the people involved, in some ways the integrity of the work we all do—and the principles we stand for—is being called into question.

It is entirely likely that readers of this book have not thought very much, if at all, about democracy reform efforts in America—still less about professional democracy reformers. Even when I tell academics that I study the public engagement industry or deliberative democracy consultants, I often get quizzical looks. What I mean by that terminology is a group of diverse professionals and volunteers who help to facilitate public engagement or dialogue. By organizing events and processes that get people talking together, usually face to face and often across divides of party, race, or class, they are midwives of a relatively new civic form with very old roots. Readers of this book have probably participated in participatory dialogues in workplace retreats or community meetings without actually noticing much about who was facilitating those processes—in part because public engagement facilitators are, by necessity, self-effacing.

Public engagement is a broad term that encompasses a variety of forms of professionally facilitated, large-scale events and smaller scale processes involving as few as ten people in a workplace or community organization. What these efforts have in common is a rejection of one-way information sharing, whether as public relations efforts to communicate to the public or as consultation efforts seeking public response to decisions already made. The new public engagement draws on principles of active interaction of a cross section of stakeholders, including sponsors, in substantive dialogue about their priorities and preferences. Such processes are often referred to as dialogue and deliberation or deliberative democracy by academics, emphasizing that they shift authority relations in the direction of political equality, entail learning among all, and may transform participants' social relationships and behaviors.

Social scientists have a history of studying odd hobbies and unheralded occupations—mushroom hunters and crack dealers and engineers and flight attendants and street vendors—to help us see the world through their eyes. The public engagement volunteers, activists, and professionals studied here, with a similar dedication to empathetic understanding, might seem odd to study as subjects in their own right. But I hope that for those who have thought about democracy as an abstract ideal, this book will paint a new picture of democracy in America. Today's democracy is a dynamic configuration produced, on one hand, by increasingly specialized professionals and, on the other, composed of cultural threads from nonpolitical realms as diverse as therapy, religion, and sports. In other words, by exploring the specific personal experiences of democracy reformers trying to do good in a world where common ground seems increasingly hard to find, I hope that we can see participatory democracy reform as something that touches all of us—whether as parents, workers, citizens, patients, parishioners, team members, volunteers, or students.

***

Many people believe that our hopes for a politics where each voice is heard should be easy to achieve by humble means, requiring little more than a circle of folding chairs, a shared concern, and hearts open to change. On closer examination, there is not much agreement about the right way to participate in American politics—although there seems to be plenty of agreement about the public's susceptibility to manipulation.[3] For those concerned about the state of democracy in America, understanding the difficulties we have in deciding what participation should look like is key to knowing what we really mean when we talk about how Americans should try to go about achieving the public good. But the fights we have over participation are also relevant to more than just citizenship in civic settings, important as that is. Increasingly, Americans face proliferating invitations to "have your say!" and "join the conversation!" In all kinds of contexts, we are asked to engage in dialogue with diverse others over questions as large as how health care should be provided and as small as whether we agree with pundits on the latest celebrity scandal.

This book looks at the expanding market for public participation across many contexts of American life, from the standpoint of the engagement experts who have caught the fire of participation and have dedicated their lives to sharing its transformative power with others. Those charged with deciding what public engagement should look like are increasingly likely to be a specialized group of professionals who design and run participatory processes like "Our Budget, Our Economy" on behalf of their clients. These individuals direct public conversations in schools, churches, public meeting rooms, community organizations, and companies. They play new roles in contemporary civic life and are uniquely positioned to shed light on the everyday tensions involved in making public engagement a reality—intimately familiar with who comes and who doesn't, who is truculent and who participates too much, what is working and what isn't.

This project takes citizen participation seriously not just as a symbolic inspiration, but as a concrete practice with far-reaching effects. Widespread enthusiasm for public engagement has led today's social entrepreneurs to develop an expansive range of methods, technologies, and services designed to facilitate nonpartisan citizen input in solving contemporary problems. But the general consensus in favor of increasing citizen input as a route to better policies or good governance diverts attention from the ways in which these processes affect decision-makers and the citizens they serve in unintended ways. Not least is the fact that increasing citizen participation often means creating new institutions, new professional fields, new government contracts, and new interest groups. Efforts to enhance public access to power have increased the number of intermediaries and experts in public life.

This book grew out of my initial puzzlement at this paradox and, as I learned more about it, my astonishment that only a few scholars paid much attention to the consequences of institutionalizing participatory practice, despite the voluminous literature on the importance of increasing citizen engagement in public life.[4] Scholars and social entrepreneurs cared very much about what was going on within participatory processes. Were participants learning new information, listening to those with other perspectives, able to get heard, and willing to change their minds? What was the quality of the decision made? Were they satisfied that they had been heard? Studying these questions meant observing these processes and their complicated dynamics up close. What I wanted to know instead was: Why are these processes taking place now? Why do they look the way they do? Who runs them? How much do they cost, and who pays for them? Do they make any difference? Why are they so popular with sponsors and the public, and why do activists seem to dislike them?[5] Answering these questions meant I would have to go beyond detailed studies of individual processes. Instead, I wanted to go to the source—those who were supplying new processes to public administrators, officials, and corporate executives fed up with the predictable fights that made getting things done so frustrating.

As a result, this book explores the passions and problems of the social entrepreneurs who design the participatory spaces in which an increasing number of decisions are made in American life. These decisions include which health care plans we should have, whether toxic waste should be cleaned up, how municipal budgets should be trimmed, what our cities should look like, and what our children should eat. Most scholars have been thrilled to observe that these topics are discussed at all and have dedicated themselves to finding more and better ways to engage the public in these kinds of dialogues. I propose that, instead of celebrating that these issues are up for public debate, we should ask a larger set of questions about the time, energy, and resources being devoted to participatory decision-making in America at this particular moment. This means thinking of public engagement not as a sacred political act, but in the context of broader questions social scientists ask about related changes in social and economic life. Is public engagement a new culture industry or field of political specialization? Are professionals and experts who work with citizens and stakeholders using similar techniques in workplaces and consumer settings? Are public engagement processes spectacles, commodities, services, and products—at the same time that they are substantive political events? Who benefits from all this participation?

By temporarily removing the moral halo from public engagement, we can understand how professionally facilitated participation evolved in recent history and why it is being celebrated now. We can also investigate how the deliberation and dialogue processes currently in vogue relate to the other participatory opportunities proliferating in a tech-enabled culture, where Americans are invited to vote on their favorite wine cooler flavor, generate homemade ads to show their devotion to precooked pasta or compact cars, and comment in an infinite number of anonymous online forums. Many political scholars would find such comparisons absurd, claiming that deliberations about storm water management or fiscal priorities create moments of shared political purpose that go against the tide of individualization and commercialization in American life. For them, dialogues on childhood obesity, with their serious topics and responsible citizen volunteers, are obviously different from clicking the Like button in shallower customer participation campaigns.

My own analysis argues that public dialogue is explicitly framed in relationship to contemporary political culture. The construction of deliberations as unique spaces apart is a routine task of their promotion by engagement professionals. Pure civic settings are in high demand in an increasingly apolitical and consumption-oriented age. These authentic political experiences, far from being alternative spaces, could not exist without the institutional contexts they claim to supersede. In this way, to understand what is sacred about political participation, we must understand how its specialness is carefully crafted, why that perceived specialness is so valuable to sponsors, and why it is so threatening to activists seeking collective, not individual, transformations. Participants' experiences with a different kind of engagement reinforce their suspicions of ordinary politics and ineffectual bureaucracies.

This is not a story of a bunch of corporate consultants out to make a buck on the back of the nation's political anxieties, nor the tale of a radical social movement brought down by the inherent conservatism of organizational life. This book describes a group of smart, reflective people pursuing and achieving social change throughout society's largest, most important institutions. As that process has unfolded, they have been remarkably successful. Public engagement reform has influenced democratic politics and work and community life beyond their wildest dreams—and it has also transformed them in unforeseen ways. The story is instructive for those seeking change anywhere, particularly for those trying to understand the ability of large institutions to absorb and deflect challenges by embracing novelty and disruption—not least because the people under study are themselves experts in organizational change and human behavior.

Those unintended consequences? I argue that public deliberation like that in "Our Budget, Our Economy," far from revolutionizing decision-making, burdens everyday people with new responsibilities without much empowerment and frames elites and industries as saviors of social change even while they don't accomplish much—despite lots of talk of transparency and accountability. Overall, public engagement reliably mobilizes individual participants to pitch in and help out, to "be" the change they want to see in the wake of catastrophic institutional failures. When citizens choose practical options that align with sponsors' budget priorities or make the kinds of individual commitments to action that public engagement produces, they make those decisions freely. But we should care because they are learning lessons that are not the lessons in civic pride deliberative democrats intend to teach. Instead, citizens are quietly reassessing the capacity of leaders and governments to make change and finding them wanting.[6] Given the massive challenges facing

America in a new century, we can't afford for the ambitions of the electorate to be defined down in this way. We face problems that individual actions alone, however noble, won't fix. Chapter 1 begins on another January morning, full of bittersweet moments and unexpected levity, as the dispersed residents of a destroyed city come together to find their way out of a national tragedy.

# PART I

## THE PUBLIC ENGAGEMENT
## RENAISSANCE

# I

## Democracy in Miniature

JANUARY 20, 2007, 8:30 A.M. The Dallas Renaissance Hotel, a salmon-skinned, lipstick-shaped luxury tower with a full parking lot on a cold and overcast Saturday. A massive ballroom with crystal chandeliers is in the final stages of preparation. Officious twenty-somethings hustle around tables outfitted with laptop computers. Community Congress III—a very important meeting to decide the future of New Orleans—is about to begin. We may be in landlocked sprawl 1,500 miles away, but 140 displaced New Orleanians are beginning to arrive from around the Dallas–Fort Worth Metroplex for a six-hour meeting that will reshape their beloved city.

Community Congress II was a big success, and CCIII is being billed as "the public's collective opportunity to review and give final input on the draft Unified New Orleans Plan (UNOP) before it is sent to city leaders."[1] The prior meeting allowed current and former New Orleanians to give input on what they wanted to see in draft recommendations for an official, comprehensive plan to direct the rebuilding of the city; this meeting is the follow-up, intended to show how the public's recommendations have been incorporated.

While awaiting our assignments, the other volunteer table facilitators and I mill around in our UNOP T-shirts; city dignitaries and special guests confer in corners. The headsetted staffers from AmericaSpeaks, the self-described nonpartisan, nonprofit organization running this event, bark instructions above the final A/V checks. A large screen on stage will display slides and video. Mayor Ray Nagin will be front and center by videoconference at today's event, demonstrating the city's willingness to listen to the people. Since public approval is so important, the design of this meeting and the phrasing of the options for discussion have been extensively piloted in practice run-throughs by AmericaSpeaks, so there are unlikely to be many surprises in terms of what this particular subset of "the people" have to say regarding their support for different recommendations in the plan.

AmericaSpeaks is experienced at handling the sensitive issues involved in postdisaster redevelopment. The organization ran a much-heralded success, the post-9/11 "Listening to the City" meeting for the public to comment on rebuilding plans for Ground Zero. A who's who of philanthropy—the Bush-Clinton Katrina Fund, Carnegie Corporation of New York, Case Foundation, Ford Foundation, Greater New Orleans Foundation, Louisiana Recovery Fund, Mary Reynolds Babcock Foundation, Rockefeller Brothers Fund, Rockefeller Foundation, Surdna Foundation, W. K. Kellogg Foundation, and DaimlerChrysler—paid for CCII and CCIII, events that are a far cry from the usual public hearing, with touches like local praline candy in the free lunches, public service announcements advertising the meeting by Wynton Marsalis, robocalls from Mayor Nagin urging citizens to attend, and even a second-line parade through the streets of New Orleans to register participants.

The funding has made a difference. Many disconnected, fragmented, and competing planning processes have debuted and then faltered over the past fifteen months on issues of funding authorization and hot-button decisions like whether the city should reduce its footprint and convert low-lying areas to green spaces. Some have wondered whether this unified effort to engage a cross section of the city and its displaced residents on the critical questions of how to regrow the city comes too late. New Orleanians are already exhausted by participating in the earlier meetings and angry about the lack of progress thus far. Major questions, such as the political untenability of shrinking the city, have already been resolved. While some of these anxieties were forestalled at CCII, as at any live event, technical difficulties and unforeseen hiccups can threaten thousands of hours of advance work. "Every detail matters" in this emotionally fraught event.[2]

As we near 9:30 a.m., participants enter and are greeted warmly at the welcome table and assigned randomly to our tables. My own table has been designated for latecomers, so I eavesdrop with envy on the volunteers who are already making introductions. Each table is outfitted with ten keypads linked wirelessly to the audience response system, but this high-tech network is also outfitted with humbler stuff for us to arrange at our spots: a table number, pens, markers, handouts, and red, yellow, and green cards to hold up if we need to signal for help from one of the roaming facilitators or the floor manager. Such a crowd inevitably attracts those seeking to provide and sell services; local community organizations and agencies are thrilled to have this far-flung group together in one room and try to remain unobtrusive while distributing informational flyers, and a village of child care, counselors, translators, sign language interpreters, and emergency service personnel stand at the ready. The air is humming with the energy of folks ready to help.

While the ballroom warms up, the same preparatory rituals are being conducted in New Orleans, Atlanta, and Houston. Smaller groups in other cities are gathering to participate by webcast. All four main sites will be connected by satellite video feeds, allowing the assembled crowds to cheer and wave at each other like fans on the big screen at an NFL game. Most participants are indeed riled up like superfans because their scrappy New Orleans Saints have made an improbable run to the NFC championship taking place tomorrow, a triumph even more symbolic because this is their first season back in the Superdome. "Saints!" cheers and "When the Saints Go Marching In" will get smiles out of everyone over the next six hours, and many attendees are bursting with pride and nervous energy in their jerseys.

On the ground in Dallas, local coordinators have been working with community interfaith groups, charities, and service organizations to ensure a good turnout and recruit facilitators. AmericaSpeaks has been tracking the demographics of registrants for weeks and has been involved up to the last minute in recruiting a group that represents the racial, housing status, income, and age makeup of the city before the storm. The first three people to sit at my table are white Dallasites biding their time as observers before the meeting begins. A twenty-something graduate student named Becky plops down and whispers conspiratorially about "colored people's time" when the start is delayed; such discordant notes characterize the awkward racial and class politics of a meeting where most of the non–New Orleanian staffers and observers are white and the former residents of the city who have attended here in Dallas are nearly exclusively black and low income. Most displaced white and upper-income homeowners have already returned to the city more than a year after the storm.

Across the sites, almost 70% of the volunteer facilitators have self-funded trips from all over the United States, Canada, and even the United Kingdom to be a part of the event. The volunteer facilitators are considerably more diverse than the Dallas officials on hand to observe and include veterans, schoolteachers, and black and white Katrina survivors, along with plenty of white out-of-towners from the Northeast like me. Facilitators used to leading meetings in other communities that tend to attract high-income, involved citizens will note to each other at the debrief after the event the unusual level of poverty and illiteracy present among participants, describing participants taking two lunches and tucking extra sodas and markers in their bags or sneaking out to drink during the discussions. In a report following the meeting, Carolyn Lukensmeyer, AmericaSpeaks' president, celebrated that in this "'hardest case' environment" where "the majority of the target audience was living in a postdisaster crisis mode," the organization "succeeded in giving equal voice to the most disenfranchised," both the poor, largely black citizens most affected by the storm and those in the diaspora who could not attend public meetings in New Orleans.[3]

Each survivor finally assigned to my own table in Dallas is black. This meeting and the one that preceded it are largely seen as do-overs of Community Congress I, a public meeting with very little coordinated outreach that engaged a disproportionate number of white returnees in elevated areas of the city. As such, the black turnout at CCIII, which we will find out is 55% across the sites, is a major improvement from earlier failed processes, even though it falls short of the 67.3% black population pre-Katrina and is slightly down from CCII. Jesse, a woman in her early sixties, sits down and immediately wonders aloud whether the feedback from this meeting will be heard. Taking his place beside her is her husband, wearing a feedcap and looking like he would rather be anywhere else. Roberta, a woman in her early fifties, and her daughter Janie, a youthful art school student in her early thirties, join Jesse in a joke. Another older man in a feedcap and overalls sits in silence next to Jesse's husband while the women laugh. Despite my entreaties, these two men at a table full of women will say little, occasionally getting up to have a smoke outside when the proceedings drag. The gender differences in volubility at my table are typical across the sites; scholars studying the process found that women participated more than men, white women more than black women, and white men more than black men, especially when racial balance at the tables was equal—certainly more common in New Orleans than here in Dallas.

Last but not least, Susan—a tornado of upbeat energy—comes to our table, snapping pictures, shaking hands, and handing out her business card. She is a caseworker for Katrina survivors in Dallas, having been employed by the Department of Housing and Urban Development in New Orleans. When the call goes out for captains to volunteer to keep in touch with the group after the meeting, she will take responsibility for maintaining contact and encouraging action after the event, collecting e-mails and sending us scores of messages about programs and services.

Everyone quiets down as the meeting begins, with formal speeches from the local facilitator and civic leaders via satellite uplink in New Orleans. A gospel choir sings an invocation. Pain and anger are acknowledged, while speakers strike hopeful notes and emphasize that the focus today is not on public figures but on the participants, who should give themselves a hand for coming and contributing. Lukensmeyer, emotional at the sight of so many people gathered, leads a visioning exercise where we close our eyes and imagine ourselves as a bald eagle flying over the city we would like to see. Gary, a white facilitator from Maryland, will later complain that the "eagle visioning was totally inappropriate" and that those at his table wistfully imagined just being able to sit on their front porches again. The first task of the day is to ask my table to think quietly and write down our "experience of inspiration" in the recovery of New Orleans. Barbara, a Katrina survivor at last night's facilitator training, asked, "Why do we have to write down our inspiration? People are tired of talking about their feelings!" The video monitor shows reports from the different sites—most say that the event itself is an inspiration.

Next, the first major test of the day is the demographics voting, where participants get a chance to try out the keypads and see "who's here today." During the voting, pop hits keyed to the theme of the vote, like ABBA's "Money Money Money" during the income question, are played at top volume over the sound system, to much laughter. The results? Fifty-five percent had participated in CCII, with similar numbers having participated at many of the other planning meetings. Those with income less than $20,000 make up 24% of attendees, 11% less than pre-Katrina levels in the city, but those with incomes $20,000 to 39,999 are here at 21%, close to the 24% before the storm. The group is asked to take responsibility for thinking of the city's younger residents and other underrepresented groups as they discuss the options today.

Susan and the rest have fun with the voting but are nonplussed by the "pomp and circumstance," and by Nagin and other officials. This running commentary and skepticism of the larger event will continue as the day goes on at the latecomers' table, despite my following the facilitator instructions to "model attentive listening" and encourage voting. I note that key points from our discussions, dutifully entered into the laptop computer and channeled to a central "theme team," are not consistently reflected in the discussion slides or the voting patterns of the larger group.

Eventually, the men do pipe up, nearly simultaneously, to share their worries about handicapped access to elevated housing: "How will that work?" A great question! Other tables shared the same concerns about the flood safety recommendations in the plan. We see "Elevating homes creates an access problem for elderly & disabled" come up on the voting list for flood safety options, and the men are more invested in the voting in this round; this becomes concern five of eight with 29% supporting it, under top choice "Bad governance could undercut speed and fairness of implementation" (59%).

Despite some boredom and cynicism around the table, Susan keeps our spirits high. I try to keep things moving and draw out the men, and as the day goes on, we will get choked up as we find out that some displaced residents have spotted lost relatives and friends, scrutinizing the video feeds and the sea of faces across the cavernous meeting rooms for loved ones. The room is beset with alternating currents of emotion, as participants listen to public officials and community organizers, hear slam poetry and stories from other participants, debate and vote on the wonkish details of policy incentives for rebuilding, stretch, eat box lunches, grouse about the lack of bathroom breaks, and commit to new actions. Those with their own transportation have begun trickling out by 2:45 p.m., as the topic turns to implementation and participants are asked to take responsibility for action on the plan. First, table participants are asked to "share some personal lessons of citizens working together on the rebuilding and recovery," hard for those in the Dallas area who are removed from the ground-level work going on in New Orleans. When asked if she will return, Janie demurs, saying that she would like to but can't justify taking her twelve-year-old son back in the current conditions.

Next, participants are asked to review options for citizen participation, thinking about which are best for "citizen interests." Participants are asked, "What personal commitment can you make to stay involved in the rebuilding of New Orleans?" and the day concludes with voting on the Citizen Participation Plan options, closing remarks, and a final round of voting on four evaluation questions about the process. When participants are asked to vote on how satisfied they are with their own participation, Janie cries out, "Why do they have to put it on us?" The group doesn't answer her specifically, but the other women quietly say they are choosing "satisfied" instead of "very satisfied." When the results are tallied, 93% of participants commit to remaining engaged. Some new options for participation, such as an annual community congress like this one, have been suggested. In a grand finale, the group receives a printed handout, still hot off the copier, reporting the votes of the day so they can share and remember the options they discussed. We hug, say thank yous, wave goodbyes to the other sites, and promise to keep in touch with tablemates, snaking our exits around the tables amid lots of Saints-related cheering and relief after a long day's work.

The headset crew is running to finish last tasks, collect keypads, and close out the meeting, and the volunteers make our way to the training room to debrief. Event pacing and politicking by public figures are shared concerns, with some worrying that the speeches were too long and the "fancy language" in the voting options was not basic enough to be understood by participants. Others note that they struggled keeping their tables on track because of the "level of anger": "People couldn't get at issues because they were still healing and so frustrated." A black male Katrina survivor in his fifties says, "New Orleans culture is social. The process did not reflect New Orleans culture. Why could we not take a real break at lunch and eat and talk instead of trying to discuss and eat at the same time?" The staffers have invested their hearts in this process but are having trouble absorbing the volunteers' pent-up criticism after helping us learn the ropes all day.

After our debrief, the facilitators are energized and eager to tell stories from their tables. We head to J. Pepe's Mexican Restaurant and chat with each other about our table discussions over sweet tea and beer before the conversation moves to politics and our own lives. Finally relieved of their headsets, the professional staff trickle in after their own debrief, looking exhausted but relieved. They are greeted with hearty cheers from the now-relaxed volunteers, who compliment them on a job well done. After goodbyes and exchanging business cards, I leave the happy hour, hoping for a Saints win. It is not to be. The fans will be crushed tomorrow, as the Saints take a 39–14 beating from the Chicago Bears.

What of the recommendations produced in CCII and CCIII? Foundations in the twenty-first century are nothing if not compulsive about evaluation and spent some of their funding on follow-up studies. Lukensmeyer wrote a report on lessons for other citizen participation processes, and a Kennedy School of Government doctoral candidate conducted interviews with decision-makers on behalf of the foundations involved. Other independent scholars studied the process as well. Before CCIII, the foundation-sponsored study found that "Community Congress II engendered 'buy-in' from both the public and their community leaders" critical to the future approval of the Unified New Orleans Plan but that "community leaders appeared far more interested in the event as a means to earn 'buy-in,' than as a way to improve the actual plan": "Substance was almost irrelevant."[4]

None of the leaders interviewed thought of the CCII process "primarily as a way to improve the substance of UNOP," and some had not even looked at the preliminary report on citizens' recommendations. As with the pilot studies, the key issue of getting the "demographic mix ... correct" meant that the preparatory, invisible work behind the scenes was far more important than what actually went on at the meetings. The AmericaSpeaks process had built into the fixed set of options room for "other" options and had taken care to point out where participants were angry or where options or phrasings were changed based on immediate feedback from the tables.

The sense that the Community Congresses incorporated critique—that the public spoke with one voice, and that that voice was heard—was more important substantively than any of the concrete recommendations, which generally followed planners' expectations of what was feasible or politically tenable. Many openly acknowledged that they needed a form of engagement that wouldn't further enrage residents already irate about wasted time in earlier meetings. A mayor's aide agreed that CCII's focus was "motherhood and apple pie": important for "consensus-building," "education," and "bringing people together," but not about substance.[5] According to Lukensmeyer, "the Community Congresses were a vehicle for restoring community and therefore hope."[6] Not least, innovations like the recruitment robocalls pioneered in this process, and the triumph over the many complex difficulties involved in producing public engagement for disaster survivors who were spread across the country, served to prove the worth of public deliberation more generally: "In addition to advancing the level of practice in the field, the Unified Plan process concretely demonstrated two key tenets of civic engagement work: that average citizens *can* make substantive and worthwhile contributions to complicated policy issues, and that reluctant decision makers *can* be effectively brought into these processes."[7]

The $14.5 billion UNOP was approved by the necessary stakeholders, and rebuilding could continue in a more effective way. Although CCII and CCIII were not going to solve long-term structural problems, they had demonstrated the potential of a different way of civic life for New Orleans. By 2011, the UNOP website was nearly defunct, and little evidence of the congresses appeared online. What of those commitments to action back at the individual level? Two hundred citizens showed up to a City Planning Commission hearing in March on the UNOP, an exciting show of citizen support.[8] Longer-term engagement was understandably tempered by the passage of time, and it was hard to keep track of people who got together just once for a singular experience.

A few traces around the Internet and continuing contacts revealed life changes and new perspectives. Dynamo Susan moved back to New Orleans by June, but her health and fortunes have plummeted by the time I check in with her a year later, in January 2008. She still has faith in the plan and carries good feelings about the meetings, despite her struggles:

> I do think that the time spent in those meetings were worth the time and effort. Those plans are long range and will happen eventually. It showed a genuine concern of the people to come together and come up with plans to rebuild our city. ...
>
> As to if these meetings and plans have affected our city in a concrete way is still left to be seen. Progress is slow and citizens are still having difficult times trying to rebuild their lives. I for one am struggling so much until I feel like a victim all over again. Agencies are not helping as much as we thought they would. There is not much empathy for the people.
>
> Yes, I am glad I participated and wish I could be more involved. My health is failing and I am in a busy demanding job that does not pay much. Also I haven't been in touch with anyone concerning the UNOP.
>
> The planning of the meeting and getting so many people involved was done well. Now if they could begin executing the plans with open acknowledgements so that the people can see what is being done and if it is being done well.

She concludes her e-mail with a quick summary of her life a year later: "I am back with my former employer at a rate of pay not adequate to maintain my household with the increased cost of living brought on by the disaster. My failing health does not afford me the privilege to go out seeking more suitable employment. ... Good luck and keep your eyes on us."

How, exactly, should we keep our eyes on Susan and the other citizens of New Orleans, willing and able to participate to improve their communities as they rebuild their lives, despite having fallen on the hardest of hard times? How should we understand the impressive, overwhelming phenomenon that is this "21st Century Town Meeting," with its foundation underwriting, civic partnerships, robocalls, celebrity endorsements, precision timing, patient circle sharing, inspirational poetry, talking heads, gospel music, earnest New England traditions, generous social services, positive psychology, constant polling, networked infrastructure, live simulcasts, quiet reflection periods, attentive listening, and instant journalism? How do we understand why this civic festival of inclusion, equality, and democracy—seemingly so hard to achieve in other contexts—is being rolled out for the poorest of the poor, in a time of fiscal and social retrenchment? As my research unfolded, my perspective on Susan's experience and on the uniquely moving elements of January 20th, not least on what they said about the virtues and failures of public engagement, would shift dramatically.

## Putting the Vanguard in Context

Many scholars have been captivated by the no-detail-too-small professionalism and gargantuan scale of spectacular multisited events like Community Congress III. Such events are so complex, involving such detailed, place-based policy histories and the sustained collaboration of so many private and public organizations, that they can provide fodder for whole volumes of academic research unpacking the narratives of their emergence and long-term effects. The Community Congresses and other ambitious participatory efforts, such as participatory budgeting in Pôrto Alegre, Brazil,[9] and the British Columbia Citizens' Assembly in Canada,[10] have been systematically analyzed as real utopian interventions in ordinary politics. Scholars have scrutinized the stakeholder power dynamics and the micropolitics of reason-giving and preference change going on in these discussions—as in the study finding that women and white attendees talked most at the tables.[11] Even when public engagement initiatives fail to influence local politics or policymaking, scholars often take the same perspective as Carolyn Lukensmeyer, arguing that such processes have significance far beyond their immediate effects, inasmuch as they help people see how wonderful engagement is in the first place and why we should have more of it, even if it is not very powerful right now.[12] It is certainly hard not to be moved by Lukensmeyer and her energetic staff, so dedicated to reinvigorating American democracy, or by the volunteer facilitators, ready and eager to help people like Susan get back on their feet.

I believe it is critical that we take seriously and think inventively about the passion public events like Community Congress III inspire, even as I argue that we should adopt a different viewpoint than prior scholars to understand fully what the public engagement industry can tell us about our public life. It is tempting to absorb the narrative that deliberative processes themselves tell, their collective feeling that we are having a self-contained moment of civic renewal, shutting out partisan bickering and punditry for an alternate universe that blends the old-fashioned civic commitment of New England town halls with of-the-moment justice-centered practices, exciting new technologies, and the evidence-driven decision-making of the twenty-first century. But this would ignore the ways in which these processes, in the vanguard of a new movement for substantive public engagement, are not worlds unto themselves—as compulsively as they try to maintain their distance. It does not diminish the many compellingly experimental deliberations, study circles, and citizen juries of the last thirty years, nor their tireless champions, to place them in the context of larger-scale trends and countertrends in American politics.

I had a ground-level view at this particular process—at similar processes I was employed as a research observer and served as a roaming volunteer—and that view is essential for understanding the lived experience of these meetings. But I argue that understanding deliberation in terms of one-time or two-time events or as interventions in a particular urban political environment prevents a wider understanding that will help us put Susan's experience in perspective. With a few notable exceptions, very few scholars have conducted sociological analyses of the strategic and political settings of dialogue and deliberation processes[13] or given much attention to the burgeoning public engagement consulting industry.[14] This is true despite the recognition that "good deliberation is not self-generating," and most public engagement processes require some form of top-down organization and facilitation.[15] We owe it to Susan to understand individual experiences in engagement processes in terms of the larger place of the public engagement movement in America's halting relationship with empowerment and popular governance.

To do this, we must study the actual sociohistorical contexts in which public dialogue and deliberation itself is organized and its practitioners make their livings.[16] As such, this book is based on five years of in-depth analysis and participant observation in the field of public engagement.[17] Neglecting the behind-the-scenes production of public engagement processes like CCIII for what transpires at their discussion tables comes at a cost. Certainly, these processes tell amazing stories that scholars are well trained to hear and describe for us. But we need to unpack the idea that there is no backstage here, that there is simply inside and outside the circle of chairs, with the chairs creating a safe, temporary space for the rest of us to synchronize our nostalgic yearnings with our contemporary values, whether or not we can make much of a change in the outside world. The captivating narratives that holistic engagement processes sell are critical to understanding how they work, but they are not the end of the story. From different angles, the impressive performances—and sometimes spectacles—of civic inclusion can look less like empowerment and more like social control.

On the one hand, we can be wowed by the spontaneity and on-the-fly changes that citizens are allowed to contribute to UNOP; on the other, we might see the numerous pilot run-throughs as evidence that the process is canned, with the participants discovering ideas and feelings that sponsors and observers have already anticipated. For some, the process's tears and songs and poetry of inspiration might be holier than politics as usual; for others, they are offensively treacly hokum that gets in the way of the real work that needs to be done. In one light, we might view the high-tech investments, shining luxury hotel, and deluxe services as well-earned signs of respect for people whose second-class treatment is a lingering national shame; in another, we might question the showy expense and discomfort of a one-time, red carpet rollout of long-deserved services for people whose child care and food needs extend beyond a single day in January. The institutional approach I use in this book does not force us to choose among these contrasting perspectives, but to understand how they can coexist.

## Studying the Design of Civic Processes

By looking at the larger field of organizations involved in public engagement, I forgo detailed case histories to examine the deliberation movement and the professional settings where deliberative innovations are pioneered. But I also look at these organizations from the standpoint of the real people like Lukensmeyer who created them, so that we do not lose sight of the human scale of public engagement events and their effects on flesh-and-blood individuals like Susan. This "inhabited institutions" approach, with its emphasis on the way culture influences and is created by people within organizations, focuses on the kinds of language people use, the models for action they draw on, and the quirks and resources they bring to their work from their other experiences.

Sociologists of inhabited institutions are interested in unpacking all of the routine assumptions and rules that structure everyday life to better understand the eternal interplay between social structure and human agency: the shortcuts that allow us to get things done, the reasons that many of our social institutions often look similar, the official instructions that everyone knows to ignore, and especially the causes when the same action produces a different result in a different place. When sociologists study organizations, we are interested in exploring the choices that seem available and desirable to people at any particular point in time, how they implement and negotiate those decisions once a path has been taken, and how they explain (or how they don't explain) whether those choices worked. We are particularly interested in the choices people make when the logics—the guiding principles for action—of their work conflict, such as when pressures to rationalize *and* democratize demand that hundreds of round-table discussions be digested for policy-makers or when holistic visioning and hip-hop bump up against decision-making. As is evident in CCIII, many logics, so instantly familiar to those of us immersed in American culture that they are almost invisible, are active in any particular engagement process.

This means that I am often interested in looking beyond the particular content of processes to understand the peculiar dispositions and attitudes that constitute civic life in the twenty-first century. I want to know what across all of these processes stays the same and how and why facilitators customize such processes for different settings. Why are they borrowing techniques like robocalling from political campaigns? What is the overall result and tenor of these meetings for the people who attend? Why do facilitators exhibit so much emotion? Why do publics generally feel so positive about processes in the face of substantial administrative failure? Why is participatory authenticity so intensely valuable and meaningful now?[18]

There is plenty of evidence in comparing deliberative events and looking at other studies of the texture of civic engagement in the United States that well-meaning political reform is not the only agenda on the table in scripted civic events. Josh Pacewicz, who studies civic partnerships in a Rust Belt city, has found that:

Civic partnerships appear much like an ideal Habermasian speech situation: people interact as provisional equals, treat one another with dignity and respect, and seek out consensus. In reality, this front-stage performance is only possible because—just off-stage—others have excluded specific actors who refuse to play along and have designed the deliberative context to crowd-out oppositional forms of civic self-presentation.[19]

To appreciate the "curtain of sophisticated practices [that] separates front-stage aspects of democratic participation from the back-stage effects of such practices," Pacewicz argues that we must look to "the actors who channel civic energies," because "economic-civic links are only obvious to those actors who structure broader patterns of community engagement, frequently not to 'regular people' who participate in civic initiatives."[20]

Although so much of Community Congress III seemed uniquely moving at the time, I have learned over the past five years that much of what worked that day was part of a standard palette of tools for deliberative events. The exuberant sports fandom as a substitute for flag-waving patriotism? Check. The New Age visioning? Check. The jokey pop ballads to make demographic discomforts go down easier? Check. The blue-chip sponsors? Check. The public vocalization of process criticisms and the showy changes made to the options? Check. Susan's motivation for action and lack of interest in or time for political mobilization? Check. Susan's and Janie's long-term frustration with leaders? Check. The celebration of the process method, and of deliberative reform itself, as a solution to our civic malaise and an alternative to failed leadership? Most definitely check.

By understanding processes like CCIII as part of larger shifts in American life, we can turn away from one-sided opinions about the thrilling alternative they offer or the cynical window dressing they disguise to marvel at the odd assemblages of American culture and politics they entail. Today's version of wise, responsible, and effective governance includes New Age wisdom circles, sophisticated digital surveillance apparatus, Gestalt therapy, homespun testimonies, strategy games, art projects, artlessly didactic videos, extensive backstage politicking, and recorded clips of 1970s and 1980s pop hits blasted at ear-splitting volume to get citizen stakeholders fired up and in the mood to deliberate. This book explains how all of those elements got into the blender of civic reform, why they are not as random as they seem, and why their results are surprisingly predictable.

Whereas most deliberative democratic theorists believe that these kinds of participatory processes should provide participants with fertile contexts for action, my research suggests that intentional efforts to activate grassroots participation from the top-down may foster more reliance of individuals on the institutions that support such actions, or more faith in individual-level efforts over collective ones. *The end result of all of these little steps to empowerment is, unfortunately, not a long journey to social justice but a tightening spiral of resignation and retreat from public life to our increasingly demanding domestic worlds.*

But the story being sold about stimulating civic engagement is certainly true on a small scale, and it's not one that its purveyors don't vociferously believe in themselves. As Pacewicz points out, "Models of civic participation have a history, and ... this history is thoroughly structured by the economy. Prior theorists have conceptualized such economic-civic relationships in scalar terms: the powerful exert economic influence, disrupt autonomous civic logics, and reduce civic participants to 'alienated ... supplicants.'... In practice, people rarely behave in such heavy-handed fashion."[21] This could not be more true or, in this case, a more important part of the argument. The story told here, like other stories of participatory life in a neoliberal world of accountability and personal responsibility, involves people who are actively embracing new models of action and new calls for social change.

The response to proliferating invitations to join the conversation is often a self-serious, diligent civic performance on the part of employees, consumers, and unaffiliated members of the public, in spite of their suspicions regarding administrator intentions. The meaningfulness of distinctively civic action is content-rich and enduring. But the ad hoc, tightly delimited citizen actions and civil attitudes that result from facilitated public engagement have restricted the boundaries of possibility in contemporary civic space. Inasmuch as researchers have a moral obligation to caring, community-minded citizens like Susan in their public engagement research, it is less to make deliberative empowerment ideals work in practice than to imagine more ambitious opportunities for the systems change public deliberation repeatedly offers, and rarely delivers, even—and especially—when it works as promised.

## Critical Engagement with Public Engagement

The broader scope of this book is what distinguishes it from other books that have made critiques of particular processes and organizations (such as in one city or in one method like the 21st Century Town Meeting) as flawed or manipulated. I do pay special attention to three high-profile processes led by AmericaSpeaks ("Our Budget, Our Economy," "Community Congress III," and "Bigger, Better, All Together," held at the 2008 National Performing Arts Convention) because doing so lets us control for process characteristics so that we can look at the difference different sets of participants (working-class African Americans in CCIII, arts professionals in "Bigger, Better, All Together") and different kinds of sponsors (foundations, private individuals, and nonprofits) can make in process outcomes.

I find that, in fact, outcomes are very similar across cases, both when processes are successful and when they fail—and this is true in a wide variety of processes beyond those facilitated by AmericaSpeaks, which itself failed to find a durable source of long-term financing and closed its doors in January 2014. The surprise announcement capped nineteen years of on-the-ground work to promote large-scale, in-person public engagement in all fifty states in a landscape that was increasingly suspicious of the proliferation of "nonpartisan" and "transpartisan" organizations, some for-profit and focused on mass online mobilization. Carolyn Lukensmeyer had already departed in 2012 in the wake of the Gabrielle Giffords shooting to direct the National Institute for Civil Discourse at the University of Arizona, citing a "toxic blame game" that "has begun to seep into public life across the country," with Americans having "lost hope" in political problem-solving and even civil discussion.[22] In the words of one board member, "the people and organizations that really care about nonpartisan, open-ended citizen deliberation don't have a lot of money to pay for it."[23] The fact that celebrated, high-profile processes like CCIII can be hard to track on the Web a few years later, and that established public engagement organizations like AmericaSpeaks may fold abruptly, makes it even more important to expand our field of vision to the place of the public engagement industry in the larger political economy and the effects facilitated public engagement does or does not have on our public life.[24]

Instead of critiquing particular processes or particular organizations, this account seeks to understand why, despite its seeming fragility, public engagement has metastasized across sectors and among vastly different groups of people because of larger macroeconomic and cultural trends in American life. Times have gotten tighter for millennial Americans, and their civic life has adapted accordingly—"down market" democracy is now faster, easier to produce, and more efficient, but it is also leaner and tougher—with less up for debate and more self-sacrifice demanded of its participants. In a time when most cultural critics are nostalgic for the sacrifices asked of earlier generations and bemoan that Americans are simply invited to shop their troubles away, these calls for belt-tightening and voluntarism in the name of community spirit may seem worth celebrating.

Ultimately, however, I argue that what we take today to be good engagement is itself the problem, even when it produces genuine empowerment. Public engagement professionals are deeply self-critical and reflexive, taking great pains to ensure that their processes are authentic and empowering. These artful processes, which scrupulously take account of human values and moral responsibilities, seem to be everything that ordinary politics and business as usual are not—but this impression is deceptive because many organizations now seek to sell themselves as socially responsible. The citizen activism that results from these processes, while real, is reliably aimed at sacrificing collectively and acting individually in service of the greater good. That greater good is framed not in terms of social and economic equality, but as preserving the fragile health of the institutions publics depend on, which have routinely betrayed this trust. Counterintuitively, it is not fake engagement that threatens democracy (publics can easily detect this and routinely reject it), but real engagement, because publics invest hope in it that it can't possibly fulfill.

In the current context, public engagement simply is not the democratic tool that scholars have made it out to be—because it contains citizen protest so effectively and creates more of itself rather than more mobilization. Many readers who lament the failings of public engagement will nevertheless condemn this argument as too depressing or cynical. I hope that by sharing the concern of deliberative democrats for social justice, but by shifting the terms of the debate from whether particular processes are good to whether they advance social or economic equality in addition to political equality, this book sparks a vigorous, critical dialogue among academics, practitioners, and the general public.

## How This Book Is Organized

To understand how public engagement can be authentically real and disempowering at the same time, we must start at the animating tensions that have structured growth in the market for deliberation. Chapter 1 has introduced a typical process and made the case for an institutional approach to understanding such an event. Chapter 2 investigates successes and struggles behind the growth in top-down orchestration of bottom-up empowerment.

Part II, "Process Evangelists: Spreading the Gospel of Deliberation," studies the ways in which deliberation professionals navigate these struggles by envisioning their work as a professional calling of spiritual awakening and transformational ritual. Chapter 3 unpacks the challenges practitioners face in professionalizing democratic dialogue, and chapter 4 investigates those cases where practitioners do not recognize such tensions, but instead assert the harmonic integration of their lives and their work.

Part III, "Civic Engagement as a Management Tool," looks at the marketing of deliberation to clients and the ways that the selling of deliberative outcomes blends business and politics, while also rigidly defending their distinctions. Chapter 5 investigates the use of arts and performances to invigorate deliberative work with authenticity and reject business logics of instrumentality. Chapter 6 looks at the authentic transformations from cynical consumers to active citizens that deliberative practitioners seek and investigates how these transformations are increasingly documented in sophisticated surveillance systems.

Part IV, "The Spirit of Deliberative Capitalism," studies the lessons that deliberation professionals claim to teach and why public resistance to these lessons is unlikely to change the power dynamics that deliberation produces. Chapter 7 looks at the kinds of activism—and the kinds of resistance—that deliberation produces in its subjects, with an emphasis on the simultaneously therapeutic and extractive goals of public engagement remedies. The conclusion puts the appealing promises of public engagement in larger context and considers the role of social critique in citizen participation and action.

Before we can begin to understand the potential of those critiques, however, we first have to understand the maelstrom of contemporary political life to which authentic public engagement seems a promising, if elusive, alternative. Chapter 2 captures the hard-won achievements of the professional public engagement field by going back to the White House, this time in the grassy sunshine of July 2010.

# 2

## The Idealists behind the Curtain

> Through the reforming generations, the hunt for the people yields large changes but small victories. The major legacies are unanticipated—the development of an administrative apparatus and the legitimation of new groups.
>
> James A. Morone, *The Democratic Wish: Popular Participation and the Limits of American Government* (1998: 9)

> It is fair to say that the deliberative movement around the globe is spearheaded by a relatively small cadre of experts.
>
> Mark Button and David M. Ryfe, from *The Deliberative Democracy Handbook* (2005: 21)

ON FLICKR, THE PHOTO-SHARING WEBSITE, is a folder of pictures of deliberation proponents posing outside the White House on a glorious summer day in July 2010. These folks know each other well and have taken turns posing individually and in a group, with many grinning while pressing cell phones to their ears—no doubt calling their families and friends while standing on the driveway of the East Lawn. Proudly wearing blue "A" Visitor tags on lanyards, they are dressed in formal business attire. Carolyn Lukensmeyer, usually in colorful woven prints, wears a gorgeous linen jacket in taupe, and Joe Goldman, also of AmericaSpeaks, has a neatly trimmed beard and matches her in a taupe and beige tie. The others have accented their outfits with reds, whites, and blues for the occasion. Martha McCoy, the petite executive director of Everyday Democracy, the organization that pioneered the Study

Circles model, used by communities all over the country to discuss topics like school reform, youth violence, and race relations, wears a gray pantsuit and electric blue blouse. Archon Fung, a political scientist from Harvard's Kennedy School of Government, looks every bit the Ivy League pol in a summerweight smoke-colored suit and red tie, with a folder of papers and legal pad clasped under his arm. John Gastil, a slightly more rumpled communications scholar who has authored a number of books on deliberative democracy, wears a sharp blue tie and flashes a tiepin with the iconic Obama Hope image on it. How did these scholars and organization leaders, all of whom have spent hundreds, if not thousands, of hours on the ground patiently listening to what everyday people have to say about life in their local communities, end up rubbing shoulders in the West Wing?

The answer has to do with the ability of engagement professionals not just to mobilize everyday people, but to organize themselves. This chapter sketches the tensions public deliberation consultants face in pursuing both of those tasks and describes the growth of the public engagement industry in response to concerns about declining civic participation and the rising power of experts in American life. In doing so, it highlights the challenges of expanding access to participatory engagement while maintaining its distinctive virtues—defending deliberation from ordinary politics and business as usual in a world in which those categories are increasingly blended.

Despite their successes, deliberation professionals are deeply concerned about the perils of co-optation and bureaucratization as public engagement becomes more popular. By 2010, deliberation reformers had made their way to the White House, but Obama's Open Government efforts had primarily emphasized nondeliberative engagement strategies like crowdsourcing. Emotions among practitioners currently range from hope to dismay about the future prospects of the field and its ability to defend from incursion by public relations firms or to prevent superficial appropriation by public bureaucracies. Sociologists Ernesto Ganuza and Gianpaolo Baiocchi, initially excited about participatory innovations in South America, now question why global leaders and international NGOs have jumped on the deep democracy bandwagon, wondering whether it "may conceal a new form of domination that has nothing to do with a new process of democratization."[1]

A progress report on the Open Government Directive shows that most of the innovations pioneered in federal government in 2009 took one of a few forms, such as online suggestion boxes for federal agency employees, Web dialogues, and contests using citizen-generated content for public service messages.[2] Public engagement practitioners have substantial concerns about the formalization of current efforts and the extent to which nondeliberative innovations like crowdsourcing are "damaging the enterprise of D&D [dialogue and deliberation]." One worries: "My fear is that 'crowd-sourcing' is compelling Orwellian double-speak: rather than the razzmatazz public *empowerment* that it is sold as, it reinforces the power of the convening authority while the public gains little in return. The enduring effect is that the public expectation of what 'public engagement' means is steadily dumbed down. Tomorrow's 'public engagement' will have nothing to do with empowerment at all. It'll just be yesterday's 'hearing.'"[3]

Public engagement professionals are not manipulators behind the curtain—in fact, they have managed to retain their idealism against the odds. But they are also pragmatic realists, fearful of the kinds of manipulation to which public engagement might be put while they try to advance its use. Most deliberative democracy scholars have focused on the growth of public deliberation as an explicitly political "movement" and highlighted its grassroots character, with much less attention to the growing market for civic empowerment and the professionals like Lukensmeyer, Goldman, and McCoy who have led the field.[4] Scholars who describe deliberation this way see the expanded use of dialogue and deliberation processes as the result of a progressive, bottom-up movement to reform politics that draws on participatory democratic movements of the 1960s and even earlier movements, such as the Progressive-era forum movement.[5]

Accordingly, some would argue that the moment on the White House lawn is the culmination of a long-time dream—the ascendancy of the public engagement movement to part of a national agenda for governance reform, all originating from the passion of a few political theorists and visionary activists who adapted the participatory strategies of the 1960s for a new age. Those strategies—of circle sharing, shared leadership, equal voice, consensus building—developed from activists' sense that their own organizational practices should match their philosophical commitments to the justice and equity they were fighting for. Critics have argued that these practices were the downfall of those movements, becoming shiny happy ends in themselves that hindered the sharp-elbowed decision-making and authoritative action necessary for reform.[6]

But deliberative democracy reformers have turned that logic on its head, seeing the practices themselves as a stand-alone mission, not tied to particular causes or owned by marginalized groups. Advancing and defending that mission has, in many ways, required these activists to pursue strategies seemingly at odds with 1960s grassroots values. The success of democracy reformers in getting to the White House was not about swelling grassroots pressure and chaotic democratic voices, but about elite networking and professional mobilization—what sociologists call "grasstops" activism. Because of these tensions between pushing for democratic voice in ways befitting sophisticated professionals who claim a unique form of expertise, many public engagement facilitators reject the terminology of movement altogether. As deliberation proponent Matt Leighninger, author of *The Next Form of Democracy*, notes, even for those who do claim movement status, *movement* has a different meaning now than in the past: "though people in this field still like to use the term 'movement' to describe their work, civic engagement has lost much of its movement flavor."[7]

Is deliberation a progressive movement? When so many practitioners reject movement language, scholars should proceed with caution, but that does not mean they should abandon the language of mobilization and collective action.[8] Sociologists have recently begun to study "awkward movements" and "social movement industries" to capture the elite memberships and significant amount of coordination that can accompany more traditional movement labels or tactics.[9] These concepts can help us to clarify and refine our thinking about the ambiguous status of the dialogue and deliberation movement and the tensions practitioners face in pursuing their goals of carving out a unique space for nonadversarial politics. The assumption that deliberation is grassroots does need further interrogation, because so much of the activity in the field is driven by elite actors—a fact that practitioners readily acknowledge. Some scholars who view the growth in deliberative democratic processes as a movement, like Mark Button and David M. Ryfe in the quote that introduces this chapter, do note that the movement is led by a core group at the top. And these concerns are by no means new, as political scientist James Morone's quote at the beginning of this chapter also demonstrates. But the ways in which deliberation professionals have navigated these tensions can also tell us something about the challenges activists face as they attempt to succeed in contexts hungry for grassroots authenticity but increasingly hostile to movements themselves.

The Obama administration's Open Government Initiative prompted a sustained effort from these leaders of foundations, professional deliberation associations, and civic networks and institutes to take advantage of a unique window for integrating public engagement into government. Not only did major deliberation leaders get an audience at the White House but also deliberative experts won roles as advisory experts to federal administrators at invitation-only conferences such as "Champions of Participation" 1, 2, and 3 and "Strengthening Our Nation's Democracy II." As one practitioner writes on a listserv, "All across the Net we see expert online communities of practice essentially involving professionals, but not everyday citizens." This elite character of contemporary deliberative mobilization at the national level is by no means unusual for contemporary social movements and in fact reflects broader shifts in which effective movement actors are increasingly institutional insiders.[10]

Field elites also tried to mobilize their own constituents in the democracy community—facilitators, educators, and supporters—to complement their networking with direct action.[11] This meant taking advantage of the opportunities the administration had created for the public to offer input on open government. Deliberation organizations and associations e-mailed their own constituencies and asked them to blast the administration's idea-ranking website with votes, thereby dominating the online process to gain input on the Open Government Directive. In the absence of much layperson interest in participating in developing technical specifications for participation, the organizations were very successful on this front. AmericaSpeaks proudly reported having authored six of the top ten ideas in the public brainstorming phase.[12]

Seeing public deliberation *only* as a political movement with progressive aims prevents an examination of the multiple tensions that have shaped its development and the institutional interests driving the market for deliberation services. Deliberation certainly has roots in the participatory democracy of the 1960s, but it is important to recognize—as practitioners do—that deliberation borrows from many fields, including alternative dispute resolution, workplace participation, New Age religious practices, and lobbying and campaigning. Investigating the varied logics and tools practitioners bring to the field from nonmovement contexts can provide a far richer analysis of deliberative practices and a more nuanced picture of its social change discourses and de facto representatives than that of a spontaneous grassroots renaissance.[13] As a start, we need to know how activism became business as usual, how a new kind of civic participation became seen as an antidote for anxieties about the public sphere, and how expectations changed over that period regarding the best way to pursue social change.

### Reforming Participation: This Is Not Your Father's Public Hearing

> Town Hall Meeting Gives Townspeople Chance to Say Stupid Things in Public
>
> The *Onion* (2007)

Public participation in problem-solving has been a reassuring civic rite since Thomas Jefferson ennobled the yeomen whose small farms stitched together new communities in common purpose. Traditional modes of participation like town hall meetings and public hearings are instantly recognizable touchstones of American experience, even for those who have never attended one. The ability to stand up and have one's say is an American birthright. Whatever else they disagree on, progressives and conservatives agree that much of the problem with big government is that it is unresponsive to citizen input. To rectify this, scholars and pundits advocate increasing more of what we venerate: citizen engagement in decision-making. All comers, from Tea Partiers to Moveon.org members, should have their say on issues that affect their daily lives. If the views of the people can be tapped more easily and amplified through new technologies and new kinds of engagement, then so much the better. The greater the citizen voice in policy-making, the healthier our civic life, and the more sensible our politics will be. Democracy 2.0 can lead us to a brighter future.

To understand the public engagement renaissance, we need to examine the origins of this movement to solve a failure of democracy—serial, three-minute monologues at a microphone—with more democracy. The late 1980s and early 1990s were a time of concern for the decline of citizen engagement in public life, as baby boomers and their children withdrew into their homes and away from the collective rituals of community life in favor of cable television programming. Americans worked longer hours, women entered the workforce in even greater numbers, and distractions within the home multiplied.[14] American Legion watering holes and citywide garden clubs—organizations lovingly cared for by the Greatest Generation—dried out and withered as their memberships aged. Robert Putnam's swan song for the lost bowling leagues of America gripped cultural commentators and community activists with a persuasive narrative of the civic decline they were witnessing.[15] Putnam argued that because people were no longer bonding within small groups, they no longer felt invested in the larger social enterprise of community building. Polling places, public hearings, and PTA meetings had emptied. Most pressingly, people seemed to have lost their aptitude for or interest in talking to people unlike themselves. Collective frustration with contentious public hearings and endless litigation had reached new heights.

On the one hand, members of the public were sick of the "decide-announce-defend" model of government decision-making, with its paternalistic overtones and undertones of backroom deals. For their part, public administrators were tired of hearings attended by the same few unrepresentative souls who could be counted on to show up and spout familiar complaints regardless of what was being offered.[16] By the end of the 1980s, holding placards on the steps of city hall didn't attract much attention. The risk of capital flight gripped industrial cities terrified of becoming the latest in a long line of Rust Belt casualties. Containing the civic conflict that might frighten multinational corporations was job one for local leaders.[17] The old protest politics didn't work anymore, for the opposition or the establishment.[18]

The crisis of confidence in Americans' appetite for public discussion prompted new efforts to bring more people to the table and engage communities in difficult, nonadversarial conversations about pressing social problems. Amid the bleak news about declining civic engagement was a quietly growing roster of collaborative and participatory experiments aimed at taking advantage of the hunger for more authentic debate and less contentious politics. Mediation and alternative dispute resolution efforts, begun in the 1970s, gained ground and legitimacy throughout the country.[19] Federal administrators fed up with endless Endangered Species Act litigation vowed to change the politics of environmental planning by bringing together environmentalists and developers to work out plans for preserving natural areas and supporting economic growth at the same time.[20] Collaborative efforts to engage the public in fixing broken social institutions like urban public schools and decaying inner city neighborhoods led to community policing and neighborhood schools councils in Chicago and other cities.[21] President Bill Clinton started up a national dialogue on race in 1994. This deep form of democracy, requiring sustained commitment and mutual listening, was a radical departure from the one-way, episodic consultation most cities conducted on public issues.

*with no results*

Scholars have noted that these initiatives were not sui generis, but driven in part by the new fiscal realities of global capitalism in the latter part of the twentieth century. Isaac Martin describes how the growth of new forms of civic engagement like town hall meetings was a result of states' needs for more intensive "resource extraction" from publics; administrators sought "anticipatory consultation" to gauge public preferences and mollify restive constituents when they had to raise taxes.[22] Josh Pacewicz describes how, in one Rust Belt city, "partnerships co-evolved with a re-orientation of local priorities towards economic development."[23] Facing disastrous consequences, local union leaders voluntarily adopted less aggressive stances, at the same time that community organizations became more dependent on community development corporations and other elites.[24] Local communities developed new partnerships as they focused on major urban projects that would boost their economies and lure corporate investment.

Deep public engagement initiatives—variously called collaborative governance, deliberative democracy, or empowered participation—signaled a brave new world of government leaders turning power over to the people and trusting their judgment. Those who took the risk found that deliberation actually worked. Although Clinton's Dialogues on Race fizzled in the wake of his impeachment scandal, they prompted the founding of AmericaSpeaks, which pioneered 21st Century Town Meetings. In the Pacific Northwest in 1993, timber companies and spotted-owl lovers called a truce in the timber wars and met in a county library to try to find common ground on forest management.[25] Los Angeles held Days of Dialogue following the O. J. Simpson acquittal to avoid a repeat of the mayhem caused by the Rodney King verdict.[26] In Boston, pro-life and pro-choice leaders were won over to the idea of collaboration as they met secretly to discuss strategies for avoiding the polarization and violence that had scarred national debate on abortion.[27] Participation and deliberation were the new buzzwords in universities, planning departments, and companies. Robert Putnam himself founded a civic engagement institute that became a model for similar efforts around the country.[28]

Public officials discovered that initiatives bringing together nonprofit organizations and businesses with average citizens tended to generate broad support from the center and disempowered the polarized interest groups that had previously dominated public debate. Clinton, George W. Bush, and other politicians made a point of showing up at celebrated examples of citizen collaboration and advertising the power they were devolving to public-private partnerships and local-level actors. The deliberation movement rode a wave of enthusiasm in the 1990s and 2000s for downsizing bureaucracy and upsizing public engagement.[29] Whether called new public management, reinventing government, or neoliberalism, centrist governance reforms in the last twenty years initiated deeper public involvement in problem-solving, with government serving as a facilitator of locally organized action.[30] Obama's imprimatur made it official, but by 2009, public participation was already integrated in policymaking at even the most recalcitrant federal agencies.[31]

Of course, such reforms address only one part of the larger picture of public engagement in policymaking, which comprises citizen participation in more formal electoral politics and referenda and unsponsored civic action not connected to formal institutions of government.[32] But many (including the Obama administration) see the dawning of collaborative, participatory, and transparent processes sponsored by the government as key to a democratic renaissance in American society. Scholar Carmen Sirianni argues: "Vibrant self-governance in America today requires that government—local, state, and federal—design policy and invest strategically and systematically in building civic capacity to enable the everyday work of public citizens."[33] Bringing back bowling leagues is not the solution to our social capital deficits. Instead, these democracy advocates are seeking to entrench participatory democracy in *formal institutions*, meaning that community members and public administrators develop the habit of working together on a routine basis according to a transparent set of rules favoring inclusion, openness, and productive agreement.[34] This turn toward explicitly nonadversarial, multistakeholder discussions—getting different constituencies in a room, talking to each other, instead of approaching administrators individually—as the solution to declining civic engagement is the result of the accelerating interdependence of formerly separate fields that sociologists have termed "multi-institutional politics."[35] A little more background on these converging and blurring forces is necessary to understand how facilitated engagement of diverse groups became the centerpiece of an agenda to restore American democracy.

## Professional Engagement Facilitation as a Solution to Professionalized Activism and Declining Citizen Capacity

> The cure for the ailments of democracy is more democracy.
>
> John Dewey, *The Public and Its Problems* (1927)

One aspect of this convergence is the extent to which activism now looks a lot like big business. The civic action that Americans are interested in undertaking and the organizations that facilitate it have changed dramatically over the last century. Beginning with the transformation of progressive movements into national interest groups at the turn of the twentieth century, citizen mobilization has become tied to professional organizations over time.[36] This concentration of power in the hands of a few, as movements rationalize their organizations and lose touch with their populist roots, demonstrates a common theme in scholarship on politics: radical ideas are inevitably tempered as they are absorbed into bureaucracies.[37] Even formerly oppositional actors have moderated their tactics as they have been allowed greater say within institutions.[38]

As social movements have become more professional and more market oriented in their interventions, average citizens have had less of a role, except in writing checks and supporting organizations' activities through e-mail petitions. Theda Skocpol believes this "diminished" form of democracy has been caused by the displacement of broad-based, chapter-driven membership organizations by Beltway lobbying groups with contribution-based memberships.[39] The disempowering effects of professionalization go hand in hand with coordination at the national scale. Even when mobilization reaches citizens where they live, it is divorced from local social networks and thereby loses a significant opportunity for building social capital. By not providing avenues for access through local chapters, organizations lose authentic connections with members, and citizens do not develop the leadership and organization skills or relationships with diverse others to organize themselves.[40]

Even traditional forms of activism have been commodified: petitioning has been outsourced to professional canvassing organizations, and a "grassroots lobbying industry" of consultants stands ready to mobilize citizens on behalf of shadowy super PACS and well-heeled corporations and interest groups.[41] Ironically, as lobbyists' influence has been curbed through new regulations, these new firms can rapidly assemble smokers' rights groups and HMO-loving patients to demonstrate the popular bona fides of any cause. In such an atmosphere, grassroots activism has become as easy and as superficial as clicking an animated "Tell Congress!" Web ad, but the skills required for sustained participation are atrophying. Scholars of citizen participation in organized politics have puzzled over the paradoxes of a largely absent public in today's increasingly participatory climate: in the missing movement for gun control in America, despite clear public desire for stricter gun control; in the myth of digital democracy, whereby participation in political dialogue on the Web is, upon closer analysis, revealed to be controlled by a small group of elites; and in the myth of the rational voter, in which democratically organized publics vote for policies that are clearly not in their best interests.[42] The wisdom of crowds is hard to celebrate when you can't get a crowd together in the first place, or when you do get them together, they are reluctant to talk to each other, or when you do get them to talk to each other, they are reading from a script handed to them by an interest organization.[43] Because of all of these factors, proponents of participatory governance believe some kind of facilitation is necessary for democratic engagement initiatives, inasmuch as citizen stakeholders are simply not able to participate in a diverse, complex, and multitiered system without some assistance in setting ground rules and preventing moneyed interests from pulling the strings.[44]    *like government agencies*

This is where professional facilitators come in. Professional facilitators increasingly run formal stakeholder engagement processes like the Community Congress described at the beginning of chapter 1. Not just de rigueur in comprehensive community planning processes, facilitated public deliberation is an omnipresent element of administrative decision-making and planning, from negotiated rule-making by federal agencies to Web dialogues on disaster response and deliberative exercises on health care. A striking one in four citizens in a recent survey had participated in organizationally sponsored, face-to-face deliberation on a public issue.[45] As enhanced public participation has become an expected part of government decision-making, the use of outside consultants who offer expertise in collaborative process, consensus building, and public deliberation has expanded dramatically.[46] Inasmuch as participation in governance can occur along a continuum from information sharing to full decision-making power,[47] public deliberation practitioners are typically private-sector or not-for-profit consultants who facilitate participatory processes that involve citizens in more intensive, collaborative engagement with decision-makers and other stakeholders than the limited consultation in mandated public hearings or comment periods. These structured opportunities to participate in developing and discussing alternatives and selecting preferred policy options may occur in addition to required consultation or outreach processes, prior to them, or in place of them. But deliberation has also become a standard practice in quasi-governmental and nongovernmental settings as well.

The field of professional public engagement facilitation developed in the late 1980s and early 1990s, building on the alternative dispute resolution and community mediation movements of the 1970s and initial successes in the environmental planning field. These collaborative innovations were intended to reduce the litigation generated by an earlier phase of institutionalized participation enshrined in the National Environmental Policy Act.[48] This "veritable revolution ... in the formation of organizations and a 'profession' devoted to the participation of ordinary citizens" has produced an extensive "organizational infrastructure for public deliberation."[49] Major professional associations in the field today—the International Association of Public Participation (IAP2, founded in 1990) and the National Coalition for Dialogue & Deliberation (NCDD, founded in 2002)—together boast more than 1,000 US members. Growth in the outsourcing of public engagement is undeniable, as evidenced by the training budget of IAP2. Demand for facilitation training from IAP2 increased dramatically over the 2000s, with the number of licensed public participation facilitation trainers tripling between 2004 and 2005 and training revenue, the largest source of income for the association, increasing 538% from 2001 to 2008.[50] One popular method, Open Space, in which participants themselves set the agenda on urgent issues, estimates 20,000 to 30,000 unique events worldwide held in the method since it began in 1985.

Most analyses of the expansive growth of deliberation have focused on the proliferation and heterogeneity of deliberative methods, emphasizing the diversity of ways to recruit participants (from random selection of small, representative groups to massively inclusive invitations to whole communities), the variety of tools and technologies on offer, and the differing purposes of different processes (from dialogues aimed at conflict reduction to citizens' juries directed to produce judgments on policy proposals). Nevertheless, most methods have similar characteristics and topic framings. Deliberative methods commonly share an emphasis on substantive input from a cross section of the public, along with the opportunity for preference change following sessions of collaborative problem-solving and active listening to other stakeholders' perspectives. Public engagement consultants typically combine a variety of deliberative, dialogic, and participatory methods over the course of a particular project. They may convene a working group of major stakeholders for a series of meetings, produce an interactive website and host a series of online dialogues, or design and host a town hall meeting where participants share ideas in small groups and then vote on the options that have been developed.

The responsibilities of the public engagement consultant typically involve all aspects of process design and implementation, including production of informational and marketing materials, stakeholder outreach prior to the process, selection of methods and issues to be addressed, recruitment of participants and small-group facilitators, facilitation of the overall process, continued communication with participants through newsletters and stakeholder management software, presentation to the client of process outcomes, and evaluation of process efficacy. Some aspects of these tasks, such as recruitment of underrepresented groups, process branding, and software design, may also be outsourced to subcontractors like opinion research firms and marketing firms for large projects, but most contractors provide the complete range of process design and facilitation services from inception to evaluation, which may last from a few months, in the case of public engagement on pandemic flu planning priorities, to ten years or more in the case of stakeholder collaborations on contaminated sites remediation or natural resource management.

Where did these new professionals come from? To find out, I conducted an online survey of dialogue and deliberation practitioners with sociologist Francesca Polletta, since the industry is so new that no one had done a comprehensive survey of everyone who identified with the field.[51] Our 2009 survey found that practitioners, typically in their fifties, arrived at their public deliberation work from a variety of different pathways, including community organizing, public relations, adult education, management consulting, and law. Practitioners draw on their experiences from all of these settings as they have constructed their products and services, borrowing techniques from participatory democracy, dispute resolution, and workplace participation and citing their training experiences in these fields as relevant to their current practice.[52] Many practitioners who are engaged in facilitation of public engagement on a regular basis nevertheless maintain footholds in other types of consulting; one practitioner, a frequent contractor for a national deliberation organization, describes how his work varies: "I wouldn't be surprised if I had 50 or 60 engagements of one sort or another over the course of a year. But you understand they vary enormously in magnitude, some of them are large [lists a four-day process with 1,500 participants and a one-day process engaging 1,000 participants in 15 cities]... but then at the same time I've got a lot of clients that are one-shot deals or coaching clients."[53]

There is no typical public engagement facilitation organization, as some practitioners work from within large departments of environmental engineering and development firms, some are self-employed sole practitioners, some have developed their practice within for-profit partnerships, and others work for major national nonprofits promoting a particular method. Half of US professionals in the practitioner survey described their organizational role as independent consultant or sole practitioner, with another 30% selecting staff member.[54] While self-employment is the norm, many individuals with private practices belong to or have founded multiple organizations to support their work, such that one firm is used for the practitioner's private coaching in deliberation facilitation, another is a larger institute in which the same practitioner is a partner who conducts research and carries out large-scale contracts for public processes, and still another is a boutique consultancy offering less high-profile facilitation services by the same practitioner to an assortment of public and private clients. On average, US professionals in the survey listed 1.7 organizational positions each. For this reason, the apparent heterogeneity in the field of public engagement organizations might be overstated by a focus on the organizations themselves. In understanding the multiplicity of individuals' affiliations, we can grasp both the usefulness for practitioners of distinguishing different types of work and the heterogeneity of individual practitioners' workload and client base.

It appears ironic that the solution to increasing professionalization in activism would be a new wave of experts in lay participation. Certainly, one could argue that the rise of the public engagement profession entails many of the trends that have so worried scholars concerned with declining civic capacity and the disempowering effects of expert knowledge. Professional facilitation is often nonlocal, as in the case of the facilitators at the Community Congress who had flown in from all over the United States to help. Such interventions may build public faith in the power of externally facilitated dialogue but fail to build locals' capacity to solve problems on their own or develop indigenous leadership skills. Leaders in the field are in most ways driving decision-making on important issues, with memberships in lesser roles as constituents to be mobilized when the moment is right, as in the case of participation in the Open Government online processes. But merely pointing out this irony doesn't help us to understand exactly why professional help is needed—this is skilled and delicate work, for which there is increasing demand from all sectors. As we will see in part II, public engagement practitioners are hired in part because they are highly aware of such tensions and know how to navigate their independence from local contexts with their support for locally driven decision-making.

## Privatized Accountability and the Widening Market for Public Deliberation

The workload of professional engagement facilitators has indeed gotten more diverse, especially in terms of the types of clients public delibera-tion consultants serve, no longer restricted to government administra-tors or community-based organizations. As activism professionalized in the twentieth century and citizen capacity for self-organization dimin-ished, the lines separating private business from the public interest have also blurred. The 1980s and 1990s ushered in an era of deregulation, privatization, and financialization, and market actors—corporations and the associations and organizations that support them—have become more powerful in relationship to local, state, and federal government. At the same time, in their management cultures and their promotional work, private corporations have increasingly adopted the civic trappings of empowerment facilitators and the solidarity of activists.[55]

Businesses have framed themselves as enablers of participatory poli-tics and even leaders of progressive reform. Private companies have been some of the most enthusiastic in jumping on the deliberation bandwagon and are often better positioned to buy the top-of-the-line services and software on offer from engagement consultants. Unilever's Dove promotes encounter-group-styled forums on "real beauty," and Shell sponsors dialogues on climate change. Media conglomerates host websites for citizen journalists to post their own videos. Participation is a valuable tool for connecting with consumers as audiences fragment, and companies are eager to harness social capital for their own purposes. One executive with the Advertising Research Foundation is quoted in the *New York Times* as saying, "With engagement, you're on your way to a relationship instead of just a sales transaction."[56] In a national study of twenty-first-century engagement, political scientist Cliff Zukin and his colleagues found that buycotting (purchasing a product to endorse a company's values or practices) was the most common nonelectoral engagement activity in their survey.[57] If traditional civic skills have declined, participatory innovations have brought into being the savvy, nimble-fingered citizen-consumer, who votes with her page clicks as well as her pocketbook. According to "digital utopian" narratives in the business press, citizen-consumers collaborate with benign corporate entities working to bring about social change.[58]

As such, corporate giants and their lobbies are now construed as part of a larger community of equally empowered stakeholders, with an interest in community politics and the public good just as, if not more, legitimate than not-for-profit civic associations and interest organizations.[59] Professional activists have themselves recognized that going directly to companies and encouraging them to regulate voluntarily can be more effective than targeting national governments whose administrations change on a regular basis; companies in turn have adopted many of these civic strategies in part because of their increased targeting by activists.[60]

Rather than pitched conflicts between unions and management or environmentalists and polluters, corporations have blurred the boundaries of public and private interests as they assume responsibility for ensuring their own accountability. Private actors have created certification standards and invested in community causes, and these efforts have not garnered the cynicism they might have in earlier eras.[61] Government is expected to bring the private sector to the decision-making table to solve public problems with market tools.[62] While this table may no longer be in a smoke-filled room, companies' ability to frame themselves as benevolent players and even leaders of participatory reform has shifted the balance of power away from government and social critics in consequential ways. Ironically, as business has become more powerful in relationship to the state, that power is increasingly understood as the will of the people.[63]

Despite the national and international scale of many organizations and associations engaged in deliberation, scholars often associate public deliberation processes with community-based nonprofits, with the exception of high-profile events conducted on behalf of governments and agencies at the state and national level (e.g., "CaliforniaSpeaks," a statewide process focused on health care reform in California). Political scientist Larry Jacobs, social policy scholar Fay Lomax Cook, and communications scholar Michael Delli Carpini argue in their book *Talking Together: Public Deliberation and Political Participation in America* that deliberation is "largely a local activity" and hardly a top-down phenomenon " 'imposed' on communities."[64] The data in my own survey support the assertion that much deliberation practice is carried out with nonprofits at the local level. Analysis of the specific categories of organizations sponsoring deliberation reveals that local governments and agencies slightly bested local nonprofits. Local and regional governments and community development corporations were most frequently selected as one of the top three sponsors for processes on which US professionals worked over the last two years, at 25%.[65] Local nonprofit groups were next, at 22% of all selections (figure 2.1). Certainly, local organizations and government actors at the community level account for a substantial proportion of demand for deliberation services.

But understanding demand for deliberation services in other sectors and at other scales is important to getting the full picture of the

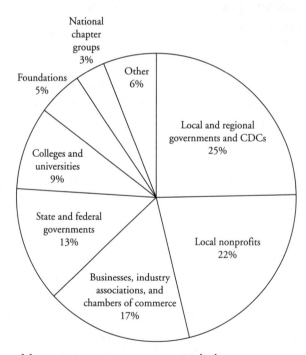

FIGURE 2.1. Most common process sponsors in the last two years, as a percentage of all selections by US professionals (2009 D&D practitioners survey; N = 660)

expansion of deliberative practice in the United States. Public deliberation consultants advertise their services to a wide variety of clients,
including private-sector clients, and nearly all deliberation consultants,
even ones specializing in the nonprofit sector, work with private organizations. The for-profit world is by no means anathema to deliberation
practitioners. In the survey, businesses, chambers, and industry trade
groups accounted for 17% of all client types selected, less than local
nonprofit groups, but not by much. Jacobs, Cook, and Delli Carpini
themselves found that deliberative events were sponsored by businesses
in 20% of cases.[66] An internal IAP2 survey found that "private sector"
actors were *primary* "customers, clients, and partners" for 16.2% of
respondents; this does not include those who selected clients of multiple
sectors.[67]

Why is this important to understanding the full scope of deliberation
practice? Private clients represent a small but important—and unusually remunerative—part of practitioners' client base. Scholars concerned
with dynamics within processes have similarly paid little attention to the
structure of deliberation contracting, in which clients with whom practitioners work directly to design processes may actually be separate from
the sponsors who are underwriting deliberation, like DaimlerChrysler
and the foundations supporting the Community Congresses for the
Unified New Orleans Plan. In describing nonpublic sponsors, Jacobs,
Cook, and Delli Carpini assert that deliberation is funded "by third
parties (government entities, foundations, and individuals) committed
to the public-interest contributions of these forums and to reducing the
costs to individuals of engaging in public talking."[68]

My own research has discovered a broader range of organizations that
subsidize public deliberation, and these groups typically fit the profile
of urban growth machine actors.[69] Foundations, community development corporations, and individual civic boosters play major roles, but
newspapers, television networks, banks and mortgage lenders, utilities,
health systems, universities, and residential and commercial real estate
developers also sponsor or underwrite public deliberation efforts on a
regular basis. The involvement of community actors heavily involved
in growth may result from the fact that growth management is often
the subject of public deliberation. Of US practitioners in the survey,
44% had facilitated on the specific topic of comprehensive community

planning over the last two years.[70] At larger scales, multinational corporations like Allianz have underwritten deliberative initiatives such as the "Tomorrow's Europe" deliberative poll, where international trade policy and other topics of clear interest to the company were on the table.

Thus far, if the deliberation literature has addressed the private sector at all, it has usually been in terms of either conflicts between market values and deliberative values or private-sector co-optation of the public sphere.[71] A substantial literature starting with Habermas documents general trends in incursions of private enterprise into the public sphere and their negative consequences on democratic politics and deliberative possibilities.[72] These scholars have been concerned that market logics are incompatible with civic life. Some critics have been extremely concerned about the negative implications of a market for deliberative processes, particularly in regard to the commodification of participatory products and services. David Mosse, both an academic and a practitioner on development projects, critiques the marketing of participatory development in a project with which he was involved: "'commodification' of participation was inadvertently helped by myself and other consultants."[73] Action researchers Elham Kashefi and Maggie Mort criticize "the extractive, incidental outputs of the consultation industry":

> This network of academics, market researchers, consultants, trainers, advisors, and public relations workers has an ever-increasing supply of new conferences, training workshops, toolkits, Do-It-Yourself Guides and How-To manuals to promote and sell; it has a plethora of fixed models of consultation that are formulaic and can be learned, packaged, and replicated without being contextualized or situated. The guaranteed output of this process is "the public view" in an unproblematic format, easily digestible by the policy process.[74]

Communications scholar David Ryfe describes market-oriented practitioners who "brandish a dizzying array of tools, guides, handbooks, and methods."[75] Political economist Erik Swyngedouw argues that, "while enabling new forms of participation," democratic governance reforms produce a "substantial democratic deficit" because "the democratic character of the political sphere is increasingly eroded by the encroaching imposition of market forces that set the 'rules of the game.'"[76]

Those who believe the market is destructive tend to assert that deliberation is inevitably contaminated by its encounter with the market. A deliberation industry is either impossibly ironic or oxymoronic. As sociologist Peggy Somers argues, "Pairing social together with capital actually threatens the very social relations upon which social capital depends."[77] These critiques have largely been speculative and focused on the specter of commercialization. Button and Ryfe indeed note that the field has "an entrepreneurial cast," in which process experts "are in the business of promoting deliberation—both as an abstract ideal and in the specific form of the models they employ."[78]

But explicit commodification of the "$5 per citizen"[79] kind common in fields like grassroots lobbying is certainly not endemic to the field. Given that deliberative processes can involve fewer than twenty or thousands of people, project expenses vary considerably, depending on the uses of technology and the extent to which participant and facilitator costs are subsidized by sponsors. Typical expenses associated with a daylong public engagement project using volunteer facilitators might include transportation, lodging, and staff time for deliberation consultants; advertising, marketing, and website expenses; outreach and recruitment costs; printing of project materials; site rental and catering for facilitator training; venue and set-up fees; audiovisual system expenses (lighting, stage, microphones, projection screens); meeting technologies (table laptops, wiring, and keypad systems); participant transportation; catering for participants (box lunches); day care, translation, and American sign language services; wheelchairs, assisted listening devices, and large-print materials; and participant stipends (often in the form of gift cards). A community forum of this sort facilitated by a leading consulting firm on behalf of local government and engaging 100 to 150 citizens would cost a sponsor approximately $40,000 to $50,000 total, with approximately $30,000 of the total paid to the deliberation firm and an additional $10,000 to $20,000 of direct costs (site rental and catering) and agency staff time.[80]

For more ambitious multicity events or multiday events engaging 1,000 to 1,500 participants, deliberation consulting firms might bill sponsors $185,000, the charge for "Bigger, Better, All Together," the multiday performing-arts-focused process that I observed with a research team of two other professors and ten graduate students. Considering the services, staff, and technology on offer, large-scale deliberative projects are a relative bargain for private sponsors; to put the $185,000 cost in perspective, the team employed to evaluate the same process billed $100,000. The 2009 practitioner survey found that the median cost for US deliberation practitioners' most recent project was considerably smaller than the figure for a networked one-day community forum, at $5,000,[81] which gives a picture of a field characterized by small local projects—the largely nonprofit-sponsored, local-level project type that has been described as predominant.[82]

However, the survey also found that the combined budgets reported by individual US survey respondents for their most recent project facilitated were $36 million.[83] Although most survey respondents (57%) were engaged in small-scale processes costing less than $10,000, a substantial minority (43%) of practitioners were engaged in processes costing more than $10,000; of that group, 17% were involved in processes costing more than $100,000. Given that the median number of projects facilitated by US respondents per year was eight, this figure demonstrates that, with a conservative estimate of annual project expenses at least in the low hundred millions, deliberation project revenue is somewhere between the much larger (by billions) grassroots lobbying industry and the comparable digital campaign consulting industry. These related consulting fields—the folks responsible for activating smokers' rights groups and Obama voters—have received far more substantial attention from scholars of participation industries in the public sphere.[84]

Although the dollar estimates for industry revenues are dwarfed by those in grassroots lobbying, the organizations served are some of the largest in the United States and internationally, the lay participants involved in formal deliberation represent at least a quarter of the adult US population,[85] and some of the decisions made—such as those over electoral reform in Canada or health care in California—can affect state and national policymaking, even if they involve only a few hundred or a few thousand people directly in actual meetings. This is very much a Fortune 500 phenomenon that has been embraced by elites and corporate executives internationally—deliberation is sponsored by the World Bank, the IMF, and the UN, as well as by the Ford Foundation, the Kettering Foundation, 3M, Kraft, Altria Group, a consortium of all the nonprofit performing arts organizations in the country, and many,

many other actors and consortia of similar stature and scope.[86] Those working in the field are oriented toward scaling up their practices to large groups, one of the reasons for their recurrent claims that they serve groups ranging from 10 people to 10,000 people. With international public relations firms like Edelman reframing their work as "public engagement" for the "conversation age" and the UK Conservative Party offering a 1-million-pound prize for the development of an online citizen participation platform, there can be no doubt that providers of products and services to facilitate deliberative engagement are facing the prospect of expansive growth in and steep competition for the public engagement facilitation market.[87]

Rather than presuming sinister motives or co-optation by private companies or other deliberative sponsors, this book investigates the reasons behind the increasing trend in private investment to actually produce opportunities for citizen engagement and the ways that market and deliberative values are being blended in actual practice. As grassroots lobbying scholar Edward Walker argues, there is far less literature on the topic of private sponsorship of engagement opportunities, perhaps due to researchers' sense that such processes are not authentic public engagement.[88] But an exclusive focus on private co-optation of the public sphere would limit our understanding of how public, nonprofit, and private-sector clients collaborate to produce public events and how political authenticity and protected civic space are exactly what public engagement practitioners are being paid to produce, for clients of all sectors. As we will see in part III, it is critical to understand how deliberation practitioners, highly conscious of the threat of commercialization, resist commodification even as they sell deliberative solutions to clients and the public.

## "What We Should Call What We Do": Defining Engagement Interventions

As the democracy reformers celebrating Obama's Open Government Initiative in January 2008 discovered, the professional work of selling the benefits of public engagement to clients and the public involves a navigation of different logics: administrative efficiency for administrators, democratic inclusion for the public. Balancing these logics while avoiding the perception of having sold out is an everyday concern and a matter of soul-searching for these reformers. Five months after the inauguration, at the "No Better Time Conference," a meeting organized by the Democracy Imperative and the Deliberative Democracy Consortium, participants have organized themselves to define their professional roles in a national landscape where *participation* has become a buzzword. Major movement leaders, including Carolyn Lukensmeyer from AmericaSpeaks, Martha McCoy from Everyday Democracy, and Pete Peterson from Common Sense California (later the Davenport Institute), mingle with local reformers and entrepreneurs promoting their dialogue software. Leading scholars of deliberation—and some "pracademics" like James Fishkin, a political science professor and founder of the Deliberative Poll—are on hand to discuss how the academy can advance the cause of deliberative democracy.

Despite the upbeat conference name, the mood on the last day of the conference, held at the University of New Hampshire, is a little dispirited. A day earlier, Peterson and others lamented the Obama administration's rollout of participatory techniques. While the transparency part of the Open Government Directive seemed secure, with online transparency movement activists elevated to positions of real power, the White House had not tapped any of the leaders at the conference for significant roles in the administration. Instead, its renamed Office of Public Engagement (formerly Public Liaison) and its new Office of Social Innovation and Civic Participation were stocked with private-sector middle managers, public relations executives, and corporate litigators. The head of the Office of Public Engagement was a manager from Google Finance, and the head of the Office of Social Innovation and Civic Participation was another Google veteran, with stints in corporate philanthropy at Goldman Sachs and the Treasury Department.

Online wikis designed to solicit feedback on open government were confusing and overwhelming, and got vote-bombed by conspiracy-minded birthers questioning Obama's right to be president. Many posts exemplified the vituperative political climate that deliberative democrats were trying to overcome with new and improved processes. In a post titled "HOW TO DELETE ASSHOLE LIBERAL COMMENTS," fd43wv gave his fellow conservatives tips on silencing opponents by using the self-moderating system designed to encourage civil discourse in the forum: "OPEN THE COMMENTS AND CLICK ON MARK AS ABUSE. ... WE HEAR ENOUGH FROM THESE ASSHOLE FAGGOTS SO START DELETING!" The administration's weak embrace of the deliberation community and the explosive rage they encountered from some segments of the public that they work to empower had precipitated vigorous dialogue at the conference.

Using their own methods, members of the field engage in round-table discussions on their framing problem: "what we should call what we do." Conversation has bogged down, and Matt Leighninger, an organizer of the conference, listens as participants critique the current names for the democratic reforms they are seeking. The ivory-tower standby, "deliberative democracy," seems holier-than-thou for the masses, and "shared governance" and "collaborative decision-making" are deemed too technocratic. Everyday Democracy is already the brand name of one of the organizations attending the conference. Other options are variously too New Agey, too dry, too progressive, or too apolitical. There isn't one term that describes all the changes they are talking about that will appeal to different audiences. Democratic participation and its varied terminology seem to have tremendous turn-off potential, which is difficult to accept within a group so turned on by its promise to transform people's lives. Leighninger, usually infectiously peppy, looks exhausted and shrugs. January's soufflé of excitement about open government was deflated in the stifling atmosphere of a stagnant economy and the practical challenges facing an administration battered by multiple crises. The fact that there is no name for what dialogue and deliberation experts do, or no name they can agree on, is actually quite important. The field of public engagement is extremely difficult to define, still developing, and diverse; this quality makes studying it interesting, and it also tells us something about why deliberative interventions are so popular. Fields still undefined can use resources from lots of other fields and can be many things to many people.

Despite scholars' excitement about deliberation as an alternative to the current state of partisan politics, distinguishing real public engagement or authentic civil society is nearly impossible, if not quixotic and out of step with the kinds of creations public engagement professionals construct and the kinds of meetings and activism in which participants engage on a regular basis, both online and off. If we were to define public deliberation as only sponsored by government or as only sponsored by local nonprofits, or if we focused only on case studies of high-profile projects like Community Congress III, we would miss many of those processes where some of the most well-funded public deliberation work is being done, with very different goals and for very different audiences. Because facilitation professionals cross all of those settings, and publics may encounter deliberation at their workplaces as well as in their community, it is important to understand public engagement as an extremely wide-ranging set of practices without clear boundaries.

The fact that public engagement can be used in any number of different sectors, sometimes at the same time, is critical to understanding its scope and significance. In her book *The Language of the Heart: A Cultural History of the Recovery Movement from Alcoholics Anonymous to Oprah Winfrey*, cultural historian Trysh Travis describes the "category-confounding complexity" of Americans' understanding of recovery: "The energies that animate it spring from religious history, from the republican tradition of mutual aid, from progressive notions of identity and community, and from secular and commercial discourses of self-improvement."[89] This blurring of different influences is increasingly a feature of contemporary life, from corporate culture to think tanks.[90] In many ways, the borrowing and blending of different discourses, logics, and sources of authority, whether therapeutic, political, judicial, or academic, enables certain cultural forms to slip into everyday life in unnoticed ways.[91]

A book investigating the blended practices and discourses that constitute contemporary Americans' civic life must define relevant terms with these complex and shifting meanings in mind. The term *public engagement* is used here to refer to facilitation services aimed at engaging the public and relevant stakeholders with organizations in more intensive ways than traditional, one-way public outreach and information. Public engagement processes can range from two-way dialogue meetings to deliberation processes that give lay participants an opportunity to learn about and discuss preferences regarding administrative decisions. The aggregated input resulting from participatory and deliberative processes provides rich information to administrators on participant preferences and, in cases where decision-making power is turned over to participants, may determine the course of organizational action. The terms

*public engagement, public participation,* and *public deliberation* are typically used interchangeably in the field to refer to the broad spectrum of
reforms aimed at intensifying public participation and deliberation in
governance, and this book uses all three terms to reflect their overlapping usage by practitioners. Matt Leighninger notes: "In common usage,
'deliberation and democratic governance' = active citizenship = deliberative democracy = citizen involvement = citizen-centered work = public
engagement = citizen participation = public dialogue = collaborative
governance = public deliberation. Different people define these terms
in different ways—and in most cases, the meanings are blurry and
overlapping."[92]

Throughout the book, I describe the organizations and people
involved in public engagement facilitation variously as a movement,
field, industry, and profession, depending on the characteristics and
subgroups to which I refer. A brief definition of these objects of analysis
and their limitations as explanatory categories is worthwhile here. I use
the term *industry* to refer to the for-profit and nonprofit actors paid
to supply public engagement facilitation services and products, such as
software, instructional materials, and audience response systems. I use
the terms *clients* and *sponsors* to describe the for-profit, nonprofit, and
public entities who pay facilitation providers for their services—the
demand side of the industry. *Client* typically refers to the administrative entity in which stakeholders have a stake and with which facilitators work to define the goals and scope of the process. *Sponsor* refers
to clients paying for facilitation and also to third parties who may
underwrite or donate some portion of either the costs of facilitation to
clients or the costs of participation to stakeholders, such as participant
stipends, child care, translation services, or venue fees. Sponsors' role
in providing direct and indirect support of stakeholder participation is
termed a *subsidy*, inasmuch as it reduces the costs in time, resources, and
capacity for participants to engage in participatory processes.[93] *Profession*
refers specifically to organizations and educational institutions offering
training and degree programs, trained practitioners paid for their work
in deliberation facilitation, and their professional associations and occu-
pational networks; *volunteer* refers to those amateur and professional
facilitators who provide services at no cost to clients and sponsors. *Field*
refers to the professionals, volunteers, and organization types just listed

but also more broadly to the academics, institutes, foundations, and other organizations that share a common language, set of practices, and interest in advancing public engagement.

These distinctions are made with the recognition that, in a contemporary landscape characterized by blending and blurring, a given organization may be a stakeholder, client, sponsor, professional institution, and field actor simultaneously.[94] A university, for example, may provide an institutional home for researchers of deliberation and train future public engagement practitioners, while it also sponsors deliberative dialogues on local planning as a community stakeholder and is a client of practitioners using participatory methodologies to conduct internal strategic planning. An analytic approach that makes strict distinctions among profit orientations, sectors, and organizational types may actually obscure the interactions and discourses centered on public engagement.[95] Actor categories used in the field, such as *pracademic* (an academic engaged in participatory practice) or *social entrepreneurship* (a combination of enterprise and social activism), reveal that distinct identity affiliations and sector domains often retain their relevance insofar as they provide readily accessible value paradigms and discourses for blending or transporting logics across multiple organizations, professions, and fields. By figuring out where those gaps and disconnects happen, as well as where they are smoothly integrated, we can learn much more about the blended settings of contemporary civic life.

## Deliberation as an Ephemeral Practice and as a Bureaucratic Form

> Public life is too important to be left solely to the professionals.
>
> Bill Bradley, from the Foreword to Matt Leighninger's
> *The Next Form of Democracy* (2006: xiii)

In its communitarian emphasis on democracy as problem-solving, public deliberation seems perfectly suited to the pragmatic ambitions and less partisan tone of a small-*d* democratic and small-*r* republican time. Public, private, and nonprofit domains of action that formerly were distinguished by their separate goals and values have increasingly centered on a hybrid field of business and politics where market

competition and public cooperation are believed to be complementary social goods. Public deliberation, as a new civic form that brings
together interest group representatives, activists, and laypersons as equal
participants in decision-making sponsored by public administrators,
foundations, and corporations, reflects both the professionalization of
activism and the reframing of corporate citizenship described earlier.
This new species of governance has found a comfortable niche in the
multi-institutional habitats of the twenty-first century.[96]

These new processes are quite literally popular with a wide swath
of the electorate, indicating that scholars' excitement over the new
public engagement is not overblown. Despite resistance in the Open
Government participation process, participant satisfaction rates for 21st
Century Town Meetings like the Community Congresses are typically
above 90 percent.[97] While social entrepreneurs have been spreading their
deliberative techniques, methods, and software around the country,
formerly fusty institutions like cooperative extensions and libraries have
been joining the participation choir and getting a new lease on life.
Handbooks and training courses try to meet the explosive demand of
local officials and community groups seeking templates for conducting
such experiments in their own cities and towns.[98] Foundations have
gotten in on the act by promoting process innovations and even letting
the public choose grant recipients.[99] Obama's top-down command
that the feds get ready for bottom-up religion on day one is no accident. Twenty-first-century participation is avowedly postpartisan,
pro-government, pro-business, pro-civil society, pro-people.[100]   *irony?*

How did the new public engagement become professionalized?
The answer, as articulated in this book, is relatively easily and seemingly without the notice of most political theorists concerned with how
to counter elite power with democratic innovations. I argue that the
efforts of public engagement professionals to protect their practice from
professionalization and commercialization—and the unintended consequences of those efforts—should be understood in reference to each
other. As politically problematic entities, public deliberation experts can
help us to understand the larger contradictions of living within institutions in late capitalism. By taking a step back from fine-grained analyses
of the discursive content of deliberations, and by placing the engagement industry in the context of neoliberal management policies and

corporate reform strategies, we can gain a better perspective on those consequences and contradictions. But we can also see how they are produced by highly intelligent, self-conscious, and self-critical agents who may reinforce elite power even as they challenge elites to change. The next chapter begins at the level of individual action and language by investigating how public engagement practitioners skillfully integrate different kinds of logics as they describe their entry into the field and the inspirations for their practice.

# PART II

## PROCESS EVANGELISTS

Spreading the Gospel of Deliberation

# 3

## Challenging Enemy Institutions

"STAND UP EVERYBODY AND SHAKE it out. We're going to give you some techniques for listening with your whole bodies and minds. Let's start out with thinking caps! Rub your ears, Julia is going to demonstrate for all of us. Doesn't that feel good? Okay, now we're going to do energy yawns and John is going to demonstrate for us up here. Rub your jaws. I want you to do three fake yawns until you do a real yawn. Okay, lazy eights! Trace those infinity signs around your closed eyes. This activates listening and your heart. Feel that stretch. Shake it out" (figure 3.1).[1] As I dutifully traced my fingers around my eyes along with 300 other people, I wondered what I had gotten myself into. My tolerance for "get to know you" warm-ups and group exercises has always been limited— and I immediately realized at my first extended stay among dialogue and deliberation professionals that I would be in for some mild discomfort. But if this felt like a familiar exercise from YMCA day camp, it was also a misleading picture of the field, and the series of impressions I would get at the conference would later be revealed, on the one hand, as critical and, on the other, as initially deceptive. As I would discover, the relationship practitioners had with New Age whole-body exercises like this was fraught with tension—and in fact caused at least some small portion of the stress that we were shaking out that morning in August 2006 (figure 3.2).

I had headed to San Francisco for my first conference, excited to explore this field and to see if dialogue and deliberation practitioners would be willing to talk to me. I was interested in studying engagement

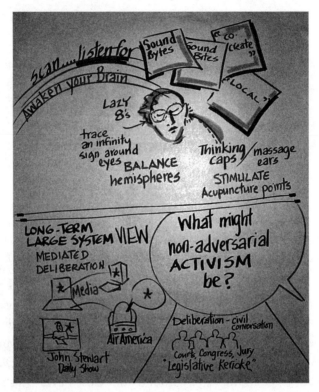

FIGURE 3.1. Professional graphic recorders illustrate portions of dialogue in real time on large pieces of butcher paper that are later posted around the room so the group can see what they discussed.
Photo by author.

professionals because of the ways in which the hype about inclusive engagement had not really seemed to match its disappointing results in my prior research. Who were these people who could maintain so much positivity in the face of frustration? At first glance, they seemed to be idealists awed by the power of deliberation—treating it as "an enchanted object, the product of forces greater" than themselves.[2] I would learn that they were also deeply pragmatic and working out their relationship to this enchanted object in front of each other—and that I would have to work out my relationship to it in front of them as well.

At the beginning of a project, the first thing one begins to discover are the cultural lifeways and behavioral dispositions of individuals in the group one is studying—what Pierre Bourdieu calls the habitus—summed

FIGURE 3.2. Using graphic recorders at public engagement conferences allows practitioners to use facilitation techniques on themselves and enables graphic recorders to advertise their services to other facilitators.

Photo by author.

up by the ways that white-collar professionals might feel comfortable tracing infinity signs around their eyes, while a group of firefighters would feel ridiculous doing so.[3] What are the "habits of judgment and evaluation" public engagement professionals use to look at the world?[4] How do their shared professional lingo and moral discourses reveal their collective knowledge and taken-for-granted assumptions about the world? Where do conflicts arise, and what do those conflicts reveal? In this chapter, I introduce readers to dialogue and deliberation practitioners through my own first total immersion in their world, supplemented with data gathered in my subsequent investigations. I discuss shared meanings, common traits, and textures of their interactions and specifically investigate the striking complexity of their conversations—those areas where they vigorously debate who they are, what they stand for, and how they go about making change while they make a living.

I find that the blending of different logics and discourses described in chapter 1, in part a result of the blurring of public and private described in chapter 2, is not always easy-going work for people at ground level. Scholars have focused on deliberation as an empowering political intervention, a reconstruction of an uncommercialized, equitable public sphere. But this is not just a problem because the empowerment deliberation produces is enacted through top-down strategies by an industry of private professionals.[5] To understand public engagement today, we need to understand how deliberation draws on logics besides those of progressive empowerment and informed citizenship—including commercial discourses, New Age self-help, and "mind cures" emphasizing the power of positivity to attract not just individual well-being, but community wealth. Despite democracy scholars' avoidance of the spiritual discourses of deliberation, these are ever-present in the dialogue and deliberation community—from eagle visioning to infinity-sign tracing.

Illuminating these connections is not enough to understand how deliberation is practiced by informed professionals. We also need to understand the contested status of New Thought positivity and New Age religiosity, and of progressive discourse itself, for those who make dialogue their profession. The power of positive thinking is not always an easy sell, and deliberation professionals are extremely wary of falling into "the New Age trap." That they care so much about balancing hope and pragmatism, and share their strategies for doing so with each other, enables us to get a sense of the seriousness and sense of humor they bring to the field.

It can also help us to understand how people acting within contemporary institutions negotiate a mishmash of logics and strategies endemic to postmodern, neoliberal organizational life. As Nina Eliasoph points out, participants in empowerment projects—short-term, state- and NGO-funded participatory democracy initiatives aimed at empowerment on a rapid funding schedule—are taught how to "decipher ... the puzzles of active citizenship in a society with an elusive, scrambled state."[6] Logics, as understood here, are coherent systems of organizing principles that guide action within market and state institutions;

Eliasoph notes that this set of principles may be externally coherent but contain internal tensions, as when empowerment projects aim "to promote grassroots, local, multicultural, inclusive and open, participatory, empowering, personalized, voluntary community."[7]

On the one hand, facilitators are engaged in explicit attempts to make decision-making more participatory, more equitable, more diverse, more responsive to lay knowledge, more creative, more flexible, and less hierarchical. On the other hand, as those charged with bringing a contained, manageable form of democratic process within the bureaucracy of existing formal organizations, public engagement practitioners are driven by the rationalizing logics of the institutions they work for— making deep democracy less messy, more formal, more specialized, more professional, more standardized, and more accountable.[8]

These contradictions matter for public engagement consultants as they develop accounts of their actions and methods and construct a stable professional identity. As one practitioner pointed out in a listserv discussion:

> Everyone who does this work of citizen engagement understands that the design of public engagement mechanisms is wrought with difficult trade offs about values that we all care about. We care about diversity and reaching those who normally do not have a voice. We care about public influence and impact. We care about informed participation and judgment ... the list goes on. Unfortunately, it is generally the case that as practitioners we must make strategic and tactical choices that try to find some balance between these often competing values. More often than not, a strategic choice about the length of a forum, the structure of a question or the recruitment tactics used to get people in a room put values that we care about into conflict.

As described in chapter 1, observing those tensions can reveal much about the fraught place of public engagement in the contemporary political landscape and in everyday organizational life. But blending and selecting from logics may also cause conflict for less obvious reasons, as when sets of cultural assumptions or class distinctions are embedded in seemingly benign terminology and practices. New Age philosophies and progressive politics were both hot potatoes for practitioners, inasmuch as they felt comfortable for facilitators but could turn off potential participants. Was that the practitioners' problem or the participants'? Debates in the field about how best to introduce concepts, strategies, and deliberative values into hostile territories were vibrant and open.

## Entering the Field

In my earlier research on regional land conservation networks, it was clear whom to talk to since major players in the region had known each other for decades and sometimes even shared office space. Entering the field, as sociologists and anthropologists call beginning a project at a new research site, has a standard set of challenges, but in this case there was no clear site to study because I wanted to study the organizations and professionals all over the country doing work on public engagement. Studying professionals who are spread out in this way offered a whole new set of issues, even as their professional networks were dense and their friendships strong. The difference was that, instead of running into each other in the grocery store or at a charity benefit, these facilitators chatted with each other on the National Coalition for Dialogue and Deliberation listserv and on webinars and flew across the country to see each other at professional meetings. I would need to become like George Clooney's character in *Up in the Air* or like the conference addict in David Lodge's novel about academic meetings, at home in the airport shuttle buses and conference hotel bars that make up the routine of peripatetic white-collar lives.[9] I started with the conference of the National Coalition for Dialogue and Deliberation, held in San Francisco in August 2006.

Studying a professional conference presents its own challenges. Everyone is colocated for an incredibly intense few days, which is very convenient, but there are multiple simultaneous events happening from morning until night, and the classic conference anxiety that something important is happening wherever you are not is even stronger when you are a researcher. First, I knew that participants would not be able to give me time for interviews; time is pressed and conference coffee shop settings and bars are chaotic and noisy—a hailstorm of interrupted discussions and hail fellows well met. Like any researcher entering the field, I planned on observing as unobtrusively as I could, but to offer something back to the group and introduce myself and my project to conference organizers, I volunteered by e-mail to help out for a few hours at the reception desk and to take photos of the proceedings and attendees.

The Parc 55 in San Francisco is a characteristic specimen of overpriced conference chain hotels in downtown locations, with its second-floor lobby, tasteless hard candies, cut-crystal water glasses, and smoked-glass chandeliers. But despite the conventional location, the software exhibits, and the standard-issue coffee breaks, the 300-plus-person National Coalition for Dialogue and Deliberation Conference is far less dry than typical industry get-togethers. No expense-account meals and regimented rounds of pontification and passive listening here. Public engagement conferences are dedicated to soliciting the active participation of everyone present, making everyone feel at home and accommodated, and supporting community building that many have waited years to bring into being at substantial personal cost.

Many deliberation practitioners are independent consultants pushing a sometimes-lonely path for change in their communities. The smiles and excitement, the announcement board, and the listening corner contribute to the feel of a cozy, exceedingly well-organized family reunion. Indeed, organization president Sandy Heierbacher and her husband, Andy, were warm presences at the meeting, as were other familial pairs, like a couple who founded a group for Jewish-Palestinian dialogue and a mother-daughter team of graphic recorders who illustrate the discussions for the larger group. The body language in the pictures I took show attendees leaning their heads on each other's shoulders, throwing their arms around each other, and laughing or grinning. Often when I asked to take a picture, the subjects would borrow my camera and take one of me and whomever else was standing around.

At many professional conferences, attendees stalk the halls with name badges decorated with ribbons indicating their officer positions and affiliations: chest decorations that are surreptitiously scanned in silent elevator rides to the next plenary. At the NCDD conference, organizers had purchased a range of ribbons participants could choose to attach to their name badges at the registration desk, including "FIRST TIME ATTENDEE," "ROCKSTAR," "ASK ME," "Hablo Español," and "HERE TO SERVE." One attendee supplemented these with homemade "LOVE CHOCOLATE" and "CAN'T STOP" ribbons. This sense of letting one's hair down and getting real among friends and strangers, of not taking oneself too seriously, made it easy to feel at home quickly.

I spent the long plane flight to the NCDD 2006 conference poring over the conference schedule and figuring out how to choose from forty-four workshops in three days. During any one workshop session, ten others were going on. Because I was interested in what was new about D&D, I tended to choose sessions that were not specific to mediation and conflict environments—many scholars have already studied the mediation field. I tried to make sure I had talked to all of the presenters at some point during the conference, and there were open houses on methods that allowed for an introduction to the various methods and approaches. I also attended a one-day preconference training on choosing methods that work, which allowed me to get a head start on the lay of the land, get to know some practitioners in an intimate setting, and gain a drive-by familiarity with various methods. Looking back, it's an indication of how well the conference was run that I could get such a wide perspective on the field in only three days.

But I needn't have worried about the typical conference habit of feeling guilty for sneaking out of a session—an act whose social shame, once one is safely out the door, is leavened by the sweet relief of forty-five minutes of life reclaimed from a droning presenter or dull topic. In fact, conferences like the NCDD's are based on the same idea of faith in self-organization that has produced unconferences, unmeetings, and barcamps. Some of the sessions explicitly abided by "the law of two feet": if you are at a session or discussion where you don't have much to contribute, go elsewhere. Having permission to move on was strangely liberating, at the same time that it encouraged those present to think about why they were there and what they wanted from the session. Although I bounced around during Open Space and product demos, I didn't leave a single session for another because the ones I had chosen were so engrossing.

Not only did the conference give me an introduction to the major methods in the field and its reigning easygoing, friendly, but direct ethos, it also gave me an appreciation of what these people dedicated to the power of conversation were like. Because they were so disarmingly open, my sense of who they were and what they cared about developed very quickly. Funny, reflective, self-critical, idealistic, they were open and generous but had the tough-mindedness that comes from a commitment to fairness. Quick to solve a problem themselves or to point out something that needed improvement, they were scrupulously attentive to power inequalities and sleights of hand. They had a therapist's unflappability in quietly absorbing difficult stories of violence and hardship but a rare resistance to hurried communications or ignoring a potential misunderstanding.

Wherever there was ambiguity or room for multiple interpretations, they immediately noticed, stopped, and asked for explanation or drew out an elaboration that could change the direction of discussion entirely. Because of this attention to subtle missed connections in conversation, dialogue and deliberation practitioners actually argue a lot, and openly, over what is taken for granted in their field, debates I unpack in this chapter in detail. Not least, because they are so deeply rooted in the everyday work of discussion, practitioners are acutely sensitive to the niceties of tone and bodily comforts. My earlier research had investigated how meetings over a shared, home-cooked meal helped collaborators to see each other in the round; this group was very attentive to whether there was cold water and whether the coffee was hot and properly brewed (the Parc 55 fell down on the job on that score, to vocal protest).

The professional consultants from California, the nonprofit executive from Connecticut, the minister from Texas, the rural development expert from North Dakota, the academic from Colorado, the foundation executive from New York City, the think tank staffer from D.C., the therapist from Virginia, the EEO officer from Nevada, the deliberation organization staffer from northeastern Ohio: what drew these diverse people together, and what perspectives did they share? A participatory art project run by a New York City artists' collaborative dedicated to "interactive public art" gave attendees at the Parc 55 the "opportunity to share your advice on D&D, life, love, or anything else" in three enormous suggestion boxes toted around by a jolly team of three. The board of suggestions, posted on a wall at the conference, contained everything from the silly ("I would like to have stuffing more often—not just at Thanksgiving") to the pointedly political to the literal and gave a useful introduction to the varied preoccupations and prevailing mindset of the group.

As cultural historian Trysh Travis points out, activities like the suggestion box may seem like calls to political and social action—small steps that might lay the groundwork for more substantive political conversations—and indeed there was political talk on the cards submitted, which provided rich grounds for conversation for those milling around. While fifteen suggestions and compliments were directed to conference organizers about keeping up the great work, improving the quality of the coffee, the cold weather in San Francisco, and the affordability of the hotel, six suggestions related directly to dialogue or the deliberation community:

- Each voice counts—I want to hear all—Let's co-create deep conversations ♥
- If you want more intimacy in your dialogue come to room 2055
- Send our kind waves into universe
- We need to talk about how our works connect with the work of people from Africa
- More dialogue, less fighting
- Use art and music to teach teamwork and cooperation

Another twelve suggestions contained recommendations for collective political change:

- Violent revolution to overthrow capitalism. Right on!
- Let's end world poverty
- Give children the power to control their own education.
- You need to set Hezbolah + the Israelis at this conference so they can learn to sit and talk in a peaceful manner
- Less propaganda, more free press. Don't believe the myth that we have free press here.
- Hold council of women + youth before making any world choices.
- That everyone in sf would ride their bikes to work
- Spend our tax $ on schools, universal healthcare and other useful services rather than preemptive wars
- National public works program for unemployed and homeless people.

- Let's all find ways to help the environment
- MORE COFFEE STATIONS, FIRE BUSH!
- To raise voting rates, Americans should be <u>fined</u> if they don't vote. Crazy? They do it in Australia and have a 98% voting rate!

Seventeen more suggestions focused on individual actions to make the world a better place:

- Check your email daily and respond brilliantly
- When you pray... Dance
- Learn to laugh at yourself
- Vote based on the needs of your neighbors, rather than your own
- BREATHE
- DANCE
- LISTEN!
- Eat and buy fresh food! Exercise daily
- Say the things you need to say to the people you love before they're gone
- HAVE FUN
- My suggestion is for everyone to reserve one night every week just for your family—"Family Night-In" or "Family Home Evening." From small things, great things can happen!
- Keep smiling! ☺
- LOVE A LOT LAUGH A LOT
- Hugs... unlimited, free
- People should talk more about the importance of love in our lives— and move that to <u>action</u>!
- MORE HATS—<u>WAY</u> MORE HATS
- I loved the guy on the street yesterday who said he was going to arrest me for looking too seriously—more reminders to smile!

I was intrigued that this conference brought together peaceful suggestions about sending kind waves into the universe, hugging, and dancing with conflict-oriented suggestions like overthrowing capitalism, ending poverty, and firing Bush. The latter, liberal sentiments were wholly familiar for a sociologist who teaches Marx to college students. But the former sentiments drew on less familiar territory like art therapy, and felt light—the "power of positive thinking" talk that Barbara Ehrenreich maligns in her book *Bright-Sided*.[10]

As I got acclimated to the world of engagement professionals, I saw these diverse sentiments reflected throughout the conference and the field. The staunch leftist politics were illustrated in the independent bookstore's stall, with handbooks and guides to dialogue and deliberation sharing space with books on socialism; treatises on economic, social, and racial justice from scholars of the left like Patricia Hill Collins; critiques of consumer culture and suburban sprawl; and older classics like Paulo Freire's *Pedagogy of the Oppressed*. The idealistic ambitions for world harmony and the notion that change begins with small actions to create happiness, love, and joy in your personal life were present throughout the conference in the stories that participants told about how dialogue had changed their personal lives such that they wanted to share that revelation with others.

I didn't know it at the time and may not have even noticed it as I scanned the jumble of mundane and lofty sentiments on the suggestion board, but the toggling there between individual action rooted in hope and structural issues requiring collective solutions is a recurrent tension throughout this book and in the field of public engagement generally—a tension that is explicitly articulated and defines the practical dispositions of the actors in the field. Balancing these productively is an everyday struggle for those trying to put bread on their own tables, and practitioners resolve those problems in different ways, by using resources from their varied experiences.

## Journeys from Social Activism to Institutional Change

I grab lunch on the first day of the conference with some new acquaintances I made through the plenary earlier that morning and the Conversation Café demonstration the night before. Rebecca is a white woman in her early fifties, recently divorced after a twenty-five-year marriage, living in Berkeley, and chatty about herself and her interests. David is shy and tall, in his early thirties, with a thatch of light-colored hair that makes him look younger than he is. Immediately we start talking about why we are at the conference and when we learned about dialogue and deliberation. David went to a Quaker school growing up but tried on many interests as he found his calling: neuroscience, hydroponic gardening, band manager. Rebecca got here by getting in a fight with her landlady over rhododendrons and going to a mediation, where she loved the process. She laughs at her revelation: "You can keep the money, I want this!" She dreams about running an intergenerational Conversation Café with her son, a documentary filmmaker.

Origin stories were extremely important for dialogue and deliberation professionals as they explained how they came to their work, and D&D conferences generally included many invitations to reflect on these pathways to the field. Before the 2006 NCDD conference, participants were e-mailed a list of announcements, including this one: "If you think you may want to create a Peace Tile at the conference, Lars and Nil suggest you 'bring a letter, photograph or miscellaneous paper items that tell a little bit about the story of how you got into the dialogue and deliberation field. Bring something personal, that you would like to share. Something that sheds light on a personal experience that propelled you into this work. You will be invited to use these items in a shared arts activity.'" In a FutureSearch exercise of "Discovering the Collective Story That Brought Us Here Today" to start off the 2006 conference, NCDD participants mapped their personal trajectories and the evolution of NCDD on a "journey wall" after telling their stories in pairs and then fours. Scholars like Eva Illouz and Carole Cain have studied the role of narratives of self-discovery and recovery in therapeutic culture, as individuals reincorporate organizational knowledge into their own self-understandings and self-presentations.[11] By listening to others tell their stories and practicing their own versions, participants develop coherent narratives of their transformation to deliberation that emphasize particular aspects over others. I noted the themes in these stories as I became familiar with them.

The origin stories of public engagement professionals reflect logics of empowerment rooted in experiences with grassroots activism in the 1960s. As the brief history in chapter 2 indicates, public engagement as a *distinct* field of practice is very young (about thirty years old), but the median age of US D&D practitioners in the 2009 Dialogue and Deliberation Practitioners Survey was 55 (N = 341). Despite its recent development as a professional field, rooting the origins of professional practice in emotionally empowering, spiritually awakening, or cognitively liberating[12] experiences in the 1960s was critically important for many NCDD conference attendees. Of the survey respondents,[13] 45% reported prior experience in community organizing or social activism. One panelist introduced herself at an NCDD conference by stating: "I am a child of the sixties and I grew up as an adversarial activist. ... The evolution of [my methodology] in our living room has been a spiritual journey of learning about what non-adversarial activism actually might be in giving people democratic voice. And that's why I do this work." This linking of New Age personal histories and 1960s-era radicalism was explicitly made throughout professional discussion settings and credited as the basis of current participatory practice.

Conference participants often referenced an "evolution" from the tumultuous 1960s. Autobiographical comments on the emergence of interest in the field connect contemporary public engagement principles to both grassroots movements and social activism following political awakenings in the 1960s. Thirteen of twenty-eight comments in the discussion following a reflective panel (as recorded in a blog transcript) were explicitly or implicitly sixties-themed, including:

> "I was there in the 60's, Participatory Democracy & the War on Poverty."...
> "Viral Spread—It all started with me going to a dialogue group."...
> "Drive for connectedness in the 60s."...
> "Motivation—What motivated each of us to make changes—My anger & dissatisfaction in the 60's over women's rights issue."

Conference participants' personal narratives culminated in hard-won pragmatism about the best strategies for "systems change." This pathway into the field was synthesized through report-out sessions as follows: "*Listening for patterns*—Emerging patterns for D & D—In the 60's—Adversary based. In the 70's—Internal Inner and personal development. In the 80s—Mediation. In the 90's—Corporations and Love of technology with Networks (the internet). 2000—Building on this—the whole system in the room."[14] Activism and political awakening in the 1960s gave way to personal discovery in the 1970s. By the 1980s and 1990s, organizational innovations in mediation and the corporate world were attracting their attention and energies, and the 2000s have been a time of bringing together and integrating all of those currents of their lives.

The transition from opposing institutions to attempting to work for them was a clear concern for practitioners and an area where they saw a need for a mature, accepting outlook appropriate to the twenty-first century. This was phrased as a movement "from being anti-institutions -> To asking how can we institutionalize what we've been about?" Large-scale systems change—the preoccupation of consultants as the dominant narrative of the 2000s—was directly linked to learning from the 1960s about the limits of activism and the additive power of evolutionary, microscale transformations. One listserv contributor describes how the education system needs to be transformed by referring to his personal experience in the 1950s and 1960s:

> Growing up in the South in the 1950's and participating in the achingly slow demise of segregation, I learned that government action was necessary-but-not-sufficient ... it took thousands of "experiments" by individuals and organizations to make it REAL. I trust the self-correcting capacity of all living systems to do what needs to be done to stay alive.

Moderating critiques of institutions and seeing public officials as human beings was part of an animating project—organizations and fields were dynamic, "living systems," worthy of respect. One panelist, an academic, cautioned: "Let's be careful about saying 'Them' when talking about government. ... Embrace the connections to other institutions no matter how much you want to get rid of them." Another, a method pioneer, said: "I've spent a lot of time with 'them.' My hope around system change—there are great people working in all these enemy institutions. ... How can we help these pioneers inside of these tough institutions to keep courage?"

In becoming professional consultants to institutional clients, participation facilitators were willing to abandon adversarial mobilization techniques and work for incremental change, but remained conscious of the progressive beliefs and social protest experiences that had inspired their personal journeys. One participant summed this up in a way that resonated throughout the conference, in theatrical summaries of conference quotes by the roving "theme team," in report-outs, and in index-card commentary on walls: "We're between two worlds—an old way which is dying and a new world which is being conceived and is emerging but is not quite here yet. This conference is part of birthing the gazelle."[15] The transcendent beauty of that metaphor was inspirational for many attendees.

In their narratives of self, public engagement professionals were careful to note an evolution of their perspectives, and a willingness to consider ideological opponents and "enemy" institutions in less adversarial ways. In vibrant, ongoing dialogues, public engagement professionals accept complexity and difficulty in their work, describing their evolution from considering institutions as abstract enemies to institutions inhabited by well-meaning and even courageous actors, not just dominant elites.

## The "New Age Trap": Negotiating Political and Spiritual Logics

While sharing their own experience as a model of the personally transformative effects of engagement was an overriding interest for many practitioners, those concerned with expanding the profession took care to downplay progressive rhetoric or practices borrowed from participatory social activism and New Age spirituality. Such discourses were often seen as overlapping but sometimes seen as usefully opposed to each other. NCDD founder Sandy Heierbacher notes that "too much idealism can really turn some people off" and describes carefully balancing her desire to make the conference fun with her desire that newcomers not read public engagement as politicized mobilization. Heierbacher describes her attempts to curb "progressivism"—and particularly associations between progressivism and the arts—for those more oriented toward conservatism or the business world:

> Our conferences no matter what we do are always going to be primarily progressive. ... We try to bring the arts in in meaningful ways or enjoyable ways without imposing it on people, making people stand up and hold hands and sing [Laughs].[16]

The language used by those who located their awakening in grassroots movements irritated many younger professionals. Cards posted anonymously on the comment wall at NCDD conferences urged practitioners to be careful of the divisiveness of progressive discourses that they might perceive as "empowering" or "grassroots," but would be read by conservatives as politically charged. How to use democratically inclusive language that would not inadvertently exclude political conservatives was the subject of numerous panel discussions and plenaries at conferences and in extended listserv debates. At one panel of prominent conservatives at NCDD's 2008 conference in Austin, featuring no less a conservative luminary than Republican gadfly Grover Norquist, the language of organizing was described as "off-putting." An illustration made by graphic recorders on "The Framing Challenge" displayed a red flag reading "SOCIAL JUSTICE" over the caption "'LIBERAL' sounding language that is troubling to CONSERVATIVE folks" (figure 3.3).

*[handwritten margin note: the purpose is to exclude conservatives]*

Even logics emphasizing democratization as a route to mutual growth occasionally clashed with a desire to tone down talk of personal empowerment in favor of the language of efficiency and usefulness that would attract mainstream clients and larger audiences. Much of the conflict revolved around normative versus rational understandings of public engagement, with some practitioners claiming the transformative power of democratic engagement as an end in itself and a larger majority seeking to demonstrate the practical uses of public engagement to grantmakers and clients.[17] On a listserv, one contributor puts those doing facilitation into two camps: "The reason we need to build new intellectual architecture is so that we can GET THINGS DONE. Chattiness to feel all 'groovy' and 'high' that we connected to some other people who share some of our worldview is not 'enough' to address the collective challenge. I think it is very fair to ask questions about getting things done and effectiveness." Banishing 1960s language was seen as necessary to be taken seriously.

On listservs for consultants specializing in Open Space, the method designed for self-organized meetings on urgent topics and often used in corporate settings, debates were vigorous about the "turn off" potential of New Age practices as seemingly uncontroversial as sitting

*[handwritten note at bottom: talk about coccooned in left-land!]*

FIGURE 3.3. Graphic recording of a conference session dialogue on loaded and off-putting language
Photo by author.

in a circle and taking turns sharing thoughts at the start or end of an event. What was the exact point at which too much idealism might turn off clients or participants? Practitioners asserted the continuing relevance of spirit, even as it might have to be toned down for people to catch on. Here, a practitioner describes a conference for fellow facilitators: "we saw, heard and loved each other. *And it isn't about a woo-woo comfy Green meme feeling.* There is power here, a latent power of the whole. We are only beginning to understand the practical power of seeing, hearing, and loving each other fully, together. To grow into that understanding, we'll need a lot more such gatherings." Another recommends carefulness about "airy fairy" language on an organizational development (OD) listserv, even while arguing for the importance of "spirit":

> I wouldn't use that as a selling point for OD services if I were targeting main stream organizations ... not because it's invalid, but because "they" tend to cancel your vote when you come off too "airy fairy." Like you, I don't think we can truly give value if we don't bring our "spirit" into the work.

A facilitator reflected on a listserv about circle sharing she facilitated—"a mind-blowing, life-altering experience"—that provoked a strong, hostile reaction from one attendee, "who was quite turned off by the whole experience." His critique: "I was at a New Age, 'open circle' conference where the questions were as flat and meaningless as possible so no one would feel excluded." She reflects,

> I have to say honestly—I totally understand this reaction. Some times "typical" open space can get into this "circle grooviness" that some how demeans people with high professional expectations. ... When first introducing open space to technical communities not used to the "circle culture" I often use theater style—they are already doing a radically different process then normal. I don't need to force "circle" on them too. I always close the day in the circle though and sure enough in good time (like by the third conference) they get the process and begin in circle no problem.

Another chimes in about the significance of the circle for him:

> The circle is not there for "its own sake" to prove equality—as I see it, it is a configuration for gathering that is deeply archetypal, with many layers of meaning and symbolism. It has the capacity to touch something within people that I agree may have been lost or driven out. In my own Celtic mythology for example, it is a symbol of community connection, hospitality and the nature of infinity (no beginning, no end).

She replies: "To these folks this [discussion of archetypal circle symbolism] is WAY 'Granola.'... They don't come to 'deeply look into one another's eyes' and 'feel the unknown space' or 'embody reality' they came together to get stuff done."

Circle sharing visibly established equality and 1960s values for many facilitators; participants who were resistant were often framed as culturally limited and in need of interventions—with practice, they would "get" the value of engagement methods. Conversely, those who resisted facilitator interventions were described as powerful people who cannily recognized the ways in which circle sharing was designed to disempower elites. The founder of Open Space points out that those who will be most uncomfortable will be those most likely to gain from the status quo:

> In my experience, the only people who have a problem with working in a circle are those who demand that their positional power or authority or superiority over the others in the group be recognized and acknowledged. People who are in positions of authority most often got there by being very aware and politically astute as well as demonstrating ability. This means that they are very aware of the significance of a circle and consciously choose that they don't want to operate in such a setting.

As practitioners charged with leveling power inequalities, facilitators struggled to find a resonant discourse and set of practices that would "open" a space for deliberation to happen without triggering cultural alarm bells and dismissal from resistant organizational cultures. Should it turn off those in power, that was what they were hired to challenge, as described later in this chapter.

Surprisingly, the tables were turned when the groups being organized were bipartisan publics rather than industry work groups. Language of noninstrumental learning seemed to diminish participant suspicions about facilitator agendas and suddenly became very useful in promotion efforts. While an emphasis on the instrumental value of engagement might appeal to administrators, highlighting engagement as a "means to an end" raised the hackles of conservatives suspicious of progressive agendas; in the panel discussion at NCDD 2008 about involving conservatives through more effective framing, participants agreed that public deliberation was "not about converting one another, but about building

FIGURE 3.4. Graphic recording illustrating a conference discussion on the "framing challenge" for conservative audiences suspicious of public engagement processes
Photo by author.

relationships that allow our hearts to open and grow" (figure 3.4). Noninstrumental, New Age language of "heart" turned out to be key to avoiding the social justice discourses that might turn off conservatives.

### Avoiding Identity Politics: The Place of Social Justice in Dialogue

> In Iowa yesterday, Hillary Clinton ... whipped the crowd into a frenzy with her new campaign slogan, "Let The Conversation Begin." This may not be the most politically correct thing to say, but I don't think that slogan's going to help you with men.
>
> Jon Stewart, *The Daily Show* (January 29, 2007)

No one with experience observing public engagement conferences would argue that equity and diversity are not important concerns for the field. Prominent theorists of deliberation have questioned whether the reasoned discourse and public speaking ability required in deliberation might subtly exclude marginalized peoples and women, but later researchers have investigated the "problem of power" and found that public deliberation can actually afford unique opportunities to people of color, the poor, and women.[18] Despite efforts to avoid "identity politics," sometimes public engagement is perceived as feminine and as conducted *for* people of color.

Diversity is an imperative articulated on a regular basis by leading organizations. Principle 2 in the collaboratively designed Public Engagement Principles Project is "Inclusion and Demographic Diversity: In high quality engagement: Conveners and participants reflect the range of stakeholder or demographic diversity within the community or on the issue at hand."[19] One of the five priority challenge areas for the 2008 NCDD conference directly interrogated structures of power in the field itself and the larger society, framed as: "How can we address issues of oppression and bias both within the D&D community itself, and throughout society through the use of dialogue and deliberation?"

Avowed commitments to equity and diversity are omnipresent, as are efforts to make such commitments real through substantial investments of resources in recruiting participants and enabling their full participation. Processes routinely provide accommodations for persons with disabilities, child care, materials in multiple languages, food, compensation, and transportation. These efforts to subsidize the engagement of those typically excluded from other forms of political participation mean that participants in deliberative events are typically more diverse than the average pool of voters, despite the much greater burdens in time and resources that deliberation imposes on participants in comparison to voting, e-mail petitions, and other forms of political participation. Facilitation firms also routinely collect data on race and ethnicity, income, gender, and age to gauge the representativeness of the group and draw attention to underrepresented perspectives.[20]

While critically important, the focus of existing research on some aspects of the representativeness of groups and on dynamics within actual processes[21] does not afford a broader picture of the complex, fraught relationship of the field as a whole to equity and diversity concerns. Interest in the relationship between deliberative democracy and structural inequalities is deep but only for a subset of practitioners, disproportionately women and people of color.[22] At a conference on public engagement and higher education, the most popular conference session was "And Justice for All: Straight Talk about Social and Racial Justice and Deliberative Democracy," but organizers noted that 80% of participants were women (as compared with 60% at the conference as a whole) and 40 to 50% were people of color (at a conference where 73% of attendees identified as white).[23] The fact that the vast majority of practitioners do not view equity and diversity as the central concern of the field was reflected in my survey data: of NCDD's five challenge areas, "addressing oppression and bias" was ranked the most important challenge by only 6% of respondents.[24] As compared with the overall sample demographics, respondents who did select oppression as a challenge were more likely to be women and more than twice as likely to be respondents of color.

The demographics of my 2009 practitioner survey reflected the privileged dimensions of the facilitator corps: 71% held advanced degrees, and 88% identified as white.[25] As Leighninger notes in describing conflicts between deliberation practitioners and community organizers, "Most of these deliberative democracy advocates, at least at the national level, are white, whereas the leaders of community organizing and racial equity are a racially diverse group."[26] Sixty-two percent of respondents were women, a disproportion not likely to be due to gendered differences in survey response rates as the gender makeup of attendees at conferences is typically also sixty-forty.[27] Specific patterns of underrepresentation within the facilitator corps were even starker. Although respondents who identified as Asian or Black/African-American were underrepresented at half those groups' rate in the wider US population, Hispanic/Latino practitioners were underrepresented in our sample by a factor of five. This underrepresentation intensified in areas of the country where the Hispanic/Latino population is higher than the national average of 15%; of fifty-two respondents from California, only one identified as Hispanic/Latino.

When I presented the survey's demographic data to practitioners, the makeup of the facilitator corps was a matter of chagrin for some practitioners. One self-identified sociologist on the public discussion website for the survey critiqued its presentation of results as "glossing over the insularity of the dialogue and deliberation crew. This community is largely a white, left leaning, highly educated, and (I am guessing) has an income generally greater than the median. ... D&D is a field of privilege." But this interest in exploring privilege within the facilitator corps was limited for the vast majority of practitioners during discussions of survey results.

Facilitators more often worry that their facilitation skills might benefit the powerful and those who hire them—a case in which facilitators' tools are manipulated to serve the powerful. In a summary report on deliberative case studies, the authors urged attention to power inequalities and the potential for misuse of deliberation:

> We argue that rather than seeking mechanisms to more effectively include the marginalized in existing deliberative exercises ("seeing marginalization through the lens of deliberative democracy"), researchers and practitioners need to take the more controversial step of evaluating deliberative democracy as a tool for undermining unjust hierarchies ("seeing deliberative democracy through the lens of marginalization"). ... Deliberative democrats need to be attentive to the risk of bringing marginalized groups into dialogue with the wrong partners.[28]

Deliberation might be in tension with important goals of marginalized groups, and the authors argue that practitioners should recognize these conflicts:

> Identity politics may have contra-deliberative effects, for example. ... We urge deliberative democrats to accept that marginalized groups may have good reasons to refuse deliberation, in some contexts, in favor of other modes of struggle. We conclude this synthesis of our cases by framing a broad challenge to deliberative democratic theorists and practitioners: to more carefully articulate the accounts of social change that underlie our commitments to deliberative democracy, so that we can more adequately justify our advocacy for deliberation as a vehicle of political equality and social justice.[29]

Given the prior emphasis in the field on whether deliberation excludes or disempowers women because of its focus on rational argument, participants not surprisingly did not see the potential gendering of deliberation as a problem of potential exclusion of men, despite attempts to raise the issue in presentations with participants.[30] But neither was

the predominantly white practitioner corps a topic many practitioners wanted to engage, believing that doing so opened up the "identity
politics" can of worms, which prevented a focus on common interests,
mutuality, and problem-solving. The response from one practitioner
challenged "old ways" of "focusing on identity," an approach that was
deemed "too disempowering:"  *huh.*

> Topics like "race" and "gender" by themselves create an exclusive,
> divisive, and even demeaning frame. (Do people really want to be
> defined genetically rather than by their choices?) Issues like race and
> gender only matter because they get in the way of something else.
> That something else is what energizes a greater variety of people. For
> the record, I'm a white middle-aged woman with a masters degree, yet
> the dialogue culture seems a bit narrow even for me to fit in comfort-
> ably. Labels cause division. Focusing on common interests instead
> leads to cohesion.[31]

Similarly, in answering a question about gender differences observed
in deliberation styles, survey respondents expressed deep discomfort in
making generalizations, asserting that "every individual has a unique
style" or that other factors were more important or precluded their
ability to generalize. Some avowed either that such differences were a
matter of "personality" or that they did not "see" or talk about gender;
for example, "I don't tend to evaluate things on gender lines" or "I don't *racists*
like to foster stereotypes." For those in the field not focused on structural inequalities, diversity and justice challenges centered on ascrip-
tive identity categories are by no means central and are even seen as a
threat to productive deliberation and forward momentum in the field.
Deliberation experts Carolyn Hendriks and Lyn Carson argue for greater
scholarly attention to the potential depoliticization of public deliberation among practitioners focused "too much on the 'process'": "the risk
here is that consultants underplay broader structural issues such as
gender, class"—a phenomenon that seems to be occurring in practitioners' sense that raising such issues can torpedo productive discussion,
even among practitioners themselves.[32]

Debates about social justice and equity certainly animated the field
in particular places and moments. But scholarship on inclusion in

deliberation has tended to downplay potential threats to the success of future engagement efforts if dialogue gets coded as women's work or, despite the predominantly white facilitator corps, as conducted when the poor and communities of color need to vent, as in the case of Community Congress III.[33] Gender dynamics vary according to the topic under discussion, with topics like engineering, toxic waste remediation, and budgeting tending to attract male participants and less instrumental topics on social harmony and community visioning tending to attract more women. One facilitator at a conference described a regional visioning process in the Southeast, where recruiters realized prior to the process that organizers had successfully recruited diverse participants, with the exception of white men.[34]

Practitioners recognized that achieving representative parity at deliberative events, despite extensive recruitment efforts, is still a major challenge with some demographic groups. But while awareness of complex inequalities coincided with the progressive strains of deliberative discourse, it clashed with the individualistic and personalized strains of that discourse—of group belonging as a dangerous threat to the individual transformations possible in deliberation. As sociologist Nina Eliasoph discusses in her work on empowerment talk across American society, diversity is limited as a frame for empowerment because it raises uncomfortable issues and differences, differences that practitioners were careful to manage.[35] Public engagement practitioners explicitly sought demographic diversity, but at the same time, marginalized groups that were organized risked being labeled as special interests or as potentially disruptive if they did not see deliberation as a useful strategy, as described later.

### "You Can Mess This Up": Outsourcing Facilitation to Process Custodians

Attempting to document the fair market value of public engagement consulting expertise was a chief concern of NCDD, IAP2, and conference attendees. If, as described earlier, practitioners had to negotiate carefully the "enemy" institutions that hired them and the association with progressive activism and social justice that might scare off potentially hostile participants, how could their services benefit sponsors and participants? Practitioners expressed concern about remaining faithful to the ideals of sharing transformative techniques while generating respect for the difficulty of creating high-quality public engagement processes that do not make the mistakes of the old models. Participants planned self-organized sessions on "How to Make a Living in D&D," "Funding D&D NGOs—Match.com with Philanthropists," and "Making a Living in D&D." One panelist at the conference claimed that people investing themselves in dialogue and deliberation are taking an "enormous risk in terms of professional positions, financial investments, and time." Connecting compensation with appreciation for practitioners' potential impact on process quality is difficult. Many methods subscribe to explicit assumptions that preclude questioning facilitation strategies, such as "the wisdom is in the room" and "whatever happens was meant to happen, whoever comes was meant to come." Such a climate forecloses accountability for process results, as this is explicitly outside the bounds of discussion.

To address these tensions, public engagement professionals justify the utility of their services by emphasizing the dysfunctions of their own clients and the dangers of badly run processes. Here, *clients* refers to the sponsors or organizations that hire public engagement practitioners to run engagement events, as described in chapter 2. Although practitioners might be sympathetic to allies and "pioneers in tough institutions," these administrators—the nonprofit and corporate managers and government officials who saw the need for public engagement run by an outside facilitator—nevertheless might have bosses who wanted to maintain control over meetings or their outcomes. When foundation sponsors were footing the bill, public officials or client organizations might have been dragged along to serve as a public engagement host. Practitioners sold their services to sponsors and clients on the basis of arguments about those same clients' incapability of properly valuing or fairly administering public engagement processes.

Debates at the 2006 conference unfolded in sessions with titles like "When the Client Is the Problem." Powerful organizations and even powerful stakeholders might try to manipulate processes to their own benefit, and participants might be angry at facilitators for seeming to work for those in power. Concerns in this vein were recorded in a blog posting during a conference session: "The issue is one of who gets to use the skills we have in this room? Servants of power—Who has access to these skills? i.e. using the skills in this room for the benefit of the larger environment and to celebrate ourselves." Facilitators acknowledged in a teleconference on problem clients that maintaining quality is difficult in a marketplace of sometimes struggling independent contractors who might take a project with an organization that was seeking legitimacy, not real change: "When I'm looking at taking on a project, I have to keep in mind that I cannot afford to jeopardize my reputation by being associated with a client that does not share my public participation values. . . . People are always going to be faced with putting food on the table versus keeping their reputation." Association with a disastrous or manipulated process could diminish the credibility of practitioners with the public—and, by association, the authenticity of engagement practices in general.

This did not, however, mean claiming a position of advocacy for the public. Public engagement professionals emphasize their professional disinterestedness, a stance of imperviousness to stance-taking that extends to both clients and stakeholders. Clients and publics are both understood as self-interested actors against whom public engagement professionals have to defend their processes. Dealing with outraged publics or organized groups used to adversarialism or protest tactics could be just as problematic for facilitators trying to bring everyone to the table. Practitioners disagreed on which were the biggest source of pressure for facilitators, with 57% in the survey reporting that facilitators "face the most pressure for particular outcomes" from those hosting processes and 43% reporting the most pressure from those invited to participate.[36] This was the highest level of disagreement among the attitudinal questions on the survey.

In comparison with the rejection of "us-them" perspectives identified by participants in describing the evolution of their personal approaches, us-them discourse predominates when discussing the protection of process quality in public engagement consulting. As a result of the difficulty of getting clients to appreciate public engagement processes, conference participants emphasized the kinds of things that can go wrong when participatory techniques are misused—and the blame in these cases is placed squarely on power-hungry, unwilling clients, typically higher-ups in client organizations who do not understand the importance of high-quality engagement.[37] Heierbacher notes this difficulty: "It doesn't seem like something that takes a complicated skill set, which it does. One of the things will be making people realize that this is something that is complicated. There's a lot of ways that you can mess this up. You really should have someone come in and help you or train someone in your office or whatever it is to do this right."[38]

For Jack Portwood, a certification course leader, the "biggest threat" to the field came from untrained administrators facilitating poorly: "a lot of things that are called public participation are not." In the conference workshop "When the Client Is the Problem," participants shared "war stories" of "bad client behavior," and the leader recommended a book on dealing with "toxic coworkers." The perspective that "the client is all wrong and that it is their fault they are off track" was described as counterproductive, but so was a perspective in which "you buy into the client's definition of the problem." Clients are understood as problematic not simply because they have trouble surrendering authority to outside facilitators, but because their organizational and personal dysfunctions prevent them from appreciating the value of the services that the facilitator is offering.

These concerns about the misunderstanding of public engagement and its misuse by clients and sponsors are reflected in a training course dialogue exercise combining one of the café techniques (rotating round-table conversations) with "cardstorming" (noting each idea that came up in the conversations on cards for sorting later on a sticky wall). In this case, nine of us in three groups discussed for an hour the Question of the Day: "What are the challenges we face in incorporating P2 [public participation] into our[39] corporate culture?" By far the most common theme (occurring in forty-two of ninety-five total cards) involved either the public, the sponsor, decision-makers, staff, or some combination not understanding or appreciating the value of public participation. Examples of this theme include "P2 not valued—not viewed as productive" and "Sponsor does not view P2 as essential or integral to the project." Sixty-nine percent of the cards on this theme referenced misunderstanding on the part of sponsors, project managers, or agency staff. This was also reflected in the second-most common theme, power struggles and control issues, as exemplified by comments like "P2 viewed as threat to status quo—we are experts" and "Fear/loss of control."

Practitioners in the field asserted that transparency and credibility require public engagement coaching and that meaningful relationships between organizations and their stakeholders require intermediaries. The trainer noted in the certification course that sponsor agencies are unable to provide the "neutrality" an outside consultant can: "[Citizen advisory] boards can't facilitate themselves and sponsors can't facilitate boards. You need an independent third-party consultant hired by the sponsor to make the process work—totally neutral. ... I know one person who has been successful as a neutral inside an agency. It doesn't happen very often that credible internal facilitation happens." Sharing authority with and empowering the lay public must be accompanied by privatizing accountability for public engagement, since clients are not credible.

As a way of demonstrating the complexity of good facilitation, one trainer claims, "I get calls all the time [for last minute facilitation]. ... They are looking for a human shield. Then they get to blame me for bad, lousy facilitation." The danger of a backlash against engagement itself as facilitated public engagement processes become more common across a variety of contexts and settings is relatively high, as described in chapter 7. Public engagement facilitators become scapegoats when processes fail. Bad publicity for a particular project can be fatal to an independent contractor's business, as one facilitator describes: "The most valuable asset that my practice has is my reputation because I'm a one man show. ... Hopefully you look as good at the end as they [the clients] do."

Despite their dependence on publicity outcomes, public engagement facilitators claim that, for them, the quality and integrity of the means justify whatever outcomes result. Their loyalty lies neither with the public nor with the client, but with the process itself. This emphasis on high-quality process causes public engagement consultants to link their unique value proposition to their lack of investment in process outcomes. An experienced facilitator leading a teleconference training on "qualifying" clients states:

> It's really hard sometimes to win the trust of the stakeholders around your impartiality, and I work very hard making it clear to stakeholders and the client that I am an advocate for the process rather than the project. Whether the project goes ahead or not is not a success indicator for me. What is a success indicator is whether people felt they were heard, not if they got what they wanted.

A considerable amount of energy at professional conferences and trainings involves venting about frustrations in dealing with clients, much of which has to do with clients not wanting to pay for the long-term, comprehensive services required for a well-tended process. Not surprisingly, complaints about the public in general are rare, but complaints about adversarial sectors of the public who reject participatory processes in favor of litigation, particularly ad hoc interest groups, are common.

In some instances, facilitators express concern about their own culpability in process failures, where facilitation turns into "facipulation"— a combination of facilitation and manipulation. One confessional account on a listserv describes "the pain of the reality" that a "beloved" method that "wasn't working" for participants had to be abandoned; the facilitator concludes: "our struggles in facilitation may manifest themselves into shadows. . . . Positionality. Judgment. And control." Much of this self-criticism regards critiquing facilitation practices, rather than critiquing the use of facilitation experts. A contributor to a facilitation newsletter asks, "How can we address the (not so) subtle application of the term 'facilitator' to lots of activities that are almost diametrically opposite to what good group facilitation stands for?" A much quoted sourcebook on participatory workshops urges self-reflection on individual practices: "most of us talk too much, dominate too much, control too much. We have to learn to 'walk the non-talk,' to shut up and to empower and trust others."[40] Heierbacher notes that coercion can easily become a part of engagement processes if facilitators are not properly skilled: "there's a tough balance between the work that we do and coerciveness. . . . If [agencies/clients] don't bring in skilled facilitators that can really handle the process, it's easy to slip back into that at certain points and it really does cause a lot of problems."[41] Public engagement professionals are clearly aware of the pressures they face from powerful clients and hostile publics, and negotiate these tensions by asserting their capacity for self-effacement as independent custodians of process quality.

### Recognizing Tensions in Top-Down Empowerment

In professional workshops and listserv discussions, public engagement professionals confront the challenges they face as consultants charged with democratizing decision-making in American organizations and empowering the public. In their discussions on the evolution of their practice, the necessity of their work, and the definition of their roles, public engagement professionals employ narratives of internal transformation from activist identities to nonadversarialism. They negotiate the perils of using New Age and progressive discourses by carefully avoiding the New Age trap and identity politics, despite their commitments to self-help philosophies and social justice. When they highlight the ways in which processes can be derailed and practices can be manipulated, public engagement professionals not only critique sponsors, but also turn critical lenses on themselves and their own investments in power. As intermediaries who come between reluctant organizational clients and angry constituencies, they debate "facipulation" and the dangers of becoming a "human shield" for the powerful.

Arguing for organizations' need to hire independent public engagement contractors involves claiming that professionalization and specialization are necessary to safeguard democratic quality, a creative blending of progressive critiques of institutions with conservative beliefs in privatization. Making the business case for expert public engagement facilitation often means denigrating organizations' capacity to engage authentically with stakeholders in the absence of outside facilitators. Public engagement facilitators claim that they no longer are "anti-institutions," but they often blame "bad" institutions and, to a lesser extent, "bad" facilitation practices for processes that do not result in empowerment.[42] Tropes critical of institutions dovetail neatly with neoliberal ideologies promoting expert private-sector management over ineffective, out-of-touch bureaucracies.

Public engagement professionals actively debate how to "frame" and "normalize" public engagement to make it appealing to audiences that are diverse in terms of politics, race, religion, gender, class, and power. They work carefully to craft shared language and images to appeal to potentially adversarial publics and sponsors when they share their expertise. The next chapter focuses on the emotional labor practitioners perform when, instead of focusing on structural differences, power inequalities, and role tensions, they emphasize how organizations share the same needs and how participants and practitioners are all alike at heart.

# 4

## Walking Our Talk

Crucially, however, belief in the front-stage performance is constitutive of
the performance itself. To avoid hypocrisy and "get goose-bumps," even
those who structure the performance must suspend disbelief and act as-if
they are only motivated by a desire for consensus.

> Josh Pacewicz, *Partisans and Partners: The Politics of the Post-Industrial
> Economy* (Forthcoming)

I still get goosebumps when I see that.

> AmericaSpeaks staffer after showing a short film on a state
> health care process at a deliberation conference

### A Cosmology of Self

I peer out the window as my plane deploys its landing gear directly over
lush Balboa Park in San Diego in early fall 2009. Although I went to
grad school here, the familiar faces I am coming to see will be at the
seventeenth annual International Association for Public Participation
Conference. It is my first time at an IAP2 conference, and I am curious
to see how it differs from the explicitly deliberation-focused conferences
I have attended over the past three years. The IAP2 is devoted to a wider
range of public engagement practices—one-way meetings to inform the
public, for instance—than the more intensive processes farther up the
"participation ladder."[1] In the past few years, "informing" has become
more out of style, and involving the public in decision-making on a
substantive level is in vogue. There are many more people who conduct
executive coaching and work that blends into public relations here, and
I am curious to what extent deliberation is valued among this more

corporate crowd. Based on the conference program, I can see that there will be more people who do public engagement work in business settings and guess that there will be more suits and ties and more men than at the usual NCDD conferences. The IAP2 is international in scope and includes lots of participants and leaders from its very active Australasia affiliate. I wonder how the tone and rhythms of the conference might differ from the familiar patterns of national deliberation conferences in the United States.

At the opening plenary on the conference theme of sustainability, about 230 people are in the audience, fully half of whom are from outside North America—a professional crowd but not many ties in evidence and, if anything, the gender balance is even more heavily female than at the conferences I am used to. Three-quarters of attendees are at their first IAP2 meeting. The mayor of San Diego welcomes us and talks about the struggles the city is facing and the necessity of getting the public over their mistrust of local government after a number of corruption scandals and fiscal problems. A sustainability expert from Australia gives a slide show about the importance of sustainability that quashes my expectations that this conference will be more businesslike and less spiritual than deliberation conferences. She starts with slides of her own home, which has no indoor plumbing, and ends her very personal presentation with poems by Marge Piercy and Mary Oliver, concluding with the foreboding final stanzas of Piercy's "The Common Living Dirt," urging us to worship the earth before we die of "overwork" or poison.

It is a lyrical but somber start to the conference, and we file out quietly to the coffee break in the mezzanine of the downtown Westin Hotel, the only living dirt in evidence in the potted ice plants in the atrium. On Thursday, Anne Patillo, the current president of IAP2, welcomed us in an e-mail that acknowledged the sacrifice many members were making to come. Those who are staying here for three nights and flying in from overseas are spending at least a few thousand dollars on registration and travel expenses. Patillo asked participants to come to the conference having thought about "what challenges you are facing in your own practice in public participation and the challenges of the current context in which we all work—climate change, global financial crisis, cultural diversity and rapid technological change." This emphasis on challenge is a lot less "appreciative" and opportunity-focused than many of the deliberation conferences I have been to.

I say hello to some acquaintances at the coffee break but head off alone to a session titled "Speaking with Confidence," led by a personal recovery coach, herself in recovery, from Southern California. I was attracted to this session because it seems a bit out of place and because I am, teaching notwithstanding, a terrible public speaker. Plenty of other attendees are there—I count five men and twenty-seven women—and from the looks of it, all of them dread public speaking as well. Lisa, the leader, introduces herself and asks us to put our notebooks away so we can be fully present—a request that, at this point in the project, I am used to heeding although it means far more work later tonight to reconstruct what happened. "What kind of communication are we hungry for?" she asks. "Heart-based, authentic communication."

Lisa teaches us about "the power of pause" and how to confront our fears about public speaking by feeling the ground beneath our feet, taking time to breathe, and engaging with our audience members by looking directly at them with "soft, available eyes" for a few seconds in turn. Counterintuitively, she tells us that too often we are eager to show that we are listening by communicating back with yeses, nods, and other cues. Instead, she asks us to practice listening fully with soft, available eyes, but without communicating anything to our partners, taking turns for three minutes at a time. I turn to Jill, a Canadian woman in her late twenties with curly dark hair. We take turns talking and practicing how to listen without communicating. This is much, much harder than it looks, for both the speaker and the listener, and each of us erupts with nervous laughter and whispers at the end of each turn. Our instructions to look like we are listening attentively, and the speaker's knowledge that she will not get any verbal or physical response to her speech, dispel any illusion of attentive listening or talking from the heart. We are talking to talk and listening to listen, and the speaker has trouble filling just three minutes with anything of substance, while the listener wills the speaker to give her something to listen to besides "um" and "so that's about it, I guess."

Lisa uses the session to demonstrate her mastery of the techniques and bristles a bit when the audience questions whether these strategies should always apply. She is also soliciting business for her coaching company, and asks us to pass around an e-mail list and to make commitments here if we want her to hold us accountable to them. I remember a similar commitment exercise at diversity training in my past life in corporate America, and I get a phone call about a week later from Lisa to ask how I am doing with my commitments. At the end of the session, Lisa shows how to "receive" our applause for her, standing beatifically and looking meaningfully at each of us in turn. I continue to get e-mails from her, and either from this session or from other e-mail sign-ups at this conference, I am suddenly on a slew of other positive e-mail lists. The electronic exultations about living my dream and awakening my inner genius in order to thrive recall the "fake it until you make it" cheerleading that Ehrenreich criticizes as "deliberate self-deception."[2]

I wonder about the "heart-based" authenticity of what seem to be self-conscious tricks for connecting with your audience. This session on building self-confidence seems oddly disconnected from the other sessions at the conference, where the business and economic development focus of public participation is much more directly addressed in sessions on how to evaluate involvement efforts conducted by a public agency, how San Diego stakeholders in a zoning process learned to respect each other, and how to map the social capital and civic capacity of communities being targeted for mining operations. The academic giving that last presentation detailed how such a process could help communities by showing them where they were weak in local leadership, and by helping the mining company she worked for see where best to spend their philanthropy dollars. Given the international focus of this conference, the social distance between the populations being engaged and facilitators was much greater than in many US interventions and led to some awkward moments. Discussions of fiscal responsibility took place in conference facilities that were several cuts above the usual Marriott fare, and the members of the association were shocked at the business meeting when it was revealed that the conference was going to be in the red. A field trip to a shopping mall built by a foundation in a low-income community of color was made in a party bus with a flat-screen television playing Black Eyed Peas videos, leading one attendee to crack, "This gives new meaning to the term limousine liberals."

Uncomfortable juxtapositions are relatively common at conferences like this one and not unique to the IAP2. How have public engagement professionals reconciled the political implications of their role in privatizing and professionalizing "everyday democracy" with their commitment to the progressive values of democratic empowerment that animated their personal lives, as described in chapter 3? There, public engagement practitioners skillfully balanced personalized empowerment and privatized accountability when explaining their pathways into the field and their work to avoid traps: identity politics among participants, facipulation on behalf of powerful clients, and too much self-identification with potentially counterproductive liberal or New Age values. Although public engagement professionals are unquestionably creative and self-critical in addressing these issues, they do so unevenly. The analysis in the next section describes how practitioners' emphasis on the sameness of organizational interests and participant needs actively glosses over the significant differences among participants, clients, and facilitators that erupted at moments like the one where, as we slunk onto the party bus blaring club music, our local hosts at the shopping center tour remarked that we could have taken a $2 trolley from our hotel directly to the site.

The active performance of the congruence of the work self and personal self is its own kind of emotional labor. It is not exactly the alienated emotional labor forced on the helpless flight attendants Arlie Hochschild describes, who must perform "deep acting" that draws on their personal lives to show concern for passengers as though they were guests in the flight attendants' living rooms.[3] Instead, this consciously avowed holistic self merges self and work completely and finally. Instead of deep acting, participants key their emotions to a constant register of heart-based authenticity—a performance rooted in the core belief that all settings are part of one world, all people have similar needs, all organizations have the same dysfunctions. With the hammer of authenticity, all the world is truly a nail.

## Holistic Selves in Whole Systems

You might also look at [_____ Method]. While it is has been used for civic participation, I adapted it pretty successfully a couple of years back to get wider input into a major initiative we were launching. I just substituted "company" for "society" and pretty much followed the plan.

Post to a facilitators' listserv

In spite of their acknowledgment of diverse possibilities and changing perspectives, public engagement practitioners far more commonly express an overarching belief that organizations behave identically regardless of their differences. According to public engagement practitioners, private and public actors are absolutely alike in their need for public participation interventions, and deliberative and participatory methodologies are beneficial for any context if deployed correctly, no matter the audience. This is enacted at public engagement conferences, where those who work with different types of clients come together to share common features of their practice and processes, and participants rarely note differences between engaging employees on health care cuts, for example, and engaging members of the public on pandemic flu priorities. It is also avowed explicitly in listserv discussions and conversations.

As the quote that begins this section indicates, elision of difference can be explicit and purposive, rather than incidental to pragmatic goals. Public engagement professionals declare a singular belief in the transportability of their methods and act it out in a way that eliminates or resolves ambiguity regarding their roles in change. They apply these beliefs in the transformative power of engagement to every possible setting in which engagement can feasibly be practiced, including the settings of their own professionalization. Here, unlike the tensions articulated in the previous chapter, a belief in the sameness of systemic dysfunctions glosses over obvious distinctions between the aims of private enterprise and public governance.

Public participation facilitators don't simply assert these similarities in the abstract. They also act to disseminate best practices in participation across state and market contexts without noting the differing practice of power in legislative and corporate settings. For those concerned with the impacts of public engagement professionals on the quality of the public sphere, this deliberate action of applying identical remedies in varying contexts for different problems has a number of potentially troubling consequences. Ironically, the institutional sameness so assiduously professed here is not thought to conflict with the professed interest of deliberation and participation exercises in recognizing and harvesting situationally specific practices and local knowledge within particular communities, discussed in chapter 5.

Business problems and community problems are promoted by consultants as similar and similarly tractable with proper facilitation: "Whether it's a few people planning a new program or a public meeting of hundreds of people, [our consulting firm] always has the same goal for facilitation: Help people move towards their goals." Another organization's website describes the achievements of a consultant: "she has initiated collaborations between highly competitive high tech companies such as Sun and Microsoft, as well as community collaborations that address issues such as youth violence prevention." One method is advertised for "groups as small as 12 and as large as 1,200 from around the world," including "a global consumer products company," churches, Maori leaders, Norwegian townships, work teams, court employees, and professional groups.

This belief that facilitation methods are equally useful for "regional treaty negotiations" or developing "a new world-wide marketing strategy" deserves further examination. As Mansbridge noted in her comparison of workplace and community participation: "The kind of democracy appropriate in a context of common interests is qualitatively different from the kind of democracy appropriate when interests conflict."[4] The uses to which corporate executives choose to put participatory techniques are typically focused on generating employee "alignment" in cases of downsizing, mergers, and restructuring—a fact readily acknowledged in promotional materials. One consultant to both the private sector and the public sector is open about these differing motivations: "In business, dialogue is an indispensable tool whenever corporate cultures merge, employee benefits change, the company's reputation is threatened, or breakthrough strategies are needed to deal with change. In the public sector, dialogue discovers the common ground needed to resolve gridlock issues or community problems."

For all the attention to the origins of engagement practice in participatory social movements, attendees noted far less often that engagement consulting also draws on practices borrowed from the field of organization development (OD) and the human relations movement—many took OD methods for granted as universally applicable to empowerment

in all sectors without noting that OD techniques were designed specifically to enhance labor control.[5] Nearly a third of survey respondents
reported prior experience in "adult education"—the group process and
individual coaching typically called "adult learning" in management
circles.[6] The claim that dialogues initiated to gauge employee preferences on benefit cuts might serve equally well in the public sphere for
resolving community problems obscures their very different power
dynamics and aims, discussed in more detail in chapter 6. Elimination
of dysfunction and management of change-averse individuals or groups
takes on different meaning in the polity than it does in the workplace.

As described in the previous chapter, facilitators were skeptical of
their clients' motives and their ability to implement public engagement
processes on their own in noncoercive ways. But by being evangelistic
about process and critical of clients, facilitators avoided the notion that
high-quality, authentically deliberative processes might actually be facilitated well by independent consultants but used to disempowering effect
by clients and sponsors. Facilitators tended to emphasize their evolution
away from adversarial approaches in the 1960s without recognizing that
their association with grassroots authenticity—their perceived resistance
to co-optation—might be valuable for clients seeking to use deliberation
for nondeliberative goals.[7]

Not least, the idea that engagement is appropriate in all instances
delegitimizes participants who seek contention or mobilization against
institutional targets, as described in chapter 3 in the case of marginalized
groups who may prefer "other modes of struggle." If citizen-consumers
are used to "choosing" among a palette of impending benefit cuts at
work, they may not ask difficult questions about whether a public project
should go forward at all when offered a chance to troubleshoot its design
flaws.[8] Public engagement professionals' work legitimizes market and
state authority by regularizing and routinizing performances of political
equality, while social inequalities go unchallenged. According to Nina
Eliasoph, top-down, episodic engagement initiatives produce lessons
for participants in how to ignore organization's "grandiose claims."[9]
Inasmuch as facilitated engagement is an increasingly dominant form
of organizing civicness across sectors in contemporary society, the work
of dealing with the gap between the promises and realities of engagement that facilitators actively avoid recognizing may be displaced on

those being engaged, a phenomenon whose consequences are discussed in chapter 7.

## Something I Am, Not Something I Do

> I think the kind of work we do is singular in that we can only do it well to the extent that we ourselves are able to show up fully and authentically. There is a great synergy here between, as you say, the work we do in our larger framework and personal transformation. Each require each; each support each. As you indicate, we need to be willing and able to articulate this. (and, in particular, hold this reality ourselves)
>
> Practitioner, D&D listserv

Practitioners themselves rarely acknowledge being pulled between competing logics, worlds, or values. In fact, in contrast to their treatment of organizations as universally alike in their neediness, practitioners emphasize that their ability to solve such problems is rooted in their own holistic processing of personal experience, rather than in professional conventions, routine skills, or deliberative engagement. An authentic presence, produced by a fully integrated, comfortable self, will reciprocally enable the authenticity and integration of the selves in the group. Facilitation is seen as an extension of their personal self-development, which integrates their own journeys described in chapter 4 with the journeys of organizations, systems, and the world as a whole. These different scales were drawn on the journey wall exercise at the 2006 NCDD conference as parallel reams of paper that marked evolution personally, in the field, and in the world—years were across the top, with room to write in important moments and events at any of these scales, with the personal in the middle (figures 4.1 and 4.2).

The development of some processes explicitly reflected this logic, such as that used by the Public Conversations Project, started by family therapists, which employed the solutions used in therapy with divorcing couples and dysfunctional families as similarly useful with dysfunctional communities and partisan conflicts. On listservs, practitioners discussed the extent to which organizations displayed psychological disorders: "Perhaps not all workplace bullies are sociopaths, but ... organisations can display sociopathic tendencies. ... So, it is not necessarily the individuals we are interested in." At the IAP2 conference, I sat down to

FIGURES 4.1 AND 4.2. NCDD 2006 conference participants participate in the journey wall exercise.

Photos by author.

lunch at a "birds of a feather" table called "family systems research in community decision-making." As in the case of facilitators who claim that organizational power dynamics are all the same, the identification of similarities between families and communities is active and assertive. Discussion at the table seesawed from work experiences to discussions of one participant's road trip to sample burgers across America with his son. In this context, learning about oneself can be applied to other people in different situations and facing different kinds of conflicts seamlessly.

Self-actualization through work in deliberation facilitation was repeatedly referenced on listservs and at conferences. One facilitator describes how she can't help facilitating wherever she goes: "Recently, I did two informal facilitation 'gigs' with volunteer groups where I am a member. I was not 'hired' to do the work—I did it because I just cannot not facilitate when the need is there. ... These experiences really do make me feel 'at home' with facilitation—it has become something I am, more than something I do." Seeing deliberative facilitation as a calling or mission resonated in conference conversations and in stories told about the transformations that occurred as former litigants or disengaged members of the public were themselves won over to the power of dialogue. The transformative power of processes is an article of faith in the practitioner community; 91% of US practitioners surveyed believed that "many people who do not currently support D&D efforts would change their minds if they could experience a single great D&D process."[10] Practitioners envision participants having the same kind of transformation many of them have already experienced, as when Rebecca discovered her calling while in a dispute over rhododendrons. The integrative spirit that led Rebecca to want to meld her professional practice with her personal life by leading a Conversation Café with her son is typical. Because barriers to entry into the field are so low, practitioners saw the field as potentially limitless and largely inclusive of their potential subjects, who could become practitioners and lead dialogues in their own communities as they caught the fire of deliberation.

In this sense, with its focus on a personal relationship to deliberation and its democratic spirit of conversion and nonhierarchical leadership, the deliberation field resembles Protestant evangelicalism in the United States—but it also blends elements of contemporary American interpretations of Buddhism. Listserv members sometimes describe themselves as "Buddhist Christian" or "Christian/Buddhists"; another recommends a website titled "Compassion: The Crazy Wisdom of Jesus, Buddha, and Other Agents of Transformation." Many processes explicitly invoke Buddhism, such as "Zen and the Art of Conflict" or "Zenergy." Spirituality, despite the fear of seeming too New Agey, is more often seen as an ever-present resource for human connection. One facilitator notes: "Every person I know who works with process comments on the spiritual aspect of the experience of good group process."

Another facilitator on a listserv takes the evangelical mission to heart; he is "always on the lookout for words and phrases that make these simple (and obscure) facts understandable, inviting and attractive to the 6.5 billion people out there who don't know they can help each other to everyday delight." The rhetoric of spiritual enlightenment is so omnipresent in deliberation practice that those working with religious organizations emphasize the perfect fit of deliberative methods with faith communities, as one practitioner describes on a listserv:

> [The Appreciative Inquiry method] is so transformational and life-giving that it is extremely well suited, in fact ideal, for use in a church setting. *I know that full well from my personal experiences.* ... There is no doubt in my mind that AI has powerful potential to revitalize churches with a positive and life-giving spirit.[11]

In their work to convert the larger society to an appreciation of what public engagement can offer, facilitators actively blended their personal narratives of transformational discovery with their belief that all different types of settings are in desperate need of similar deliberative transformations.

Rather than the destructive "othering" of putative enemies and ideological opponents that deliberation practitioners work against, I argue that this process is akin to *selfing*—seeing all others as on an equally compelling mutual journey to personal authenticity and heart-based self-fulfillment. This empathic identification with everyone is certainly well-meaning on the part of public engagement professionals and an understandable aspect of their attraction to the work of engagement. Just as Nina Eliasoph emphasizes the distant bureaucrat as the bogeyman in empowerment projects, the enemy of deliberative practice is "the expert mindset," one that engenders critical distance, judgment of others, and hypocrisy.[12] At the IAP2 conference, one presenter relates the story of a client with this mindset, but even here, there is empathy for the client in the expression that the expert mindset is one that we all have to struggle with internally:

> Decision-makers taking that expert model. We have an example, a horrible example, my colleague's working on a city council project on water. And an elected representative just came out and said, "The broader community is a bunch of morons and they don't care." If someone can say that—and I'm sure it was taken out of context—it's a reflection of the way that we can all jump into the role of expert and people don't want to involve the public, and then it's not a wonder that they don't want to engage in our community involvement process.

While practitioners are forgiving with others as they struggle on their journeys, they are strict about the extent to which that journey must involve an ultimate congruence of beliefs and practices.

One practitioner on an OD listserv argues, "If an issue causes you to contradict your values, you are either not true to yourself or you need to change your values. If you are not willing to change your values to be consistent with what you honestly believe to be right, then you're guilty of hypocrisy, you just haven't been convicted yet." Such a project involves authenticity and heart because "what we perceive has everything to do with what we feel. There is no OD objectivity that can resolve this, because such a resolution implies that any of us can be purely intellectual." The practitioner who expressed the quote at the beginning of this section elaborates on "the possibility of individual and social transformation taking place synchronously and feeding each other," emphasizing the problem of expertise, the role of spiritual awakening, and the importance of emotional authenticity:

> As I got further into this work, as well as deepening my own personal awareness, I began to see THE critical practice as the ability to show

up with full awareness in the present. I began to see my group work as facilitating this at a group or social level. In a way, I saw that it was possible for the group body to experience the kind of authenticity I was discovering on a personal level. (This is the core goal in many personal spiritual practices, notably Buddhism.) We need to (and, in fact cannot avoid this) do this work of connecting with and acting from the present at all levels of our experience. Much of the problems in society come from people living vicariously, through representation, through material reality, through quantitative measures, through what they are told by scientists, professionals and other "authorities." We have been disconnected from direct experience coming to believe that our ideas (or, even worse, other people's ideas) are more important than we ourselves.

Just as practitioners emphasize the similarities of whole systems, they also express the importance of bringing holistic, fully integrated selves to their work and to their lives, in order to coax out the whole selves of other persons and organizations. In the words of one listserv member who credits Buddha with the insight: "the deepest transformations begin with the self." As we will see in chapter 6, achieving those transformations in others becomes a business, not a spiritual, imperative.

### Walking the Talk as a Symbolic Performance

> Facilitators and the organizations that train and support them are critical to most processes, yet they cannot themselves be completely democratic and deliberative.
>
> Archon Fung, John Gastil, and Peter Levine, "Future Directions for Public Deliberation" (2005: 3)

Building on the selfing described in the prior section, it is critical to understand the tensions public engagement practitioners face through the signature element of their professionalization: the extent to which all activities and discussions within these contexts are conducted using participatory practices. The assertions of organizational sameness described here are not simply a matter of self-interested management consultants seeking to expand their business. By using the methods they promote, public engagement practitioners provide the ultimate affirmation of the utility of their practices across all conceivable contexts and the leveling of their expertise through its application to themselves.

Rather than actually encouraging reflexivity, this is a ritualized aspect of public engagement practitioners' self-image. In "walking the talk" (figure 4.3), public engagement practitioners frame themselves as subject to the intentional structuring of power enacted in deliberative projects, despite the fact that they are highly verbal, sophisticated professionals well schooled in managing diverse audiences.[13] Enacting the universality of their methods—and the accompanying denial of their power as those responsible for structuring process—is not simply a case of creatively linking logics and practice. Performing the resolution of these tensions in front of each other is also symbolic and self-reinforcing.

Because this activity is so pervasive, a few representative examples demonstrate the performative work of engagement professionals to use "best practices" while reaffirming their personal humility and collective professional identity. Dialogue experts routinely engage each other

FIGURE 4.3. Graphic recording from the 2008 NCDD conference of a discussion about "walking our talk" on bias and inclusion

Photo by author.

in elementary icebreakers, drawing exercises, and other techniques designed to break through to resistant audiences and demonstrate equity by soliciting contributions from each member of the group. Typically, such warm-ups set a positive tone through the Appreciative Inquiry method, in which participants are invited to contribute ambitions and possibilities. One facilitator on a listserv discussion about cultural resistance to appreciative warm-ups describes their implicit messages: "I call an activity 'touchy-feely' if it doesn't seem related to the purpose of the event, and seems to be some kind of remedial exercise, as in, 'I'm not sure you can carry on a normal conversation if I don't break down the barriers to social interaction that I assume you must have … you poor sad non-interactive creatures.'" The power dynamics encoded in public engagement methods are rarely stated so baldly, but expected resistance from participants to the admittedly forced icebreaker validates why facilitators are there—to move groups to do things and say things they don't necessarily want to, for their own good.

Public engagement professionals perform subordinate participant roles through the adoption of icebreaker techniques, even in situations where they already know the purpose of the meeting and are immersed in constructive conversation. At a conference session following a reflective panel at the 2006 NCDD conference, the facilitator hushed the group, which was loudly and energetically discussing the panel at round tables, to draw trends in the field silently with markers for five minutes and then go to another table to explain their drawings. For an observer not habituated to public deliberation conferences, such a directive seems obtrusive, given that everyone involved is perfectly capable of—and many are certified in—pursuing inclusive conversations. But within the context of perpetual demonstration of methods, silencing a substantive existing discussion of complex social trends based on a shared experience in favor of a method designed to tap unexpressible feelings is entirely expected, if not always obeyed.

Often, the performance of participatory methodologies is quite literally a form of playacting that looks far more like surface acting than the deep acting Hochschild describes.[14] At an icebreaker exercise in a one-day training session, the facilitator chastised us on reconvening for being so caught up in discussion that we failed to come up with our two hopes to report to the group. A participant responded irritably, " 'The two things' are so typically seen as an incentive to talk that you should have emphasized that you actually wanted them." By willingly playing laypersons in need of engagement facilitation despite their participatory expertise, public engagement professionals demonstrate that no one is not in need of their interventions, including themselves.

Public engagement practitioners see their own use of participatory techniques as a critical part of their commitment to avoid hypocrisy by walking the talk. One conference participant avows, "NCDD was by far the best conference I have ever attended. It was 100% isomorphic and congruent with our practices." Sample comments on the NCDD conference website echo the importance of living the processes being discussed:

> There we were, a bunch of process geeks, and some others, and we were invited into a living exhibition of process, in which we were participants who brought life to the processes with our words, gestures, and images, and in that living made wonderful personal and professional connections.
>
> This was one of the most compelling and engaging events in which I have ever participated. It modeled the values that I associate with dialogue and deliberation. It made me feel connected to a whole movement.

The latter commenter's claim that modeling values makes them feel connected to the movement illustrates the extent to which such activities are symbolic practices that reinforce public engagement practitioners' collective identities. Emotionally, participants describe their experiences at the conference as "exhilarating," "very replenishing," "nourishing," and "life-altering." Such claims speak to the ways in which professional conferences and professional development activities for public engagement practitioners provide a restorative group culture and serve ritualistic functions of maintaining collective identity.[15] These performances, in which public engagement professionals collectively enact the alignment of their work with their discourse, help to preserve grassroots identities despite their expert roles.[16]

Conferences are not the only sites for such demonstrations, however. The authors of a report coauthored by numerous leaders in the field refused to credit who had, in fact, participated, because the document was produced in a way that reflected its topic:

> This is a collaborative document about public deliberation. *It was created in a way appropriate to its subject matter.* It does not have named authors because it emerged from interviews, face-to-face discussions, and a mode of collaboration called a "wiki" (in which many people edit one document online). We do not have a precise count of the contributors, some of whom were anonymous, but the number certainly exceeds 35.

Collaborative writing, of course, does not necessitate total denial of authorship, and it would have certainly been possible to list the known authors involved in developing the document.

At times, walking the talk means not talking at all. On another listserv, a facilitator argues, "As facilitators, it is not our role to give the answers... we are there to make an atmosphere in which all parties understand each other." When facilitators talk about "holding space" in the Open Space process, they emphasize the extent to which they need to "do nothing":

> I think as communities learn how to live into Open Space they need "the facilitator" to do less and less ... until capacity becomes distributed in a community and they understand collectively how to get the most out of the form for themselves and also not to enclose it—well they still need a facilitator to create space and invite them into it and to hold it.

The founder of Open Space argues, "If we really get it right we won't need extraneous processes to become fully what we are—self-organizing critters." Listserv discussions about how to effectively efface oneself are common. A facilitator talks about the necessity of giving oneself over to the group: "I am pretty clear in my own mind and heart that I am present to serve the needs of the client and their work together, not to meet my own social needs." One practitioner contemplates the way Buddhism provides lessons for letting oneself go:

> One of the teachings of Buddhism, as I understand it, is that the Ego has to "go." The destruction of the Self—the skin-encapsulated ego-identity that transacts with "the other" (the (I-it paradigm)—is, as I understand it, posited as necessary to achieve enlightenment. (I prefer to think of it as the dissolution of the Self and its merger into the higher collective super-self.)

Another facilitator quotes Christopher Alexander on the facilitator role: " 'It is their presence in the whole, and the fact that they are helping the life of the whole, which gives them their individual life.'. . . What I am seeing here as an inside-out truth, is that in a group we do not lend the group our individual life, it goes somewhat the other way round about. What gives us our individual existence and life is our presence in the group, our helping of the group; in turn the others helping the group give us life." A practitioner observes:

> I suspect that the task for us, as for any human being, is to learn how to be fully present, open our eyes and learn to do less, namely observe what is and BE fully with our immediate experience. . . . This means being fully present when we are sitting, walking, designing, facilitating, reflecting. . . . It is also not surprising that being fully present is the core task of every reflective spiritual practice; enlightenment is nothing other than simply being fully in the moment.

By emphasizing that they must play a subordinate, practically invisible role and that through this role they gain their self-fulfillment as an individual, facilitators put the groups they facilitate "in control"—a position that, as we will see in part III, does not describe the power dynamics at play in facilitated deliberation.

The selfing that occurs in deliberation practitioners' performances often involves self-effacement of this kind—denial of credit, of expertise, and of power in order to empower others to discover their true selves. Facilitators described struggling with giving up power for personal reasons in the section on facipulation in chapter 3, but this self-effacement is also a necessity for their professional work. The facilitator humbly abnegates her whole self for the greater good, an act with precedents in religious practices of Buddhism and Christianity. By invoking their spiritual humility and authentic struggles, facilitators are using the tools of religion—like Hochschild's flight attendants who employ techniques of method acting—to "hold space," while problems of power and inequality are individualized as inadequate integration of authentic selves.

Public engagement facilitators use every opportunity in their interactions with their peers to demonstrate their complete commitment—and that of the field in general—to empowerment by walking the talk. As the next section discusses, this activity disguises the extent to which power inequalities, and the makeup of the facilitator corps, show that public engagement facilitation is not open to everyone, and not every facilitator, however well-meaning, can empathize with the struggles of the populations being engaged.

## Politicizing and Depoliticizing Engagement

A month after the IAP2 conference, I flew to Toronto to attend the Canadian Coalition on Dialogue and Deliberation's (C2D2) conference, which included local teenagers and residents of the city's public housing as participants. Despite the use of deliberative practices in deliberation practitioners' professionalization settings, including members of marginalized communities throughout the programming of a conference on deliberation was highly unusual. It reflected the willingness of Canadian practitioners to be far more open about their affiliation with left-liberal values and their empathy with social activism. Indeed, one panel was a participatory game that taught us activist strategies for mobilizing Canadians against the abuses of a hypothetical mining company in Papua New Guinea, nearly 180 degrees from the IAP2 session where we heard from an academic working for one such company regarding how to assess marginalized communities' social capital. How could these two conference sessions belong to the same field? Perhaps these different perspectives were simply a result of a different community of actors? But no, many of the same faces I saw in Canada were familiar from previous conferences.

By picking particular elements of a conference stream, one could focus on different aspects of public engagement entirely, and avoid the tensions between the urge to empower and the urge to professionalize. Conference plenaries brought these groups together in ways that synchronized their thoughts and actions, demonstrating the power of dialogue to enact change and the ways in which practitioners walked their talk and faced the music. Rather than seeing these practices as signs of deep reflection, I began to realize that they were also ways of performing that reflection collectively.

There were places where the actual gaps became evident, as when an evening session at the C2D2 conference, intended for First Nations youth to discuss forced internment in native schools, was scheduled to take place in a bar. The sting of that offense was addressed in an emergency plenary session for the whole group, which prompted tears in the audience and on stage, as First Nations youth rapped about the hurt caused by legacies of alcoholism and drug abuse. One participant who worked in the Canadian government chatted with me on the final morning of what had been an exhausting few days. We discussed what he thought had and hadn't worked at the conference. He thought the session on the power of participatory budgeting in Toronto public housing—letting tenants decide how to use a portion of the agency's budget—was "disingenuous" because it was clear that tenants were limited to the same small portion of discretionary funding year after year: "If it's been working, then why haven't they increased [the share of] funding for tenants to decide?"

We talked further about the conference, and he expressed his surprise that the organizers did not do a good job of integrating the tenants, many of whom were clearly struggling with limited incomes and painful disabilities, and the practitioners, animated by the conference's opportunities for professional development. Tenants packed some sessions, and others were exclusively filled with practitioners, a phenomenon that reflected self-sorting by both groups. The students' talkback was too intense for him: "There are people who claim to be specialists in this field who couldn't deal with integrating some of the participants who were in a different place. I was telling my girlfriend last night, that I didn't know, I don't have a good way of phrasing this, if I have a right as a WASP to have found the conference not as helpful for me because it was not restricted to the people I was interested in talking to." He pauses and repeats the question, almost plaintively, "As a WASP, is it okay that this wasn't useful for me?"

Admissions of failure to identify with others were rare, and developed out of the extraordinary circumstances of the conference, but they illuminate the extent to which using practices on each other is a relatively foreshortened way of enacting the challenging realities of inclusive public engagement. Often, such efforts fall short because so many practitioners have been brought together because of their shared discourse and approach, which prompts easygoing conversations that don't require much expert facilitation. During a demonstration of the fishbowl method typically used in high-conflict situations, the instructor in the IAP2 training course started shouting inflammatory statements about 9/11 because we, the trainees, were not getting hot or "emotional enough." The facilitator hoped to provoke some strong emotion to demonstrate the method's effectiveness at defusing such emotion, but the intended effect was lost on the twelve trainees, as we recoiled in silence from the bilious statements and loud shouting—so out of place in the hushed hotel conference center in the Alexandria, Virginia, historic district. In the latter case, there is simply not enough neediness in the professional public engagement field to make engagement interventions practically useful. In the former case, in which actual people from marginalized groups were invited to join the professional community at the C2D2 conference, their different interests and needs created substantial disconnects that were hard to talk about except in sotto voce conversations.[17] The lived experience of these silences—the disconnect between teenagers' tragic experiences with alcoholism and adult professionals' taken-for-granted assumptions about the universal appeal of conference happy hours—was painful for both.

Sandy Heierbacher from NCDD wondered in an interview about the ways in which members of the field sometimes weren't aware of their capacity for excluding others and refused to acknowledge such problems when challenged: "They don't even realize how New Agey they sound and you just know that anyone who's there who's a conservative is just thinking, 'Oh my god, what did I come to? What is this?' So I cringe a little bit." Her husband, Andy Fluke, interjected, "In their defense, they're coming from communities where that's the normal language. That everybody in their community speaks like that." Sandy responded:

> But it's something that we want to try to educate the field about that. Somehow. The importance of paying attention to your language. But it's so hard, because *if you called anyone on it, they go into denial about it. Total defensiveness. They don't see it* and they don't—Ugh! It's really hard to point it out. ... And that's how it is in a dialogue or a deliberation process. You've got all those different people with all those different views together and you've got to create a safe space for that. Which I wonder if some of the people in our field really know how to do. They say they do. They really think they do. But I don't think they are doing that.

When practitioners did not walk their talk, pointing out such issues was difficult—perhaps made even harder because of the threat to self-image that not walking the talk would mean in a community that valued it so highly.

How did the reflexivity enacted in deliberative rituals and routines depoliticize the events within? I argue that practitioners' reflexive discourses and use of their own techniques on each other is a companion to the self-criticisms they make in chapter 3. In fact, the meaning of these strategies often outweighed the meaningfulness of their results, as at the listening without communicating session where everyone was struck with nothing to say, or when an existing dialogue was shushed so we could quietly draw our individual inspirations. Active advertising of self-abnegation, of the powerlessness of facilitators and their holistic, Zen approach to converting others, downplays the kinds of power deliberation facilitators enact on behalf of sponsors and the kinds of exclusions deliberation might produce, as described in part III. Using their own practices on each other depoliticizes those practices as tools of powerful actors and helps facilitators to resolve uncomfortable tensions in their work, as they assert that everyone is equally in need of engagement and seeking similar forms of self-fulfillment. As facilitators, what they do is simply "hold a space" for a group to become authentic in reflection of the facilitators' own authenticity. This authenticity represents an emotional state and orientation to the good work practitioners do more than it represents faithfulness to particular values or identities. The habitus of dialogue practice and the selfing public engagement professionals perform on themselves and others—seeing others through the lens of their own preoccupations with harmony and integration, and seeing all institutions as equally problematic in their management of power—are critical to the way they produce public engagement for powerful sponsors.

Part III builds on the awkward encounter that concludes this section to see how practitioners define authentic participation for sponsors and stakeholders in deliberative processes. In this way, we move from a close-up investigation of facilitators themselves to a careful analysis of how they interact with clients and participants. We start by looking at how they market "real engagement" to their clients in chapter 5, and in chapter 6, we consider the kinds of transformations of participants they seek to produce.

# PART III

## CIVIC ENGAGEMENT AS A
## MANAGEMENT TOOL

# 5

## The Arts and Crafts of Real Engagement

The last temptation is the greatest treason, to do the right thing for the wrong reason.

T. S. Eliot

Powerpoint slide, IAP2 Public Participation Certification Course[1]

BY THE TIME I ARRIVE at the International Association of Public Participation's Certificate Training course in Public Participation in Alexandria, Virginia, in June 2007, I have gotten a good introduction to the public engagement field. From Sandy Heierbacher's inspired leadership to Carolyn Lukensmeyer's progressive idealism, from the older activists in Northern California to the libertarian and conservative good government types from Southern California, I have a sense of where all of these diverse people find common ground and where they experience frustration in advancing their work. The course will be a chance to engage in a five-day intensive training, to see a different place where the field comes together to consolidate knowledge, and in this way, it will be somewhat like the other one-day trainings I have done—introductions to various methods through their application in teaching settings. But in other ways, this course will be different, especially because it has been designed to give the official line on public engagement from the IAP2. Public engagement is, indeed, work, and practitioners must commodify what they do to sell it. I am familiar with public engagement professionals' struggle to balance activist and expert identities as democracy professionals, but I am eager to learn more about how they resolve the tensions of top-down engagement in their event design and facilitation consulting work.

Jack, our fifty-something leader, is a highly experienced and sought-after facilitator on difficult processes, with the take-charge manner of a Beltway bigshot but a self-deprecating sense of humor. He tells us a story about his daughter resisting his questions as a child by saying, "Don't participate me!" As he teaches, his Blackberry will buzz throughout the day with important business, and his no-nonsense demeanor will lend the proceedings gravitas, as we painstakingly wend our way through an information-rich workbook for full-day sessions, stopping for lunch breaks in swampy June heat that ripples off the red brick of Alexandria. About half of the eight to ten attendees are highly experienced public engagement professionals, looking to get the official credential but not in need of a lot of facilitation training. For these folks, the course materials are preaching to the choir about the importance of doing public engagement right. During the evaluation on the final day of the course, one of the experienced facilitators will admit that this program has reinforced what he already knew but that "there's nothing you said that I didn't agree with 100 percent."

The others are much younger, junior staff at consulting and engineering firms in their twenties, sent by their companies for the $1,500 course. Jack will point out that the reason these organizations have sent young employees is that they don't value public engagement expertise and tend to put their most inexperienced staff in these positions. In fairness to these trainees, they are extremely interested in proving themselves and doing public engagement right, even in difficult environments—and Lillian, one of the youngest trainees, talks about pushing her company to let her come. Mostly from the area or on expense accounts, many are looking to learn what they need to know as efficiently as possible and are not interested in socializing at night or relaxing much—everyone steps outside and quietly takes business calls during the breaks to manage the work they are missing by being here. We do get to know each other over the long hours of the class and over our lunches. On the last day, when I thank the group for tolerating an academic in their midst, Jack will quip that I have "almost acted normal," and everyone will laugh.

Given that most of the participants and Jack have lots of experience in regional planning, transportation, and environmental work, I feel at home during our discussions since my dissertation involved regional conservation planning in three US cities. Jack is adamant that participation not be for the sake of public relations, and this reflects a lot of what I learned in that project about public resistance to showy official participation processes. I also learned the difference an astute facilitator sensitive to local context could make in a community planning process, and Jack and the other older attendees are clearly those trusted facilitators.

The class itself has a bit of the energy and lack of urgency of driver's ed or Sunday school. We do some group work and use processes on each other, but the exercises where we act out being antagonists and then college roommates at a public meeting, or pretend to be public engagement facilitators on a rail expansion or landfill project, proposing issue framings and designing process brands, have the hokey feel of role-playing exercises everywhere. We play "telephone" to demonstrate the distortions in secondhand information, but the sentence "Toxicologists say leachate is leaching into the groundwater" makes it around the room nearly perfectly.

Repeatedly, Jack focuses on the importance of respecting the public. Against those who complain about NIMBYism and the usual suspects, he says, "We need to really value the people who come to the table. We treat them like pains in the butt rather than people trying to improve their communities." On the "Communications for Effective Participation" day, after discussions about how to defuse difficult situations (if someone proposing a speed bump project talks about "killing children," reframe as "You're concerned about child safety"), we go over some basic rules of thumb: be honest, apologize when you do something wrong, acknowledge raw emotions. Charlie, one of the younger attendees, says, "It sounds like these are just saying, 'Be human.'" Jack replies, "Yes! Isn't it sad that we have to state them explicitly?"

The group agrees, but it doesn't seem as if anyone in this crowd needs the reminders. These professionals are hungry to the point of impatience for Jack's stories of how he has handled problems and challenges in his own work. The experienced consultants want to know Jack's strategies for client management, which are particularly tricky in public engagement because facilitators' success depends on adopting a neutral stance toward the client's goals in order to earn the public's trust. This task is made more difficult by the fact that public engagement consultants are usually hired to facilitate at the last minute, when the client has already made a mess of things or gotten embroiled in an explosive conflict that is probably headed to the courtroom. Based on his own experience of working with public agencies, he advised that organizations were fearful and deceptive in their dealings with the public:

> If you want to portray yourself as perfect, everyone will perceive you as being an idiot. Over time, we lose credibility. I wish I could put an alarm in clients' conference rooms for when someone says, "We can't tell people that." That's exactly what you need to tell them! Withholding information and massaging other information—and then they sit there and say, "Why don't they trust us?"

Jack acknowledged that the "first rule of consulting is to make your client happy." With organizational attitudes like those he described, he said, "If I go in and say your values are wrong, they're not going to be happy. As a P3 [public participation professional], I am sometimes going to be in conflict with the client." Jack talks about unscrupulous people who will take jobs he won't and admits that he loses jobs because of this: "But they're not worth getting. If I do get it, I have to move the agency to a different place, and move the public to a different place."

For the choir in the course, and especially for the experienced consultants, the interest of clients in public engagement was a challenge they sought to manage through reaffirmation of first principles in courses like this and by maintaining strict standards about which jobs they would take. Public engagement practitioners must behave throughout processes with respect, integrity, and an authentic interest in transforming clients' attitudes and the public's attitudes about collaboration, compromise, and the larger good of the community. Although we were here to learn the basics of public engagement, what we were being taught was that there wasn't a foolproof formula; really valuing people's participation required genuine interest and caring, not checking off a set of boxes.

Concern about the ethical integrity and substantive work required to produce real engagement was a matter of professional survival in the field as a whole. One consultant describes in a participation facilitation journal what happened when, against his better judgment, he accepted a last-minute facilitation job for a public agency: "The public solidified their view that the agency was disingenuous. The client confirmed its suspicion that the public was irrational and bitter. ... This was not public participation. This would never help our client or the stakeholders ever learn the value of real public participation."[2] Notably, the consequence of this meeting was not that the client and stakeholders did not reach a decision on the environmental issue, but that poorly managed participation would not help clients and stakeholders appreciate the virtues of well-run public participation. Jack acknowledged regretfully: "What's happening all over the country is people are having more bad experiences, which makes it hard for us. This is what harms our profession is when these things get called a 'town hall meeting.' "

This threat was palpably real. Trainees had lots of experience cleaning up after lousy processes that did not adequately engage the public, that tried to engage the public in inappropriate settings (when there wasn't much interest, or during emergency situations where authoritative decisions were needed), or misrepresented what areas of input the public actually could influence. Participants in a cardstorming conversation café exercise during the certificate training recognized: "Bad experiences/ history w/ bad approaches" or "mixed" experiences were obstacles to the appreciation of public engagement. In the D&D practitioner survey, 33% of US practitioners chose "sponsor misconceptions" and 27% chose "participant misconceptions" as one of their top three challenges; another 27% chose "participants' past experience with poorly-facilitated processes."[3]

The prior chapters have largely discussed the tensions facilitators feel as democracy professionals and how they try to resolve these for themselves. But what happens when practitioners have to convince sponsors and the public that the public engagement they facilitate is both empowering and useful? How do they resolve the business imperatives of their work with their firm ideological commitments to good-quality engagement? As described in chapter 4, practitioners assert that deliberation is something they "are," not something they "do." Practitioners take a similar approach when it comes to thinking about what they do as something uncommercial and uncorrupted by conventional business values. The discourses invoked by practitioners as protecting the civic spirit of deliberation draw on social critiques of capitalism. Nevertheless, these critiques are ones that business organizations have already effectively integrated into the logics of the contemporary workplace.[4] I argue that this has a dramatic impact on the format and style of deliberative interventions, as the power of art, music, and spontaneous transformations becomes central to what transpires in facilitated public engagement. Real engagement is not oriented simply to letting the public vent or getting the public to endorse sponsor interests. Real engagement involves taking the public and clients to a "different place," producing a transformative experience that aims for understanding, trust, and human connections, rather than manipulation or cold, rule-bound information processing.

Beginning in this chapter, we transition from a focus on public engagement professionals to a focus on the market for public engagement. Many deliberation scholars have asserted that we shouldn't really think about public engagement consulting as a market—or if it is, that the market is minor and affects only a small corner of the field, which is largely not-for-profit. As described in chapter 2, this is a misunderstanding of the substantial amount of nonprofit and for-profit business in the field conducted for clients from the public, private, and nonprofit sectors. Contrary to scholarship that minimizes the market characteristics of deliberative democracy, this chapter describes how engagement practitioners are consistently preoccupied with managing the relationship between their civic passions and their clients' business interests, and with describing to each other their successful negotiation of this relationship. In these descriptions, professionals relate how they distinguish public deliberation consulting from business as usual—and especially from crass commercialization or high prices that might threaten access to their services.

Understanding this activity better can help us see how the experiences of public engagement practitioners illuminate the challenges of living within twenty-first-century institutions, with their increasingly collaborative stances and increasing willingness to engage in self-critique and adopt social values and discourses, positions I argue in chapter 7 can actually absolve organizations of responsibility for shared social problems. As we will see later, the anticommercial, earnest language practitioners use to define what is distinctive about their work is in fact borrowed from the business world itself, which has moved from the "Do the Dew!" rebel stance that Thomas Frank describes as "hip as official capitalist style"—corporations mocking conformity, bureaucracy, and the man in the gray flannel suit—to a new emphasis on earnestness, community, and "caring, sharing values."[5] Gone is the appropriation of public cynicism about ad pitches—the knowing, countercultural stance that asserted corporations were in the vanguard.[6] The retro values and uncynical enthusiasm of square, upright citizens are the new cool. Earnestness and authenticity are in high demand as cynicism about market and state failures has exploded.

Scholars have generally viewed these trends in terms of lifestyle politics and middle-class consumption: consumers seeking "nostalgic, neo-traditional and explicitly local solutions: the slow, the natural and the authentic."[7] But the celebration of the artisanal simple life, of "back to basics, place-based nostalgia," is not limited to eco-chic products like the fair trade coffee and sustainably harvested fabrics that deliberation practitioners drink and wear with pride. Public engagement itself is consciously crafted as an artisanal, local phenomenon as a way of testifying to its organic roots, an aspirational product that enables harmonic convergence of win-win values—environmentalism, spirituality, wellness, and the good life. It is by no means an accident that public engagement practitioners take pride in producing processes that use the visual and performing arts and reject conventional business values, even as they embrace the social responsibility of the clients who hire them. Clients like Whole Foods, the corporate juggernaut that symbolizes the McDonaldization of environmental consciousness, have embraced deliberative processes for their employees, and this demonstrates both the company's enlightenment and its commitment to contributing to "whole systems."

Public engagement is a market, but it's a market for a sacred thing, the way yoga and organic foods are, which means that practitioners must constantly make reference to the preservation of that sacred value in product design and consumption. As we saw in chapter 3, practitioners' interest in changing enemy institutions meshes well with neoliberal managers' interest in privatizing and devolving governance. Public engagement practitioners, in critiquing the conventional business interests and cynicism of their clients, may be genuine, but they are also drawing on critiques these clients have already appropriated and commercialized as new sources of value and distinction in a crowded marketplace. In other political spheres, similar trends have produced a premium on handmade campaign signs over commercially printed ones and handwritten letters over e-mail petitions. Just as Jack's tips distinguished the caring professional from the remote expert, producing a process that looks and feels homemade, and that produces rough-hewn results from humble amateurs, is a practiced art. The "social value" of dialogue is a readily identifiable product with political and economic benefits for sponsors, even as practitioners take pride in scrupulously rejecting political and economic logics as "fossil values."

## A Community, Not an Industry

A primary element of public engagement consultants' work involves framing their professional roles as antithetical to market values. Scholar-practitioners Carolyn Hendriks and Lyn Carson assert that the deliberative consulting field represents a "community of practice" "richer than just a 'marketplace.' "[8] As a concept adapted from management consulting, "community of practice" is an ideal entry point for considering the ways in which business discourses provide resources for deliberation practitioners to make sense of their values and to integrate explicitly moral sensibilities into their work.[9] Practitioners themselves indeed feel comfortable adopting this terminology for their own expert field; US survey respondents resisted the terminology of "profession" (10%) and especially "industry" (1%), with respondents overwhelmingly preferring to call the people and organizations leading dialogue and deliberation efforts a "community of practice" (57%).[10]

A central norm for the deliberative community of practice is that promoting individual methods or products should take a back seat to the larger mission of convincing others of the social value of public deliberation. Field leaders and practitioners criticize an overemphasis on marketing individual processes. Sandy Heierbacher, the founder of NCDD, notes that, while her organization provides a forum for people to share techniques, it is important not to let evangelists excited about one method dominate the conversation: "You don't want to give them a soapbox to just talk about their method all the time. They have to have the NCDD philosophy, what's going on in the whole stream of practice." At conferences, practitioners derided the "peddling" of methods possible among those more attuned to their own success than to promoting the larger benefits of dialogue and deliberation.

This resistance to marketing of methods and organizations sometimes takes the shape of policing those perceived as too commercial or flashy. In one vigorous debate on a deliberation listserv, a facilitator claims: "[Large methods organization] seems to miss the heart of real democracy, settling for selling the appearance of democracy. ... They have certainly been expert at attracting funding for expensive projects, promoting their organization and publishing slick (and by appearances, expensive) publications and reports." Another facilitator speaks more generally about the whole field: "Too often I see the D&D community, conflict resolution community etc wanting to take conceptual material out into the world and market solutions like products."

These anticommercial approaches to the deliberation marketplace include critiques of conventional economic markets. One practitioner comments on a listserv on the harmony of the individual and collective good, as opposed to a market orientation:

> When we take responsibility for what we love, it is an act of service. In practice, pursuing what someone loves comes from their deepest (or highest) selves. And because we all draw from the same stream, it seems to always mean that the good of the individual and the good of the collective are both served. Were economic markets operating from such a deeper place, I suspect they might look a lot more like Open Space.

Resistance to rational calculation is noted in a report on the challenges of pricing deliberative outcomes: "There are those involved in participation who resist economic evaluations of participation on the grounds that cost-benefit analysis and other related techniques would tend to ignore the intangible benefits of participation, oversimplify the issues and potentially reduce the space for innovation and experiment by concentrating effort on those activities that can easily be measured."[11] Practitioners take pains to emphasize the incompatibility of participation and economics and to advance democratic values in ways that protect deliberation from market contamination and prevent the "commodified nightmare" feared by deliberation industry critics.[12]

Given facilitators' outspoken beliefs in public deliberation as a route to such "more than profit" outcomes as democratic empowerment and community capacity building, practitioners use anticommercial, often religious language to describe their compulsion to share their knowledge, products, and services with the world at large and critique those perceived as violating this code. In direct opposition to rational logics of commercial or professional interests, these descriptions emphasize the irrationality of consultants' missionary zeal, intellectual property sharing, and extensive voluntarism. As described in chapter 4, those who have pioneered particular methods are especially evangelistic about their anticommercial intent, constantly advocating their uniquely transformative power while handing out self-published guides, free software, and how-to cards. The free marketplace ethic of a dialogue and deliberation professionals conference borrows from the open source and free culture movements, with which there is some crossover among tech-inclined attendees.[13]

While some conference participants quantify the price of their products for for-profit clients or set up exhibitor booths, they also avow that, for nonprofits and local communities, they are willing to give away their products and software free or at reduced cost—as their intent is not making money but spreading the word about the transformative potential of deliberation. One website that sells facilitation services also showcases "a voluntary world-wide Network offering public, non-profit and NGO [method] processes and training for whatever people can afford." In the introduction of *Open Space Technology: A User's Guide* (and at its website online), the developer of Open Space, Harrison Owen, foregrounds the extent to which his enterprise subverts contemporary business logics:

> One thing must be clear from the outset. Open Space Technology is not the proprietary product of H. H. Owen and Company. This is not a matter of altruism, or as some might suspect, pure madness. ... The creation of OST has been a collaborative project involving perhaps 1000 people on four continents. ... The reality is, Open Space Technology is a World Product. There is also the practical matter that a number of people, in a number of places, are already using Open Space Technology without my say-so or sanction—a situation in which I profoundly

rejoice. ... Please join me in what has been, and will continue to be, a marvelous co-creative adventure. ... Please share what you discover and we will all be the richer.[14]

In a similar vein, the author of a manual on twenty-one participatory workshops welcomes sharing the intellectual property in his text: "In the spirit of participatory sharing, anything in this collection can be photocopied or translated ... if you want to translate the whole book, whether or not for commercial use I shall be delighted. ... Anyway, whoever you are, if you can, enjoy. Do better than I have. Make up your own 21s. And please, share them around."[15]

This spirit of giving extends to voluntarism in the field. In the practitioner survey, 55% of US professionals doing paid work also report volunteer deliberation work; 13% of self-identified US practitioners do volunteer work only.[16] National deliberation organizations with seven-figure budgets may solicit the volunteer time of professional facilitators and paid consultants, providing no support for travel or accommodations for those who simply want to have a role in democratizing public discourse. Calls for volunteer facilitation go out regularly on facilitation and deliberation listservs. In their own sharing of intellectual property and their voluntarism, the deliberation practitioner community emphasizes a principled rejection of instrumentalism and greed in favor of a spontaneous spirit of collaboration for the collective good.

Nevertheless, the rejection of conventional business logics is by and large easy because social values are already a part of business discourses, a phenomenon practitioners recognize in referencing the value of social entrepreneurship and the benefits that businesses can reap for society. Just as they viewed all types of organizations as similarly dysfunctional and in need of deliberative facilitation, they also believe that all types of organizations have a "positive core"—a key assumption of the Appreciative Inquiry method—and can help to produce dramatic, positive social change. Whereas the prior chapters described the difficulties, tensions, and sheer emotional labor required of practitioners working in contemporary organizations, the next section describes the ease with which practitioners adopt antibusiness discourses even as they talk about the social value of corporations—because these discourses are readily available in contemporary organizational culture already.

## Social Profits and the Co-creation of Change

> Did I want ACE Hardware to get their materials through their distribution system as fast as possible? Did I want the Hanford Nuclear Waste Isolation Program making the best decisions possible? Do I want a school system to transform the way kids are learning? It's the same change process for me.
>
> Contributor, facilitation listserv

Despite the ways in which they invoke community values and police marketing and commodification within the deliberation consulting industry, practitioners do not reject the private sector itself. A near-unanimous 97% of US practitioners surveyed believe "the expanded use of deliberative methods in the corporate sector (with employees or customers)" is "good for the field."[17] This was by far the highest level of consensus on any of the attitudinal questions in the survey. In understanding the virtue of spreading public deliberation in all kinds of sponsored settings, sectoral context is not salient for practitioners. One listserv member articulates this widely shared sentiment: "Of course, while facilitators are not exclusively involved in public engagement (most of my work is corporate) I think the same principles apply ... its about engagement ... the venue is irrelevant." This perspective echoes the claims about institutional homogeneity made in chapter 4 and reflects that of many public sphere scholars, who have called for investigating the civic possibilities of nontraditional civil society settings.[18] Indeed, sociologist Nina Eliasoph argues: "Just because they are in a state agency or a market setting does not mean that people cannot speak and act civically."[19]

If commercialization of practices and products is anathema to the noninstrumental goals of practitioners, those promoting their products also emphasize that their interests are far broader than simply facilitating nonprofit- or government-sponsored processes involving citizens. Harrison Owen states that his role in promoting Open Space is to advocate for its wholesale adoption across all sectors in the interest of process improvement: "If I have a vision for Open Space Technology, it is that it become rather like accounting: something we all must do because it works, and because it is useful." This belief is consonant with Carolyn Hendriks and Lyn Carson's positive vision for the future commercialization of deliberation, in which "market competition reduces costs and 'deliberative experiments' become status quo."[20]

Leading practitioners like Owen hold a steadfast conviction regarding the applicability of participatory techniques not just in public settings, but in organizational and business settings of all types. In the practitioner survey, the top selection of five "most important challenges facing the D&D community" (developed collaboratively by NCDD conference attendees) was "making D&D integral to our public and private systems," at 35% of US respondents.[21] As that phrasing indicates, rarely, if ever, are businesses, civic organizations, or government invoked in different breaths as promising recipients for deliberative interventions. This reflects the frequency of business sponsorship and the variety of sectors represented in typical client portfolios; 45% of professional US practitioners in the survey ranked businesses, industry associations, and chambers of commerce as one of their top three most common sponsors of processes conducted over the last two years; by comparison, state and federal government was ranked as a top three sponsor by 35% of professional US respondents.[22]

Going beyond the celebration of the benefits deliberative democracy can bring to the private sector, many deliberation consultants argue that the private sector contributes social profits and civic benefits to the rest of the world. An announcement on a dialogue and deliberation listserv promotes a free online course in Appreciative Inquiry Summits by the developer of the method, David Cooperrider:

> David's founding theory ... is creating a positive revolution in the leadership of change, helping companies and communities around the world discover the power of strength-based approaches to planning, empowerment, and multi-stakeholder collaboration. David's most recent passion is an inquiry into "Business as an Agent of World Benefit"... where *every social and global issue of our day can be viewed as a business opportunity* to ignite industry leading eco-innovation, social entrepreneurship, and new sources of value.

One discussion on an Open Space listserv broached the question of the essential harmonies of open space and markets:

> Maybe the free market is actually an enormous Open Space, but we just don't know what the question is yet. Maybe, because this

enormous Open Space has no clear starting point or ending point, it is taking us a long time to hear one another and realize that we are all connected, and that we really do have a common question. Maybe we are just starting to discern the underlying question that called us to participate in this enormous Open Space. Maybe that question is: How can we share resources equitably on this small planet? Or simply, How can "separate selves" live together in peace?

Harrison Owen replies: "It is all connected, it is all interdependent— and although a particular market may have a beginning and an end— the great market place in the sky never sleeps. . . . And so we have particular markets, and only those who care show up (usually), and if they don't care, they leave (Law of Two Feet). For some people Sow Bellies and Corn is the thing. If that is not your cup of tea—move on."

The treatment of clients of all kinds as potential change agents extends even to traditional progressive and consumer movement enemies like tobacco companies—as demonstrated in a session run at an NCDD conference by the head of corporate social responsibility at R. J. Reynolds Tobacco Company and the company's facilitation consultant, a coauthor of *Chicken Soup for the Soul at Work*.[23] The session, called "Try Living with a Giant Bulls Eye Target on YOUR Back," emphasized the development of empathy for different perspectives—including that of the corporate managers and consultants sponsoring the deliberative process: "Session participants will see through the eyes of the director of corporate social responsibility and the external facilitator. Feel the positions, content and emotions expressed by diverse groups ranging from public health officials to tobacco farmers, elected officials to everyday citizens." Although few attendees smoked, many noted that this session was one of the best of the entire conference; it forced them to open up to those actors they may have judged unfairly and placed outside their circle of civic concern. As we will see in chapter 6, phrasing emphasizing empathy and compassionate feelings for the process sponsor is by no means unusual in public engagement processes. Deliberation is promoted as serving the good intentions and practical needs of corporate, nonprofit, and public clients, even traditional enemies of progressive causes, and these are not assumed to be mutually exclusive.

Practitioners bring communities and business growth together in a positive context of mutual benefit in deliberative processes. A primer on public engagement concludes:

> The work should thus always operate on two levels simultaneously: On one level it is about addressing a concrete problem. ... On another it is about building what philosopher John Dewey called "social intelligence"—the capacity for a democratic community to communicate and collaborate effectively in order to solve its common problems and enrich its public life.[24]

One consulting firm describes its mission as to "support our clients in creating organizations and communities in which people, profits, and the planet thrive." Such claims are not limited to deliberation consultancies that work primarily in the private sector. Even national deliberation organizations most focused on state-centered reform advertise their interest in working with global companies and private organizations to solve pressing problems. AmericaSpeaks, whose mission was explicitly oriented to democracy and public citizenship,[25] promoted its "21st Century Summits" to industry and associations to try to drum up new sources of business. In a chapter of an edited volume, *Diversity at Work: The Practice of Inclusion*, AmericaSpeaks' founder Carolyn Lukensmeyer, Margaret Yao, and Theo Brown argue that dialogue and deliberation is ideal for private enterprise:

> Private groups that practice inclusive decision making see the same benefits as in the public sector: better decisions are made, and the lives of those who participate are enhanced. Indeed, if inclusive decision making is widely practiced in private sector workplaces, there may be even greater benefit than in government. People tend to have more immediate concern for the business, organization, or institution they are part of than they do for public policy issues; not only that, they know more about it. This means that in some ways it is easier to tap into the vast energy, insight, and wisdom that business and private organizations have available to them.[26]

Just as scholars like Nina Eliasoph have argued that civic possibilities may be possible in nonpublic spaces, public engagement practitioners by no means rule out empowerment and social benefit in business settings.

This is not simply wishful marketing. Privately sponsored deliberation processes routinely call into question the virtue of profit seeking and the sustainability of growth, asserting "the end of economics as we know it" and questioning the "dogma of materialism," for example.[27] Samples of graphic facilitation used in sponsored settings and displayed at deliberation conferences (figure 5.1) reveal celebrations of civic and community values in contrast to old ways of doing business, as in descriptions of "a learning organization"[28] with "shared ownership" for a Kodak visioning process and a Unocal event that emphasized civic outcomes of deliberation such as "courageous conversations," "doing whatever it takes together," and "creating shared meaning."

I discuss the outcomes of these processes in chapter 7, but for the purposes of this chapter, the question is not the extent to which processes actually produce social capital benefits, creatively challenge convention and social injustice, or empower stakeholder critiques of sponsors that deliberation scholars would judge authentic.[29] High-quality public engagement, by whatever standards evaluators choose to measure it, is being produced for clients whom practitioners know have economic interests in public engagement. This has much less to do with clients'

FIGURE 5.1. Sample of graphic facilitation of a deliberative meeting regarding a coalition between Unocal (since merged with Chevron) and Fielding Graduate University, which offered a graduate degree program in deliberative democracy
Photo by author.

interest in creating social harmony for the good of the larger system than in public engagement's emergence over the past three decades as a useful alternative to other strategies—primarily on issues they believe will or may devolve into expensive litigation. Jack is characteristically blunt on this issue: "The cheapest lawyer makes twice what the highest paid P2 [public participation] consultant does. Some P2 consultants charge $350 an hour. If you're charging over $200 an hour, then that's the stratosphere. Lawyers are getting $350 an hour straight out of law school!" In their discussions of protecting public engagement from clients, practitioners readily recognize that what clients really want is what was described in the course as a "buy-in process in sheep's clothing," not stakeholder empowerment.

A better question regards how the melding of civic rejuvenation and organizational problem-solving can resolve such tensions. If true stakeholder empowerment happens to be a more effective and efficient route to buy-in, then clients will learn a valuable lesson about letting go and trusting deliberation to harvest the wisdom of the people. The following sections of this chapter describe how consultants celebrate the uniqueness of their craft through carefully customized, artistically inspired processes, which don't just shift clients' values, but transform participants as well.

## Crafting Boutique Processes

As the prior section describes, practitioners themselves see their calling as fundamentally oriented to social values in all of the organizational contexts they serve. But how do practitioners reject conventional business logics in their actual work? Practitioners emphasize that good public deliberation, as opposed to fake public participation, is distinguished by long-term, artfully designed facilitation substantially customized to the needs of individual clients and particular communities.[30] Practitioner Joel Mills's take on "Designer Democracy" deftly summarizes this viewpoint.

Mills argues that the key to the civic renaissance going on in public engagement is a "localized democratic vernacular"[31]—place-based cultures of participation and institutional designs that respect this. Similarly, IAP2 training materials emphasize customization and

context. One leading independent facilitator describes his projects: "Every single one of them has its own complexity to it, and
every single one—none of them are cookie cutters and none of them
are pre-designed. They're all sort of unique in one way or another."[32]
One practitioner's website emphasizes the "art" of meeting client needs
through good process design: "The organization is our canvas." Another
website announces: "We do not offer the same prepackaged solutions
to everyone. Our services are tailored to address the unique challenges
facing each and every organization."

The demanding settings of designer democracy should reflect the
local setting, in contrast to the hollow public rituals represented by
standard hearings and contentious politics, wherein citizens are treated
as passive customers. In describing "Authentic Public Engagement vs.
Business as Usual," one leading organization lays out the connection
between inauthentic forms of politics and business:

> At worst, cynical, empty public relations gestures prevail, as in the
> rigged "town meetings" that are so common these days. With partici-
> pants screened and questions carefully controlled, such counterfeit
> engagement contributes mightily to the cynicism that is so prevalent
> among citizens today.[33]

Here, the civic spaces of ordinary politics are framed as contaminated by
virtue of being mass produced for passive consumption, with "cynical,
empty" PR on government's side mirrored by "cynicism" on the part of
citizen-consumers.

Designer democracy, by contrast, is led by "a host of organizations
that are assisting communities with cutting edge processes which are
custom-made to fit local contexts," such that "communities are actually
branding their unique civic processes as a special feature of community life" with names like "the Hampton Approach" or "the Arlington
Way."[34] Wealthy foundations in the field pride themselves on their
role in promoting and studying top-of-the-line "Cadillac" processes in
comparison with more workaday "Volkswagen" events.[35] While by no
means the norm in facilitation practice, designer processes produced by
boutique consultancies and sponsored by wealthy foundations are the
state of the art, command the highest premiums in the field, and are

highlighted repeatedly as models of good practice in conferences, trainings, and scholarship. The National Research Council's definitive report on public participation in environmental decision-making devotes two of nine chapters to the importance of understanding the contexts of the decision-making and community setting prior to designing a public engagement process.[36] Practically, this takes the form of extensive individual conversations with community members and stakeholders prior to deliberative design, a subject covered intensively in the IAP2 public participation certification training.[37]

Researchers of deliberation introducing case studies emphasize the novelty of the projects they study and the diversity of deliberative methods available. Organizational scholars Monique Girard and David Stark celebrate the "extraordinary heterogeneity" of the "socio-technologies of assembly" used in the participatory processes for post-9/11 redevelopment planning.[38] High-profile processes like the British Columbia Citizens' Assembly often emphasize in their own materials the novelty and innovation they represent: "We are here to invent a new way to engage citizens in the practice of democracy."[39]

Indeed, an initial survey of the field reveals what seems to be a thriving proliferation of diverse methods. *The Change Handbook*, billed by its editors as "The Definitive Resource on Today's Best Methods for Engaging Whole Systems," lists sixty distinct methods, from Ancient Wisdom Councils to the World Café method.[40] AmericaSpeaks staffers Joe Goldman and Lars Hasselblad Torres inventory ten potential methods available to administrators interested in engaging the public: "21st Century Town Meeting®, Deliberative Polling, Large-Scale Online Dialogue, Citizen Jury, Dynamic Planning Charrette, National Issues Forum, Constructive Conversations, Community-Wide Study Circles, ChoiceWork Dialogue, and online Small Group Dialogue."[41] To add to this palette of methods, specific processes using particular deliberative methods are customized for their particular settings, leading to the development of Mills's "localized democratic vernacular."[42] AmericaSpeaks' trademarked "21st Century Town Meeting®" technology has been used for "Listening to the City" (Lower Manhattan redevelopment), "Voices and Choices" (Northeast Ohio economic redevelopment), "Community Congresses" (the Unified New Orleans Plan), "We the People" (Owensboro, Kentucky, community planning), and "CaliforniaSpeaks"

(California health care reform). For deliberation practitioners, branding each individual process with a unique name enhances stakeholder recognition. In the facilitation certification course, trainees were advised in the day-long module on Communications for Effective Participation that creating a unique identity for individual deliberative processes is critical to becoming recognized as a credible, honest "broker of information." This process diversification tied to place-based contexts is not simply a matter of branding, however.

A unique project name indicates customization of the process or method for unique local communities, and best practices in deliberation are typically tied to individualized process design according to the unique contingencies involved in particular issues and for particular communities.[43] High-quality processes "get clear on their unique context, purpose and task, which then inform their process design," in contrast to "poorly designed programs" that "do not fit the specific needs and opportunities of the situation."[44] Deliberation consultancies advertise this sophisticated level of customization, which requires a considerable amount of innovation, ingenuity, and improvisation, as part of their added value. AmericaSpeaks' report on the Community Congresses, for example, described "carefully selecting music and images that reflected local culture."[45]

Firms emphasize "event management that is customer focused, efficient, and flexible." Mills describes "the dramatic spread of custom-made deliberative processes" using diverse methods responsive to local political cultures:

> On the local level, designer democracies have proliferated in the United States as the application of a variety of processes has produced unique democratic products. In one sense, the U.S. has become a "Baskin-Robbins Democracy," except that instead of just 33 flavors, we have thousands of boutique democracies each reflecting a unique civic culture and tradition.[46]

Certainly, heterogeneity, innovation, and improvisation are part of the story of dialogue and deliberation practice in the United States, and responsiveness to local contexts and unique issues represents a critical aspect of the expertise sold by deliberative consultants. The metaphors of painting, food, and fashion and the local cultural resources described in this section are not the only way deliberative processes are made authentic and ineffably unique. As the following section describes, deliberative transformations are enacted through artistic interventions that celebrate the human spirit.

## The Transformational Power of Art

> Critique is an essential part of capitalist production. The ability to express one's opinions in public allows the system to verify itself as democratic. Through such means, it is able to generate its own critique and then quickly neutralize it. Within the neo-liberal spaces of contemporary art, thereby some opinions not readily acceptable in other public places can be displayed but the politics easily contained.
>
> Geoff Cox, "Democracy 2.0" (2010: 61)

Sociologists have been some of the most active in arguing for the importance of art in social change.[47] These scholars assert art's expressive, emotional, liberatory, and even redemptive power—art can bring subaltern communities together, frame common experiences in transformational ways, and communicate powerful messages. Certainly, art can be powerful, as demonstrated by the strategic uses of visual art, dance, and theatrical performance in the women's movement, antiapartheid movement, and AIDS activism.[48] Popular cultural traditions like music play roles as symbolic resources and "political mediators," as in the use of work songs in the labor movement and spirituals in the civil rights movement.[49] Recent research on contemporary movements like Burning Man and Culture Jamming has, in line with the arguments asserted by activists, described the arts as a democratic and democratizing practice; by engaging nonartists in production, participatory art contests passive consumerism and creates a new domain for movement activity.[50]

But assuming the intrinsically mobilizing potential of art would prevent us from understanding how the "power of art in deliberation" is itself a social construction with political implications. Researchers in this vein have questioned assumptions about "the inherently political function of art" to investigate how claim making about the political potential of art is a "specific cultural project" subject to contestation.[51] Art may empower and demobilize, sometimes simultaneously.[52] Beliefs about the social transformations possible in art and about the value of art in "culture change" are used in particular contexts that relate amateur artistic production to authentic empowerment and real engagement.

Engendering a spirit of co-creation and noninstrumental, one-of-a-kind vibrancy within public engagement often takes the form of integrating the visual and performing arts into processes. Graphic recording of dialogue, musical performances, drumming, collaborative poetry performances, individually painted Peace Tiles, and Playback Theatre can captivate participants' senses. Creative process design should engender the creativity of participants as well; a facilitator dedicated to advancing the use of the "expressive arts" in facilitation describes how "people from all over the world participate in these transformative programs, awakening their creative juices and discovering the authentic self." One consultancy argues that its services are:

> An engine for creativity. From beginning to end, our work is infused with the use of multiple intelligences, principles of emergence and the power of play. An exciting environment with engaged participants is created when all of these elements "fire" at the same time leading to unimagined creative results in record time.

Slick commercialism is contrasted with the authenticity of participatory, artistic, customized processes unique to particular contexts.

In part, the use of art is thought to improve the quality of dialogues by providing a powerful new source of information, helping those who are visual learners to envision new solutions or get a grasp on complex data. Professional artists may be used to design such materials. One consultant on a conference call says, "What I try to do, what helps me is to have a visual representation of the whole and its parts. Right now, I'm in my office looking at a map we're using for a critical government project [on water use in a large watershed with multiple rivers and tributaries]. I'm working with a graphic artist to make overlays that show the interrelationships. We need to have some method of visually demonstrating the interrelationships that we're working on and the other activities that are going on around it. You have to look at it in relation to others. I can't do that personally without visualization. I think graphic artists and people who create visual guides for the time frame and geographic frame does help." Similarly, graphic recorders illustrate dialogue processes on large reams of paper as conversations occur, creating eye-catching, colorful images linking key points from conversations with arrows and illustrations (figure 5.2).

But, as scholars argue with respect to the use of art in social movements, art has other functions as well, and having participants—nonprofessional artists—use art to express themselves draws on tropes from art therapy, helping participants to connect with and share their own emotions.[53] In line with processes' goals of encouraging authentic, human connections and heart-based communication, drawing is intended to tap inexpressible feelings and values, forcing participants to use their creative "right brains" instead of their analytical "left brains." Conversation Cafés provide crayons and butcher paper to encourage doodling, whereas more formal exercises use drawing to produce, for instance, illustrations of a front page of a newspaper in an imagined future. The humble materials used—markers, pipe cleaners, yarn, crayons—put participants into

FIGURE 5.2. A graphic recorder illustrating "community of practice," a favorite term in the field
Photo by author.

a childlike setting of play rather than work. In the training course, Jack recommends getting participants out of a meeting room and into on-site tours and demonstrations, using their hands and bodies with models, games, and skits as much as possible. Participants also have the experience of contributing a piece of themselves by creating art, reaching a deeper level of engagement than simply listening silently or voicing support for others' views. Posting the art on the walls of meeting rooms provides an opportunity to tour others' self-expression and feel heard and seen. Art for art's sake is very much the point in these processes. The result of this art is sometimes aesthetically underwhelming, as in the art made of recycled objects at one NCDD conference (figure 5.3), but it can be strikingly beautiful, as in the Peace Tiles that are the core of one group's process (figure 5.4). The quality of the art supplies typically dictates the final result.

Storytelling and poetry are often part of public engagement events as well, a direct challenge to critics of deliberation who argue that deliberation privileges those who can communicate rationally—the idea being

FIGURE 5.3. Art made from recycled materials at an NCDD conference
Photo by author.

FIGURE 5.4. Peace tiles displayed at an NCDD conference
Photo by author.

that the force of the better speaker, rather than the better argument, wins. Instead, emotional slam poetry, peppered with expletives, and passionate forms of storytelling such as Playback Theatre, an improvisational process where participants watch reenactments of their own stories, inject the power and spirit of performance into events that might otherwise be dry or dull. As sociologists Francesca Polletta and John Lee argue, storytelling is an important form of input in public deliberation, and process consultants highlight the power of inspirational stories by encouraging testimony during breaks and providing a sensory experience of the inspiration that processes evoke through the use of choruses and music.[54]

Practitioners report that art is remarkably transformative for participants and useful for developing breakthrough innovations. One international facilitator describes a process for 460 members of a telecommunications company, following a merger in an extremely competitive environment, combining graphic facilitation, "live acting performance to open up conversation subjects, and a round of a percussion workshop, all which added great value to the whole process." The facilitator reports, "It was amazing how the group started to melt into transcendental conversations. ... I think that through the world café, our world has a better chance to face the coming challenges of food, water, resources, climate, or any sustainability concept that deals with the human capacity to face and solve challenges in innovative ways. Succinctly speaking, this world café was an extraordinary human encounter to see innovation possibilities being born that lead to hope and positive attitude to an uncertain future in which we all take part."

The art often becomes the story of the process, especially as it is crystallized in visually arresting demonstrations of collective creativity, such as quilts or murals of tiles that can be displayed and transported to new contexts. At the 21st Century Town Meeting described in chapter 7, during which performing arts professionals discussed the challenges the performing arts field faced in a tough economic landscape, the pop music played during keypad voting inspired two participants to do-si-do at the front of the room. This spontaneous dance was captured on video and promoted throughout the summary wrap-ups of the event to demonstrate the spirit of joy and self-expression the process evoked. People engage, and out comes something unique that wasn't there before. For public engagement practitioners trying to produce a "culture change," art is a powerful representation of culture.

Although the use of expressive arts is a regular feature of deliberative interventions, these stories about the civic possibilities of art are also promoted through particular methods organizations, consultancies focused on art, and arts advocacy organizations like Americans for the Arts and Animating Democracy that make the case for art as a form of civic engagement. Creative citizenship is reconceived as tapping innovation within ourselves. One facilitator organizing a series of dialogues on improvising democracy at city hall invites "artists of various persuasions" and "the innovator or artist within us all to be present as we interpret various themes around citizen engagement and the future of this city." The idea that arts and crafts are valuable for the creativity and collaborative innovation they can stimulate is repeatedly invoked as a justification for artful interventions in public engagement.

Given that one of the projects I studied in my research focused on the performing arts and that, as described in chapter 7, many professionals working in the performing arts rejected the notion that their art would actually be useful for advancing their interests, more questions need to be asked about the political potential of this art, rather than simply assuming that the use of art in deliberation mobilizes participants. What kinds of empowerment are described through the use of art? How does spontaneous creativity link with the duties and responsibilities of political citizenship? The answers are not as obvious, and not as divorced from commercial contexts, as the discourse about artisanal processes in this chapter makes it seem.

## Rejuvenating the Civic Spirit through Carefully *fakery* Crafted Process

Public engagement practitioners manage the tensions in their work by endeavoring to make their work as authentic and real as possible. This involves minimizing their role as industry experts and sponsors' roles as powerful economic actors through the use of concepts like community of practice, co-creation, and social profits. When designing public engagement events, they emphasize the importance of community cultures of participation, strategize about branding with local place names, and customize processes for the particulars of each situation. Most important, they argue that their customized processes employ art to power participants' innate creativity.

This literally *crafted* public engagement draws on the playful, noninstrumental character of art and the authenticity connoted by localism. Artful dialogue releases participants from competitive, anxious mindsets and enables them to achieve higher levels of expressive potential as individuals. As the next chapter describes, the reason pipe cleaners and silly hats have become tools of adult self-expression has much to do with the types of voice and empowerment on offer in facilitated deliberation. Art may be associated with creativity and spirit, but art-infused process design is routinized and linked to predictable kinds of civic outcomes. That these elements of individual participation and action are increasingly documented as key to economic accountability and efficiency will be investigated in greater detail in chapter 6, as we explore the transformation of passive consumers to active citizen collaborators.

# 6

## Activating Empathetic Citizens

It's never too soon to think often and think more about the business
of facilitation.

Practitioner, facilitation listserv

Some people say, "Talk is cheap." We say, "Conversation is cost-effective."

Practitioner, D&D listserv

BY 2011, I HAD REACHED THE final stages in this project of what sociologists call theoretical saturation: the point at which I was intimately
familiar with the predictable patterns of the deliberation world, and
further research yields little new information. Although I had identified
deliberative routines and regularities, I could hardly have imagined how
much the larger political and economic landscape would have changed
in the United States in five years. Ironically, the devastation of American
cities, the crisis in America's employer-run health care system, and the
financial malaise gripping the country improved the fortunes of public
engagement practitioners. Gone are the 2006 conference sessions titled
"How to Make a Living in D&D"; new opportunities and new demand
have shifted listserv discussions to how to leverage the current crises to
promote deliberation. On the NCDD listserv in July 2010, in a post
titled "On 'Marketing'. . .," Pete Peterson of Common Sense California
(later renamed the Davenport Institute) related how the "new normal"
of slashed budgets had caused demand for public engagement from
California city managers to skyrocket: hard times mean that "the time
has never been better for this field." Public engagement professionals
suddenly look like manna from heaven to these strapped administrators:

In this important time, exists a group of trained facilitators, who may be perfectly placed to come alongside these local officials as they seek to make decisions of a scope they just never taught you about in policy school. My organization works with these folks on a daily basis, and is advised by a group of them regularly. While many might be looking "for cover" from the public, that doesn't mean they don't understand that legitimate conversations about service prioritization and land use aren't important. As the Mayor of John Steinbeck's hometown of Salinas told me, "The civic engagement process and the introduction into the civic arena of 'deliberative democracy' is essential at this time in California. The gap between service expectations by the public and the public sector's inability to deliver those services needs to be bridged."

Peterson argues that traditional activism can't work because there are simply no resources to be redistributed; the desires of Grover Norquist (his fellow conservative and copanelist at the 2008 NCDD conference) to drown government in the bathtub seemed to have come true. Public deliberation is "essential" because it can provide "credible" retrenchment processes and produce "community building" and "opportunities to participate in actual solutions" in troubled times:

The methods of Alinskyite community organizing will be almost useless in this context—lobbying or coercing cash-strapped city halls for increased services will be met with blank stares from half empty cubicles.

What many in this field (and on this list) are fully equipped to do is to help public officials make informed decisions, and lead credible processes that not only prioritize service delivery options, but, if done well, create a "space" where community-building might take place.

This is what I mean by "marketing"—that in approaching your local city hall, county capital, special district, describing your work (if you can truthfully) as consulting on public discussions around service prioritization and public problem-solving. While "dialogue" may be a part of this, what I am describing is more along the lines of choice-making, and providing opportunities to participate in actual solutions (beyond decision-making) when possible.

Peterson wasn't the only one finding new forms of recognition and appreciation for the credibility of his work. Popular media from the *Economist* to politics blogs in 2010 trumpeted the work of pracademic James Fishkin, inventor of the Deliberative Poll, for providing a model of deliberative democracy with the promise to cut through partisan sniping and media misinformation. Joe Klein asked in *Time Magazine* whether deliberation was the deus ex machina to get us out of the mess we're in: "What if there were a machine, a magical contraption that could take the process of making tough decisions in a democracy, shake it up, dramatize it and make it both credible and conclusive?" Deliberative polling, Klein writes, seems like a promising answer:

> Given all the noise afflicting the country, this might be a productive moment for deliberative democracy. "It works best when you have hard choices," Fishkin says. ... "If you give people real choices and real consequences, they will make real decisions. ... People are tired of the elites telling them what to do," says Fishkin. Perhaps it's time to turn that process upside down.[1]

The *Economist* was more skeptical, but still enthusiastic, proclaiming that Web-based deliberation could promise "Ancient Athens online."[2] In a time of new normals and tough problems, deliberation received wide support from a variety of sources, both for its ability to provide more legitimate decision-making processes and for its capacity to inspire "virtuous" citizen participation.[3]

At the same time, sociologist Gianpaolo Baiocchi, then at Brown, was puzzled by the wildfire-like spread all over the world of participatory budgeting, which had begun as a set of administrative reforms proposed by leftists in Pôrto Alegre, Brazil, in the 1980s. At first the adoption of participatory budgeting in the 1990s in other Latin American countries was an exciting and heartening development for scholars like Baiocchi. Then it became the hot new "tool"—no longer a set of administrative reforms proposed by neighborhood activists and labor parties but an "international policy device." Baiocchi thought the popularity of participatory budgeting as an administrative strategy needed to be explored. The second decade of the twenty-first century may signal the beginning of an era of decline, and credible, values-oriented engagement—the hallowed practice of democratic citizenship, in artisanal form—is in hot demand.

This chapter explains the relationship between the declining economy and the rising fortunes of public engagement through the shared features of public engagement as it is practiced today. While the prior chapters have explored the professional development of public engagement consultants and their efforts to design contextualized processes that produce authentic deliberation, this chapter investigates the sociohistorical contexts in which public engagement is being produced, marketed, and sold to clients. Processes may have lots of differences from each other, but what commonalities do they share? Because I am looking at the forces driving similarities across deliberative settings—the design of deliberative processes, the topics of deliberative interventions, the outcomes promised to sponsors, and the tools used to document and sell them—the evidence used in this chapter focuses more heavily on survey data and comparative content analysis than the more fine-grained ethnographic detail in the prior chapters.

In chapter 5, I argued that practitioners aggressively police their work to avoid commercialization and commodification, rejecting old business logics as hostile to the unique community values deliberation is about. As we will find in this chapter, public engagement processes look much alike beyond their surface differences, both in terms of their design and in terms of the uses to which they are put. The market for deliberation looks like the market for other forms of top-down empowerment more generally and has been subject to the forces of standardization typical of developing fields. As sociologist Isaac Martin has argued, the Great Consultation—the explosion of deliberative interventions over the past thirty years—deserves study in terms of the root causes that drive sponsors to seek out specifically deliberative solutions.[4] Larger forces have shaped the very existence and development of public dialogue and deliberation.

When viewed from this perspective, public engagement in each sector is most commonly used to solve problems of economic development, to ameliorate the harsh consequences of contemporary capitalism, and to legitimate decisions to raise taxes and cut services. But this is not simply because authentic processes have been co-opted by clients seeking consent. Public engagement professionals actively use business logics and business tools themselves for advancing the moral purposes they seek, when they define corporate practices and discourses as critical to validating the credibility of their work and the good social transformations it produces.

In contrast to chapter 5, in which practitioners critiqued business values and the failings of a consumption-oriented model of current politics, practitioners in this chapter nevertheless invoke contemporary corporate models of grassroots accountability as providing resources on which to reframe citizen expectations and produce authentic attitudinal and behavioral change. Economic efficiency, fiscal responsibility, and positive climates for business growth are framed as the "common good" to which publics should aspire. Whereas art was a powerful tool for producing noninstrumental transformations, management software and information systems quantify and track the production of civic responsibility. Accountability measures—common throughout contemporary society—are key to validating the self-actualizing, expressive performances enacted in deliberation as morally rigorous and worthy of serious consideration.

Much other research on empowerment initiatives in the developing world and in the United States has noted similar patterns, in which business priorities for fiscal discipline dovetail with assessment of individual-level empowerment and community building. Work on neoliberal aid regimes has noted the powerful alignment of discourses of grassroots civic action—people doing things for themselves—with economic development and dramatic cost savings: win-win scenarios of political and economic growth going hand in hand.[5] Microfinance in developing countries links economic profitability and growth with women's empowerment and liberation from traditional values.[6] Sociologist Christopher Wetzel studies the training industry that works with tribal nations, providing professionalized, business-friendly evidence of local empowerment.[7] Nina Eliasoph's work describes the peculiar shape of civic interventions in the United States, which "have to please multiple, often distant, usually hurried audiences [and] needed to prove to all these audiences that they were genuinely grassroots."[8] Documenting the informality, inclusivity, and spontaneity foregrounded in the prior chapter has to be done rapidly to service immediate demands for change, all of which influences the work of consultants and participants, and the types of solutions processes produce.

The view of business logics as civilizing—as providing a moral underpinning for social action—has precedent across a number of settings in which increased political equality has served as a balm for decreasing social and economic equality. But the particular form this takes in deliberation is worth explicating in detail because of the ways these justifications—overt and explicit in marketing to clients— are invisible in the deliberative democracy literature. Deliberation scholars have paid extensive attention to the heterogeneity and messiness of deliberation as a civic process, as described in chapter 5, and ignored the reasons that variety of authentic expression is valuable in the political economic contexts in which deliberative interventions are deployed. Deliberation is *also*, and often, a standardized best practice used to achieve particular goals of cost-cutting and social control, while producing legitimacy for sponsors. Deliberative processes are only one potential solution to sponsors' economic and political aims, and they have become a preferred option in hard times for particular reasons. Demonstrably authentic, voluntary deliberation can provide "action for change without resistance"—not just forestalling citizen contention, but producing citizen action in directions aligned with sponsor goals. Deliberative scholars and practitioners have generally argued that deliberation can be a truly deep, authentic alternative to neoliberal governance if conducted in the right way. This chapter argues that public deliberation is valuable in contemporary governance *because of* the specific form of individualized activism it reliably enables.

### Best Practices for Real Engagement

While academics generally emphasize the extent to which deliberation processes look significantly different from the standard public meeting, this focus on the novel character of deliberative events prevents analysis of how and why the design of deliberation is substantially similar across contexts. Deliberation processes may have unique elements, but they also exhibit the isomorphic characteristics typical of developing fields.[9] Much activity in the field is oriented to standardizing deliberative interventions and extending their reach. Isomorphism as studied by sociologists describes the social processes of diffusion, convergence, and standardization that shape fields so their organizations and people increasingly look, act, and sound alike. Internal practices begin to resemble each other through the shared pursuit of good business strategies that reduce individual risk and collective uncertainty—whether through conformity to principles, standards, training regimes, and formal rules or simply by imitation of successful organizations within fields.

Much of this activity involves protecting the authenticity of deliberation from co-optation and misuse by unscrupulous actors, while making sure that deliberation can be measured, packaged, and accessed by those who need it. Quite understandably and explicitly, deliberation organizations want to distribute their practices and methods widely, such that successful methods are replicated in other communities and mistakes are not repeated. Sandy Heierbacher, the executive director of NCDD, described in a 2006 interview this future trajectory for the field: "Eventually it should follow the patterns of other fields where the more accepted methods of practice will stand out and others that aren't as embraced people will start migrating away from them and those who are pushing them." Formalized trainings for process design and implementation are offered not only by professional organizations and methods organizations, but also by organizations like the Kettering Foundation's National Issues Forums Moderator Trainings, leading to the consolidation of facilitation principles and techniques. In the 2009 D&D practitioner survey, 248 US respondents had participated in at least one training program. Of the trainings selected, five had participation levels of more than 20% of all trained respondents. More informal sharing of logics and practices occurs in the many professional forums within the field, including conferences, webinars, networking activities, listservs, and journals.

The effort to develop tools that work across many different contexts contributes to the emphasis within the public participation field on developing best practices, a trend that has led to industry-wide concentration around a few high-profile methods whose processes have been proven to produce quantifiably effective results. Foundations have provided grants for the study of best practices within particular methods, university centers and nonprofit institutes are explicitly "dedicated to building and improving best practices in public engagement,"[10] and, not surprisingly, professional associations have been especially active in publishing handbooks of best practices and developing sets of core values and measurement tools for practitioners.[11] These guidelines are intended to make good engagement easier to implement and have contributed to spreading processes across a wide variety of settings.

In the case of participatory budgeting, which famously was introduced by leftist social movements, political sociologists Ernesto Ganuza and Gianpaolo Baiocchi describe how early diffusion as a set of comprehensive administrative reforms gave way to more widespread adoption as its "polyvalent appeal" was apprehended by administrators of all stripes: "PB attracted international attention, becoming a best practice that was taken up by a number of international networks. Now, it traveled as a politically neutral device, one that could improve governance and generate trust in government."[12]

Examples of more intentional and formalized diffusion of practices include fieldwide guidelines for practice developed collaboratively in the Public Engagement Principles Project, an effort led by NCDD to create a common template of elements required for real public engagement.[13] Multilateral initiatives like the Open Government Partnership are explicitly devoted to formalizing commitments and sharing best practices.[14] Ganuza and Baiocchi note that a wide range of mechanisms enabled the "fast policy transfer" of participatory budgeting: "dozens of international exchange programs, literally hundreds of conferences ... several NGOs that promote and help implement it." Its success in travel has created opportunities for even wider diffusion: "In this case, the travel itself has made PB into an attractive and politically malleable device by *reducing and simplifying it to a set of procedures* for the democratization of demand-making."[15] This has been the case not in spite of, but perhaps because of, the "weak impact" of participatory budgets themselves on administrative governance beyond Brazil—participatory budgeting's ease of diffusion has become its success story. The authors argue that participatory budgeting has "plasticity that comes from its apparent political neutrality and low institutional profile. In the majority of cases in Europe, PB required no institutional reforms or changes." In other words, rather than transforming politics, participatory budgeting has become a useful tool for legitimizing existing systems with redistributive bona fides.

Practitioners have developed performance standards within a third sector and public context to produce the commensurable outcomes that they often reject when describing deliberation as worthwhile and transformative in and of itself.[16] Ganuza and Baiocchi note this outcome in the case of participatory budgeting, in which "one clear consequence of the transformation of PB into a best practice has been the marginalization of social justice principles that inspired the initiative in the first place" in favor of "economic efficiency" and "increased revenues."

It is critical to understand not only the forces driving deliberative processes to look strikingly similar, but also what substantive content is shared across cases to understand why deliberative processes look as they do and what other interests standardization might serve beyond good business and process improvement. As described in chapter 1 with respect to Community Congress III, many of the elements that look spontaneous in processes—the slam poetry, the local touches, the recognition of an unpopular option or the addition of a new option suggested by a participant—are routine occurrences in a limited palette of frequently used practices. Initially, the deliberative methods marketplace looks crowded, and some aspects of design-like participant selection vary substantially, but the actual deliberations look remarkably similar up close—not surprising, given that deliberative theory foregrounds a number of key principles of reason-giving conversation.

Just as standard public meetings have a readily recognizable format that is routinized across contexts (officials on a dais, rows of chairs, an initial presentation, a microphone and sign-up sheet for individual comments), so public deliberative forums, while less formally structured in terms of room layout, have predictable routines and formats that are instantly recognizable for veterans (round tables; a movement, art, poetry, or visioning exercise to get started; an initial discussion to decide core values and procedures; break-out sessions; a return to the large group; "popcorn-style" reports and process summaries; and a reflective finale).[17] Most public deliberative processes incorporate some combination of discussion aids such as table facilitators, talking sticks, sketching on butcher paper, strategy games, or index card sorting in small-group dialogues. For large groups, high- or low-tech tools such as keypad polling, "dot" voting with stickers, or online voting aggregate the results of small-group dialogues.

Additionally, despite the frequent categorization of Appreciative Inquiry as a unique method, other deliberative methods generally employ its explicitly positive and opportunity-focused philosophy, in line with a belief that constructive processes must focus on strengths and future-oriented possibilities.[18] This accounts for the fact that many processes, even those that aren't explicitly described as community visioning processes, include a visioning exercise at the start to challenge participants to adopt a positive mental orientation open to imagination and creative thinking. While a democratic vernacular may be developed in the visioning processes conducted across the country, the success of deliberative process diffusion means that attendees of Imagine Chicago may find recognizable touchstones in Envision Carlsbad, Imagine Austin, and other Imagine or Envision [Community] processes.[19] The same holds for attendees of local processes run by national consultancies.

This correspondence of process methods occurs independently of standardization through the promotion of toolkits and deliberation guides. Given that process customization like that described in chapter 5 is resource intensive and time-consuming, many organizations offer off-the-rack or ready-made products that provide public deliberation process expertise at low or no cost in exchange for minimal event management services or flexibility. These can be products like the Meeting in a Box Community Dialogues offered by one consultant:

> Meeting in a Box Community Dialogues replace top-down models of public education (town hall meetings, expert panels) with two-way dialogues in which citizens become partners in solving problems. A Meeting in a Box is a specialized kit that includes video and print materials, a detailed process guide and feedback mechanisms. The kit enables leaders, their representatives, local organizations at all levels, and others to conduct two- to-three-hour community dialogues in which people work through the most compelling arguments quickly and get directly to the heart of a matter in a more constructive way.

Everyday Democracy (formerly Study Circles Resource Center) and Public Conversations Project offer standardized informational materials and templates for conversation, including a discussion guide for "Fostering Dialogue across Divides" of all kinds, such as abortion and interfaith relations, in addition to guides on typical community problems like "racial equity, education, student achievement, neighborhoods, youth issues, poverty, growth and sprawl, diversity, immigration, police-community relations, and criminal justice." Because the need for deliberation capacity in marginalized communities is high,[20] the expansion of standardized, low-cost tools and resources to organizations and communities that could not otherwise afford consulting services is recognized within the field as a positive development. Of US respondents in the practitioner survey, 87% agreed or strongly agreed with the statement "expanded access to standardized deliberation tools (community dialogue kits, best practice guidelines, issues and training guides, e.g.) is enhancing dialogue and deliberation in America."[21]

Conventions of deliberation facilitation conveyed across multiple different training settings include managing expectations based on what is up for debate in a particular decision-making process, encouraging discussion of values rather than positions, involving ordinary citizens to counterbalance the power of activist groups or interest group professionals, and organizing dialogue in small groups to encourage active listening and speaking among all participants. The focus of these different strategies on managing contention so it does not get explosive, dominated by particular vocal minorities, or mired in pitched battles gives public engagement a return on investment distinctive from that in litigation or public hearings. But these standard elements also make public deliberation deliver predictable results for sponsors, as later described. Evaluation systems ensure that deliberative interventions are real and high quality, reliably yielding the citizen empowerment and community action they promise.

## Sharing Social Responsibility for Fiscal Crises

Isomorphism is typical in professional fields, so the fact that deliberative interventions look similar is not at all unusual in an accountability-obsessed era. Although some critics have argued that uniform performance standards have negative effects, in institutions from hospitals to education, the benefits of checklists for surgical routines and benchmarks for grade-level work are clear. A sterile environment and a well-educated citizenry are worthy goals we can agree on, even if we disagree on how to create allowances for unique patients or students. But very little attention has been paid to the uses to which deliberation is typically put and to the outcomes it regularly promises, even if scholars have been preoccupied with replicating and measuring outcomes like education and civic capacity building. In fact, my survey research and content analysis have found that deliberation is typically used for particular topics very frequently, and a much wider set of outcomes are promised than simply mutual learning or civic spirit. These topics and outcomes are linked to business discipline—the moral virtues of thrift—to a much greater extent than scholars focused on civic and political values have realized, in part because civic outcomes are sold alongside fiscal ones as linked priorities.

Businesses are not just seen as capable of producing social value, as described in the previous chapter, but also as offering resources that can help the social profit realm. Much of the literature on deliberative democracy has focused on improving process design, and enhanced process design is a major selling point for the added value deliberation consultants provide to sponsors.[22] In promoting these contributions, practitioners assert that professionally managed democratic interventions can artfully revamp civic space currently polluted by a consumer orientation. Pete Peterson asserts that "governments themselves are to blame" for disengaged publics' unrealistically high "service expectations":

> Beginning in the mid-1980s, the "TQM" (Total Quality Management) craze in private industry found its way into the public sector, and a new language of "service provider" (government) and "customer" (citizen) followed. Government no longer was something to participate in, but something to pay for. We, as citizens, have too easily taken on this role as "customer," believing our taxes are just the price we pay for the services we desire, whether filling potholes or teaching children.[23]

If chasing business trends got government into an uncivic mess, new corporate models of accountability and devolved responsibility can reframe citizen expectations and produce "authentic" attitudinal and behavioral change.

Critiques of business as usual, familiar in the private sector, have also been adopted in the public sector. In the "Authentic Public Engagement vs. Business as Usual" report described in chapter 5, this consumer model is explicitly critiqued: "To the extent that citizens are considered at all [in business as usual], it is usually as consumers or clients of government." A new workshop for public officials facing budget challenges teaches that from 1970 to 1999, the model of government that prevailed was a "vending machine" model in which "customer satisfaction" dominated; 2010 to the future is the age of "community as partner" and "citizen accountability."

Inasmuch as performance measures and accountability standards are employed to make a business case for public deliberation, the moral virtues of accountability are typically framed in terms of fiscal responsibility. In selling its management services, AmericaSpeaks claims that it is "the leader in managing large public events that ensure effective citizen engagement *and wise use of resources.*"[24] A report from the United Kingdom, "Democracy Pays: How Democratic Engagement Can Cut the Cost of Government," defines the contrast between fiscal responsibility as a civic and legal imperative for administrators and good governance as a moral imperative for societies:

> Usually, the case for stronger local democracy is framed in moral terms, and this is entirely appropriate. Citizenship is a moral as well as a legal construct, and widening and deepening democratic engagement is a worthwhile cause. However, given the fiscal crisis and the demands of front-line services for public funding, *making the moral case for work on this area is not sufficient.* This is why it is also important to make the case that better democracy produces better governance and reduces costs.[25]

Notably, business principles such as return on investment (ROI) are not framed as a contrast to the art of democracy, but as wholly compatible outcomes of the noninstrumental creativity unleashed in deliberation. For example, a consultancy highlighting creative output at "record speed" advertises that "participants are not only highly productive, they also generate a common language and have a shared experience working together in deep collaboration." Progressive blogger Digby, writing about the Our Budget, Our Economy deliberations, noted that this linking of social justice and fiscal responsibility was expressed throughout the day: "Turns out there's nothing to worry about. David Walker just said, 'Fiscal responsibility and social justice are not mutually exclusive.' Whew." In facilitated deliberation, creative participation is framed as civically productive *and* profitable, and the moral value of democratic governance cannot stand alone.

In the marketing of deliberation described here, business process improvement, labor control, and increased revenues are promoted in addition to the "social profit" goals of education, community building, and empowerment. Figure 6.1 shows the outcomes defined for sixty processes described in quick summaries in the *Change Handbook*, one of the leading resources in the field. While empowerment and engagement received a number of mentions, education and community building were mentioned as outcomes much less frequently than business goals of

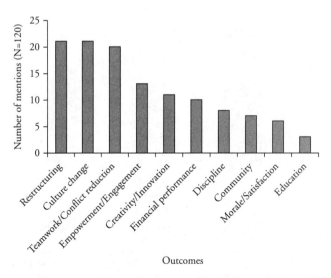

FIGURE 6.1. Outcomes advertised in sixty "Brief Examples" in *The Change Handbook: The Definitive Resource on Today's Best Methods for Engaging Whole Systems* (Holman, Devane, and Cady 2007)

restructuring, conflict reduction, financial performance, and labor discipline. Results like these suggest that political scholars are not getting the full picture of deliberation as it is practiced and that deeper investigation of goals like culture change and restructuring are needed.

The topics to which deliberative interventions are typically addressed, and their problem framings, provide evidence for the economic and social control outcomes sought through the application of deliberative dialogue to administrative policymaking in authentically deliberative, high-quality processes. These processes may indeed give members of the public substantive input or decision-making power and may have simultaneous benefits like education, innovation, and community building. But ignoring their other aims obscures why deliberation is such a popular solution in the current era. I focus here on the three most common topics on which US practitioners surveyed facilitated in the last two years: "education and youth," "comprehensive community planning and visioning," and "organizational development and human resources" (see figure 6.2). While problem-solving is undoubtedly collective in deliberative dialogue on these subjects, these complex issues are

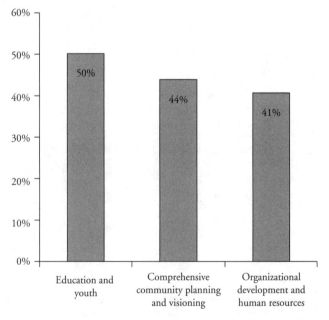

FIGURE 6.2. Percentage of all US respondents who facilitated on the three most common topics over the past two years (2009 D&D practitioners survey; N = 334)

typically framed in terms of economic development and community quality of life rather than equity or justice. The construction of powerful interests as stakeholders, when combined with an emphasis on economic growth, tends to favor participant actions and decisions aligned with the interests of institutional sponsors.

The most common topic facilitated over the last two years (by 50% of US survey respondents) was education and youth, a broad category with a rich history of participatory governance and collective action, as in the National Youth Administration, the Neighborhood Youth Corps, and the movements of the 1960s.[26] Nevertheless, the emphasis on youth development in the 1990s and 2000s focuses on youth development as an issue of economic development, not equity or political claim making. According to MIT sociologist Xavier Briggs, currently serving as vice president for economic opportunity and assets at the Ford Foundation, "An earlier era might have classified this work simply as redistributive social policy ... and public goods provision. ... But a growing focus worldwide on developing high skills, the shared benefits of a healthy population, and other imperatives makes it possible to tie the well-being of a community's children and youth to its economic competitiveness and 'quality of life.' "[27] Grants to organizations for children and youth-related projects increased an inflation-adjusted 88% from 1996 through 2001, outpacing overall growth in foundation giving.[28] In a study of 100 local youth organizations, Nina Eliasoph notes that such programs reject the paternalism of the past by serving disadvantaged children in "empowerment projects" that produce a particular type of "civicness." When youth discussed civic issues, they typically focused on actions they could take to prevent becoming a social liability, like avoiding drugs and jail; teen participants became "accustomed to being treated as 'problems' " in empowerment projects.[29]

Deliberative processes focused on youth similarly involve corporate and foundation underwriting of local efforts to curb at-risk youth's socially and economically destructive behavior, rather than to address structural inequalities. One practitioner states when interviewed on why so many projects focus on youth: "It's the one where you can get little things done. It's doable to get action on." The most high-profile deliberative effort on behalf of youth has been AmericaSpeaks' town hall meetings on "Shaping America's Youth" (SAY), part of an antiobesity campaign sponsored by Cadbury Schweppes, Campbell Soup Company, FedEx Corporation, McNeil Nutritionals, NIKE, CIGNA, and ConAgra Foods.[30] Literature for SAY's Iowa Citizens' Summit on Childhood Obesity notes that the process will "emphasize health-promoting steps that can be taken immediately." The larger goals of summit sponsors as stated in the participant guide are "lowering the cost of care" by "getting children and youth more physically active and eating a healthier diet."

Altering poor children's behavior was an explicit focus of statistics cited in public flyers for the event: "More than 30% of low income 2–5 year olds are at-risk for [being] overweight or overweight." The participant guide notes that obesity disproportionately affects the poor and people of color and that "obesity-associated annual hospital costs" for youth have tripled: "Prevention in childhood is the one viable approach that will ensure that a smaller percentage of American children will become overweight. To avoid the personal, societal, and medical costs of excess weight in the future, we must confront the adverse social norms and environments that our children face today." The framing of poor children's obesity as an economic development issue critical to the rising costs of health care and of behavioral and cultural modification as the sole "viable approach" forecloses alternative framings, such as justice framings focusing on poor children's food security and overall health.

In addition, an emphasis on changing "adverse social norms" suggests that corporations and government officials can play a primary role as change agents in community problem-solving, not as powerful economic and regulatory actors but as "stakeholders" and "partners" with "clout" among consumers. The participant guide specifies that corporations can help communities solve their own problems by investment in social marketing efforts "to advocate products and activities that encourage healthy lifestyles. ... Employers and advertisers can distribute media messages that continually reinforce the basic principles of movement, exercise, and good nutrition, and offer role models for children."

In themselves, dialogues like the Citizens' Summit serve as examples of successful empowerment campaigns to their participants, demonstrating the educational potential of cross-sector cooperation. Certainly, deliberation at these events may address structural inequalities or regulatory solutions, and education is one form of meaningful social change. But their episodic nature, emphasis on immediate individual action, and focus on powerful actors as constructive collaborators produce a narrow message about the viability of social action: youth need to be "shaped" into socially and economically beneficial forms, and "the basis of the plan *needs to be* actionable steps that each of us can take and promote today and tomorrow."[31] Just as empowerment through self-discipline is fostered in youth organizations, in deliberative dialogue on youth issues, social action is channeled toward community-oriented cultural change, not mobilization targeting national actors.

While topics like youth are linked to economic development, deliberative processes also directly address the fiscal, environmental, and social hardships that macroeconomic trends associated with neoliberal restructuring and competition for growth impose on local communities. In the practitioner survey, when individual topics were combined thematically, the most common category was urban planning, development, and budgeting, at 31% of all the topics covered in the last two years.[32] Forty-four percent of US practitioners in the survey had facilitated on the specific topic of comprehensive community planning over the last two years—the type of forum where growth management, local economic development, and community quality of life are on the table.[33]

The ongoing economic crisis has made such discussions, and the deliberations over trade-offs they involve, particularly pressing, as described at the beginning of this chapter. Administrators' desperation to manage the impacts of severe budget cuts is matched by the serious, emotionally fraught tone of difficult deliberations about which programs and services must be axed. A series of 2009 dialogue workshops in Philadelphia called "The City Budget: Tight Times, Tough Choices" asked participants to work through thirty choices for closing a $200 million budget gap, distinguishing between "low hanging fruit," "no way, no how," "shared pain," and "gut wrenchers." More than 440 individual written contributions were made on a "wailing wall." The dire phrasings of these choice exercises may seem to contradict the appreciative framings standard in the industry, but the language of toughness applies empathically to the hard tasks of administrative decision-making.

The Tight Times, Tough Choices process report describes the evolution of participants from cynicism to empathy:

> Over time, most participants warmed to the task and grappled with trade-offs and competing concerns—for protecting the poor and the vulnerable, for providing programs that would support youth development and for the business climate. And they began to realize "everything has two sides" and "we're damned if we do and damned if we don't." In some cases, this led to greater empathy for the work facing the Mayor and his budgeting team.

Avowedly tough processes structure opportunities for venting of public anger alongside dialogues that shift the practical responsibilities of project design and budget management, at least hypothetically, to the public.

This means that participants are put in the shoes of public servants and develop empathy for their challenges. One project report describes this sort of outcome: "72% of participants agreed that doing the Choicebook helped them understand the tough choices [the Health Agency] has to make about health care." Participants may also change their perspectives on the level of taxation they are willing to accept. [impose on others] The Tight Times, Tough Choices report related the participants' conclusion: "We can't declare a bunch of services off limits [to cuts] without agreeing to tax ourselves to raise money for those services."[34]

Conversely, participants may develop empathy for business stakeholders' resistance to taxation. James Fishkin reports to a deliberation listserv on the outcome of a statewide deliberative poll called "Hard Times, Hard Choices" in Michigan: "It is very striking that when the people grappled with the state's economic problems, they moved to raise the taxes whose pain they directly feel (the sales tax and the income tax) and they moved to lower the taxes they feel only indirectly (business taxes, presumably to stimulate jobs). ... The whole state in one room faced up to the state's difficult choices." Practitioners often reported that they could count on processes to produce solutions that were politically moderate and not dominated by grandstanders; in a conference session, one leading practitioner "guaranteed," based on her own experience observing health care deliberations over a decade, that no deliberative dialogue on health care in the United States would end up endorsing a single-payer model.

Similar reframing of management challenges and the limits of executive authority obtains in processes aimed at deliberative dialogue among employees and organizational stakeholders. Among US survey respondents, 41% had facilitated on organizational development and human resource issues over the past two years; this was the third most common topic selected—more common than health care, climate change, and other popular topics.[35] Like community-based processes on local fiscal crises, privately sponsored deliberation on organizational development also focuses on the direct emotional, social, and economic fallout of corporate restructuring, downsizing, and cost-cutting. The choice to use deliberative methods in these settings typically occurs in the context of managing contention or dysfunction arising from mergers, layoffs, and labor conflicts, which explains the emphasis on business process improvement, restructuring, teamwork, and culture change as outcomes sought in the *Change Handbook*. In certification training and in a conference session on dealing with "problem clients," practitioners noted that they were usually called in as a last resort after attempts at internal employee engagement or with nondeliberative consultants went awry.

Listservs feature discussions about facilitating on behalf of companies looking to manage the disruptions of corporate restructuring and cuts. In response to a post about how to reduce errors in a struggling housing-related industry where employees are "too tired, worried or disgusted to do a good job," one practitioner emphasizes collaborative solutions: "Survival as a functioning business capable of a strong come back requires compassion and a 'together' approach." Coming "together" meant having greater empathy for customers instead of sharing concerns about the industry downturn: "They all need to put themselves in their customer's shoes. What does the error or omission mean to the customer? What would it mean to them if they were the customer? *It's easy to point the finger at the economic crisis* but in good times and bad the only source of income for any business is its customers."[36] Another listserv member describes a research project on the mood and attitude adjustments required to achieve success in projects, with the goal of providing "a tool for project managers to align the mood of their project team with the project objectives." Such moods are generally chalked up to "the culture," as when a facilitator on a listserv describes the need for appreciative perspectives "so that constructive forces will not remain masked and suppressed (by the negative bias) of the problem oriented and envious culture."

Facilitation firms have developed specialized products for common management problems that produce labor conflict or demoralization of this sort. Viewpoint Learning in San Diego facilitates the aforementioned "ChoiceDialogues for Health Viewpoints," in which employees discuss preferences for health plan cost-cutting, for example. These collaborative exercises to allocate scarce health care dollars resemble processes developed for citizens in public settings, such as AmericaSpeaks' "Tough Choices in Health Care" (Maine) and "California Speaks: Working Together for Better Health Care." Like the role-playing on tough choices in municipal budgeting, processes in which employees temporarily inhabit the role of benefits managers encourage empathy for the difficulties of executive decision-making. Employees are asked to share the burden as equal stakeholders in the co-creation of change; employee performance is tied to their empathy and level of concern for collective over individual interests.

One listserv contributor describes this as follows: "AI [Appreciative Inquiry] is the perfect tool to generate alignment within an organization because alignment stems from compassion. If all members of the organization care about the work that they do and the well being of each other their performance, in any way that one cares to measure it, is exemplary." Appreciative solutions to economic crises typically focus on creative generativity on the order of turning lemons into lemonade. One handbook takes this quite literally, encouraging those marginalized in a downbeat economy to see hardship as an opportunity, through the examples of a microbrewery that sells Bailout Bitter and a Utah woman's successful "home tending" business "as the home foreclosure crisis leaves whole neighborhoods almost abandoned." In engagement initiatives for organizational development and community planning, communities and employees in crisis are often asked to put a brave, appreciative face on their losses, competing with their similarly depleted peers in other organizations and communities to decipher the best way to turn "social issues" into "new sources of value."

Overall, large-scale public deliberation processes are typically used for problems such as coping with benefit reductions, managing budget shortfalls, and mitigating social issues and labor conflicts that impede private-sector growth and local economic development.[37] Just as Logan and Molotch assert that urban machines promote growth as a community good to the exclusion of alternative values, deliberative topic framings suggest similarly constrained notions of economic growth as the route to "social profit."[38]

These framings take large-scale structural challenges affected by macro-level processes and cultivate small-scale behavioral solutions on which participants can act right away. These civic and fiscal outcomes are not idiosyncratic, but predictable and measurable. One consultancy points out that they are "able to systematically and repeatedly bring out the highest levels of thought, performance and collaboration within the organizations we serve." How, exactly, are civic qualities of authentic engagement like deep collaboration, shared experience, and improved civic capacity measured and linked to fiscal accountability? The next section demonstrates that the quantification of authentic engagement entails tracking the transformation of stakeholders from demanding consumers to active citizen partners.

### Tiny Expectations: Culture Change as Attitude Adjustment

As discussed in the prior chapter, practitioners promote transformational conversions as a testament to deliberative quality. Converting stakeholders from demanding consumers to civic partners is indeed an explicit goal of deliberative sponsors across sectors, but I argue that these transformations are framed as morally worthwhile not only because of their self-actualizing dimensions, but also because of their fiscal implications. In a wide variety of settings, stakeholder preference change is linked to improved surveillance, greater worker and taxpayer discipline, and enhanced organizational legitimacy. The cost savings reaped through these results are generally framed as contributions to the collective good, inasmuch as they reduce conflict and contention and render publics more tractable in efficient ways. According to Anthony Zacharzewski, the founder of the Democratic Society, an NGO that promotes participation in government in the United Kingdom, "Intensive information-based democratic engagement could enable councils to, in Richelieu's metaphor, pluck more feathers with less squawking."[39]

As such, the forms of action empowered by deliberation may provide authentic engagement opportunities at the same time that they reduce cultural conflict.[40] Bad citizens are reframed not as loud citizens but as expensive citizens, and citizen action is not repressed outright but channeled in structured venues where nonparticipation or exit is framed as uncivic behavior.[41] Deliberative participation is virtuous not on its own merits but because it changes the attitudes of individuals regarding their own role in change; instead of "let peace begin with me," this discourse focuses on "let action begin with me, through a shift in my own thinking about who is responsible for what." A report on deliberative training offered to public administrators highlights the transformational nature of authenticity on the part of government bureaucrats: "Civic engagement involves 'culture change' and 'authenticity.'... There are inherent tensions in the idea of government sponsoring citizens to do *what citizens need to do for themselves.* When this tension is handled well, public administrators are acting ... 'authentically.'"[42] On a listserv discussion about change in the workplace, a practitioner argues:

> Until we can shift our own ways of thinking, we won't cause a shift in how businesses operate.
>
> But what is it in our thinking that has to shift?
>
> Let's take a page from Gandhi who said, "Be the change you wish to see in the world."
>
> Or another more mundane example: "Think and act like an owner."
>
> Both represent what Joel Barker and others called a "paradigm shift."
>
> In the first case: You want things to change? It starts with you.
>
> In the second case: You want engagement and empowerment?? It starts with you.
>
> Want to shift the thinking?? You start.

As we will see, the linking of "mundane" business change and social change on the Gandhian scale is extremely common, as is the admonition to "think like an owner," in both public and private settings.

Measurable effectiveness is typically defined through cost savings; how these cost savings are articulated is generally in terms of, as one listserv member puts it, "pay now, or pay later." This was elaborated in the same discussion thread as "time to effectiveness" or "the time spent undoing, redoing and selling—nobody really measures that ... upfront investment has long term payoffs." Jack joked in the public engagement training, "There is never enough time and money to do it right, but always enough to do it over." He also noted a different economic benefit of government agencies investing in deep engagement on issues that mattered to the public: "If you spend it in the right places, people will pay attention and trust you as an agency to do the other stuff." On one listserv, a practitioner reports that sponsors "attribute the lack of protest over the rate hikes to the extensive public outreach and involvement process that the city undertook ... the city spent about $75,000 on the 14 month process between staff time and consultant fees, but he feels the results warrant this investment. The city council really respect the need to go slow to go fast on these weighty issues." Deliberation is constituted as a more manageable form of citizen empowerment than not empowering citizens and hoping that they don't squawk, increasing litigation and erecting costly obstacles to governance and project implementation. In his "Democracy Pays" report, Anthony Zacharzewski argues that "there is a good deal of evidence that greater democratic involvement in decision making leads to lower costs."[43]

Administrators and managers sometimes worry that deliberation will empower demanding consumers and organized interests, but deliberative proponents argue that these are exactly the reasons to undertake a proactive deliberative process:

> Officials fear that the demands of the public, both for spending and for information, will be insatiable. They worry that pressure from special interest groups or self-interested voters will warp the messages coming through. ... Officials ... often assume that more democratic engagement will lead to more demands for greater spending, with citizens not considering the trade-offs. In fact, practical experience suggests that consultations where citizens are given opportunities to discuss issues and wider scope to make trade-offs produce much richer and more thoughtful results. ...[44]

This claim mirrors sociologist Isaac Martin's finding that the expansion of "anticipatory consultation" is driven by increases in state resource extraction.[45] Not least, deliberative processes may save time for administrators by forcing organized activists to engage in small-group discussions with nonactivists, diluting their voices and minimizing their access to the press and high-profile targets.[46] Deliberation organizations in the United States similarly promote the ability to solicit the engagement of not the usual suspects, but those not yet mobilized: AmericaSpeaks advertised their "unique strategies for engaging a demographically diverse group of unaffiliated citizens to participate in your public forums." Ganuza and Baiocchi note that the key transformation in participatory budgeting as it moved from a leftist reform to a management tool was to "de-emphasize ... the role of existing associations and their leaders in favor of the individual citizen."[47] Authenticity here is linked to being an amateur lay actor, removed from politics as usual.

Practitioners argue that once engaged, citizen stakeholders in facilitated deliberations will abandon self-interest for co-creative solutions aimed at collective benefit; AmericaSpeaks claimed on its website: "A comprehensive engagement strategy can transform your participants into stakeholders with sustained involvement in your project." That deliberative consultancies advertise such outcomes is no surprise, given the substantial academic literature on the social benefits of deliberative democracy and the ways in which deliberative culture creates new civic capacity.[48] However, I argue here that such benefits are explicitly and actively linked by practitioners to cost savings and fiscal discipline, *at the same time* that these practitioners argue for their civic benefits. One consultancy advertises: "We look for concurrent results in not just performance and economic prosperity, but also in individual well being and societal contribution." A practitioner on a listserv reports the "magic" of Open Space: "It has been a common experience in Open Space that work groups achieve levels of performance they can hardly believe. A hard nosed AT&T executive once called it 'magic' when his team managed to accomplish in 2 days what they knew 'must' take at least 10 months. Were this to have happened just once, that would be interesting, but in my own experience it is almost common place ... the high level of performance becomes almost overwhelming."

Practitioners articulate the ways economic outcomes are achieved by describing disciplinary containment of existing or potential challengers, using the language of decreased resistance or reductions in cynicism. Decreased resistance can take the form of greater willingness to accept cuts in public budgets or in workplace benefits, in addition to greater empathy for the tough choices administrators face. One consultancy's website asserts that "leaders need to know how to involve staff in decision-making. Staff involvement, *not just superficial consultation*, is key to tapping into what they know and winning their enthusiastic support."[49] This more authentic form of engagement may require "new techniques for reinforcing group commitments, and shifts in organizational culture and norms." Zacharzewski argues that "the more involved people are in democratic discussions of financial matters, the more they can be relied upon to support targeted cuts" and the greater their "tax morale," or "willingness to pay tax."[50]

The social learning and collaborative listening that occur in sponsored deliberation reliably cause participants to adopt less self-interested outcomes, and these are routinely highlighted by both deliberation practitioners and deliberation scholars in process evaluations and on deliberation listservs. Zacharzewski reports that such processes can help administrators distinguish entitlements that are truly "off-limits" from less sacred cows, engendering greater administrative flexibility: at the end of one process, "participants had expressed a willingness to cut several high-cost areas of expenditure, such as highways maintenance, libraries, museums, and residential services for older people. . . . It is worth noting that the directions in which opinions shifted did not follow a pattern of self-interest or prejudice."[51] The results of deliberative "choicework"—dialogues that ask participants to playact making difficult budgetary choices—may reflect shared preferences and a willingness to sacrifice, but they also have value for administrators to the extent that they provide efficient feedback on which administrative goals are feasible and likely to be accomplished with the least amount of resistance from stakeholders and advocacy groups. In this sense, deliberation can help administrators anticipate or counter resistance, and large-scale deliberations typically go through a number of pilot iterations with focus groups to diminish the potential of topic framings to provoke contention.[52]

But decreased resistance is simultaneously paired with an increased proclivity to "positive" forms of civic mobilization. Advertising copy on one consultancy's website claims: "Cynicism and resistance are replaced with a renewed sense of discovery, possibility, commitment, joy and positive action." Similarly, Appreciative Inquiry is promoted as "a collaborative strengths-based approach that is proving to be highly effective in thousands of organizations, colleges and communities in more than a hundred countries around the world. The AI approach heightens energy, sharpens vision and inspires action for change without resistance." Genuine processes will yield not only genuine enthusiasm for administrative goals but activate citizen stakeholders to help achieve them.

The extent to which deliberation can prompt citizen accountability such that citizens actually are willing to assume ownership of functions previously performed by administrators reflects neoliberal governance principles of devolved and individualized responsibility for collective outcomes. These civic benefits are extensively highlighted in deliberation marketing and are discussed on listservs as motivation for strapped administrators to resort to deliberative solutions. Anthony Zacharzewski argues that "deeper democratic engagement can increase productivity, both in pure economic terms, and in terms of 'civic productivity'— where neighbourhood and social civic action replaces higher-cost state intervention."[53] In a listserv discussion on quantifying the benefits of deliberation, one practitioner reports from the front lines:

> We are finding agencies becoming interested in our work because their budgets are being cut so much that they need to find truly different and more effective ways to get their work done. They can no longer pay for inefficiency. They are having to make huge cuts in staff, which means depending more on community collaborations. Paying for process to get community engaged is cheaper than paying for staff.

The civic transformations reaped in deliberation entail attitudinal and behavioral changes predicted by deliberation scholars, and these outcomes are enthusiastically promoted to clients as both fiscally and socially responsible remedies for a challenging economic and political landscape of post-crash capitalism.

Nevertheless, the marketing of deliberative solutions as enhancing reputations and advancing conventional social control functions, despite the explicit questioning of social control functions and authority within deliberative processes, suggests that the deliberation market serves client interests by achieving regulation quietly. For example, the use of Open Space Technology, with the injunction in the technique that the civic space created entails free choice among participants to take charge of their passions, involves predictable tensions in a private setting. "The essence of OST is invitation," and one of the four principles is "whoever comes is the right people," but participation is typically not optional in sponsored deliberative settings. As such, two practitioners on a listserv discuss how to frame a compulsory event as optional:

> I am currently working with such an agency to prepare an invitation for "all staff" to come to the annual "retreat day" which will be held in OS ... this has traditionally been a compulsory attendance event and the sponsor is having "serious fun" working through the implications of "invitation"—and I think that this is the key part of the process—get the question and the language of invitation right and the rest will happen—regardless of the implicit or explicit requirement to be there.
>
> This day is usually called All Staff Meeting and is mandatory. Their question to me is how do they balance the mandatory nature of this meeting with the "invitation" approach of Open Space that sounds optional.

The fact that it is important to clients and practitioners that stakeholders undertake deliberation in an authentically voluntary way reveals the extent to which sponsors seek to create spaces that both look and *feel* authentically civic rather than businesslike.

The citizen transformations reaped in authentic deliberative processes may be no less real or civic-spirited for being in the direction of support for administrative goals, but the extent to which such projects redefine the collective good in terms of how civic discourse and citizen actions reflect administrator priorities and economic efficiency deserves further scrutiny. Simply determining which processes are "real" or "good" deliberation versus which are "fake" or "bad" will not suffice, inasmuch as the value of processes for clients stems from the social authenticity, civic productivity, and demonstrable accountability they are able to claim.

## Ancient Athens Online?

*tyrannical authoritarianism.*

Budget crises were, as the beginning of this chapter argues, front and center for municipalities and governments by 2010. But new approaches to involving the public on budget crises were being deployed by everyone from the mayor of Los Angeles to the *New York Times*, in upbeat terms that challenged participants to try their hands at the "Los Angeles Budget Challenge" and the *New York Times's* Budget Puzzle offering "O.K., You Fix the Budget." The mayor's website asked:

> How will you balance the City's budget?
>
> The Mayor of the City of Los Angeles is given the responsibility by the City Charter to develop a budget plan that must be presented for City Council consideration by April 20th of each year.
>
> This year, the City of Los Angeles will be challenged by many issues, including declining revenues, increased service demands, and soaring City pension contributions.
>
> As we begin the planning process for Fiscal Year 2010–11, I invite you to help me develop my proposed budget by participating in the Los Angeles Budget Challenge where you will be asked to make some of the tough choices necessary to balance the City's budget.

The elements described in this chapter are all here: presenting the fiscal crises of contemporary governance as a fait accompli requiring shared sacrifice, putting participants in decision-makers' shoes, asking them to co-create solutions by making tough choices. The difference? The budget survey required participants to select particular options that the mayor clearly favored to balance the budget—and the evidence of public preferences harvested from this survey exercise could clearly be used to endorse these solutions.

Online participatory budgeting processes promise sponsors the ability to scale up their budget work to larger audiences, but they tend to eliminate the deliberative element, with individuals choosing their own preferences after reading educational text rather than listening to their fellow citizens' perspectives. Despite participatory budgeting's substantial acclaim as a deliberative method, the rapid explosion of budget calculators worries deliberative proponents, who anticipate that such efforts might be manipulated for sponsor gains but might also affect public enthusiasm for deliberative solutions. The Kettering Foundation asked on their Facebook page: "What do you think: are budgeting exercises like these what we would call 'deliberative choice work'? If not, how are they related?" Tim Bonneman, an expert on online budgeting software, asked: "So is the *Budget Puzzle* in its current form deliberative? Hardly." Even Pete Peterson, who was so excited about the promise of local government adopting deliberative tools, was concerned about the Los Angeles budget website. Asking "Is LA's Online 'Budget Challenge' for Real?" he argued that:

> There are definite "Good", "Bad", and "Ugly" aspects to the initiative. ... Participants should quickly realize that not everything is on the table ... because the Mayor says so. ... To structure an online engagement in a way that forces participants to choose it is, obviously, not straight pool. Related to these issues, there is an ugly, though understandable, "middle choice" or "Goldilocks bias" to the site. Throughout the survey, I found myself, when faced with "do nothing" and "cut everything" options, choosing the "just right" middle ground for no policy-based reason. ... The real "challenge" for all these projects will be to ensure participation is not biased nor wasted.

Such questions raise the issue of unintended consequences resulting from the diffusion of public engagement technologies and standards across contexts. Managing and synchronizing these transformations in citizen performance involves standardizing them and commensurating them, not just so they can be sold but so they can be entered in databases and tracked from project to project. Online deliberative methods are commonly used by 24% of US facilitators in the practitioner survey.[54] But the uses to which deliberation choicework, forum, and stakeholder management software are put are nearly invisible, despite a great amount of attention to the virtues of software and Web applications in scaling up deliberative interventions and creating a new Athens online. It is critical to put this activity in the context of other technologies for empowering and activating citizen action because, like best practice guidelines, technologies and software cross the boundaries of these fields swiftly and easily. Practitioners on listservs frequently discuss concerns about threatening, confusing, or selective appropriation of deliberative terminology and practices, such as "America Speaking Out" (an interactive conservative website not affiliated with AmericaSpeaks) and the Coffee Party, ostensibly nonpartisan and interested in deliberation but explicitly political (and questionably left-leaning) in orientation. Scholars and practitioners have critiqued fake participation and collaboration, but the line between deliberation and deliberation look-alikes may be increasingly hard to discern.[55]

The rapidly proliferating software platforms that are becoming a standard technology in the public engagement field are similar to the digital media platforms used in contemporary political campaigning, a "technical infrastructure" combining front-end interactive websites with back-end database tools that "extend practices of professional management," according to Daniel Kreiss, a communications scholar who studies digital campaigning.[56] Far less attention was paid to the surveillance capabilities developed in the Barack Obama campaign as compared with the democratized participation it inspired, in part because front-end participatory functions are so aggressively celebrated and back-end management functions are by nature hidden from public view. In digital campaign applications, interactive software harvests participants' personal information and that of their friends and combines it with other databases, allowing campaign organizations to "leverage social networks, intimate details, and psychological processes for institutionalized ends" (by combining participant data with voter registration and census information and reselling such information, for example, or storing it for future campaigns) in ways that are invisible to participants.[57] Not only are such initiatives and techniques described as holding exciting potential for public deliberation on listservs and at deliberation conferences, as in a plenary on "Social Media, Social Movements and Democratic Participation" at a 2009 practitioners' conference, but also many technological applications of social media apply across deliberative and nondeliberative engagement settings.

Because online and offline deliberative dialogue projects require registration and collection of demographic information to ensure representativeness, participants surrender their personal contact information and reveal their demographic profiles when participating. Such information can be used to facilitate the engagement and participation of groups underrepresented in project registrations as the day of the event nears; practitioners described undertaking additional recruitment efforts with Hispanic and Latino populations and with white men prior to processes to ensure effective representation.[58] Once at a networked meeting, anonymous demographic information is collected again through keypad polling and can be linked to participant responses, providing sponsors and clients with critical data on preference differences across stakeholder groups and demographic categories.

*v. creepy*

Although national-scale information management of deliberative participants by government agencies and large firms is still in its developing stages and not standardized across agencies, issues related to maintaining the privacy of stakeholder information and engaging stakeholders who prefer to remain anonymous are already emerging in listserv discussions and webinar presentations in the field, on topics such as "Why You Need to Know about Stakeholder Privacy." Stakeholder management software guides project administrators in gathering and using information about stakeholders, tasks that resemble political strategies of opposition research and stakeholder profiling to anticipate and neutralize potential resistance: "identify your activity's stakeholders and understand their needs"; "prioritize the stakeholders"; "map their profile," including assessments of their "perceived power, proximity, and urgency"; "develop an engagement strategy"; and track "changes over time as you update and review the SH community at major change points in the activity." Software is advertised as supporting "the assessment of each stakeholder's support for the project (either positive or negative) as well as their receptiveness to messages about the project," which facilitates "a tailored communication plan" that "keep[s] the project and its key stakeholders aligned."

The use of the term *alignment* is not unusual in online discussions among practitioners, with some version of *align* occurring in 11% of all files in the listserv database.[59] Even when stakeholder information is offered by participants and shared with the community after it is collected, such alignment of institutional and stakeholder interests has a disciplinary character in the sense that stakeholders in many cases are not equal collaborators with sponsors. In some cases, power differentials are extreme, as in the conference presentation on how to map community social capital through engagement in indigenous communities on behalf of international mining companies; when asked by fellow practitioners whether such information could be used to identify communities less likely to resist mining operations, the practitioner doing the presentation avowed that she believed it was used only to help communities develop their social capital and provide guidance to the company on how best to gain impact from their philanthropic investments.

Comparisons with the new technologies of surveillance used in grassroots lobbying (the mobilization of targeted groups of stakeholders, typically by industries and organizations seeking to prove public support) and digital campaigning are worthwhile because deliberation consultancies use tools and techniques drawn from both for activating and managing engagement with deliberation participants. To promote political activation following deliberative process participation, AmericaSpeaks distributed postcards preaddressed to participants' lawmakers at the end of their CaliforniaSpeaks health care town meetings, for example—a standard technique in grassroots lobbying.[60] Although they may not itemize cost per participant as grassroots lobbying consultancies do, AmericaSpeaks evaluated and publicized deliberative process efficacy by comparing percentages of legislative contacts made by CaliforniaSpeaks participants with a control group of nonparticipants.[61]

Public deliberation professionals discuss emulating privately administered public discussions, such as Oprah Winfrey's self-described "global conversation about consciousness," a live interactive webinar series sponsored by Skype, Post-It, and Chevrolet on New Age self-help writer Eckhart Tolle's book *A New Earth*.[62] No doubt, a series of lengthy discussions taking place over ten weeks and bringing together millions of people from more than 125 countries is quite a feat in the world of public deliberation, where bringing a thousand people together is a major achievement. Given the private sector's superior resources, it is not surprising that high-tech innovations relevant to deliberation may be pioneered in the private sector and cross over to the public sphere. Public deliberation consultants face competition from other communications and political consulting fields seeking to harness "Public Engagement in the Conversation Age" for their own purposes.[63]

Of course, prior to the development of software platforms, experienced facilitators conducted similar information-sharing and monitoring functions by hand. In the public participation facilitation certification class, extensive attention was given to the necessity of meeting with all potentially interested stakeholders prior to conducting public deliberative processes so that when projects are underway, there are "no surprises." Nevertheless, new technologies integrating deliberative events with communications and research strategies have significantly enhanced the scope of finely targeted deliberative process management and the scale of ongoing engagement monitoring. As in other forms of online and offline labor premised on interactive technologies (electoral canvassing, interest advocacy, etc.), participants at deliberative sessions voluntarily contribute intellectual property and personal information in ways that can enhance the surveillance and management capabilities of aggregators and sponsors.[64]

## Diffusing a Deliberative Culture of Accountability

This chapter has discussed multiple different kinds of diffusion: the diffusion of best practices from business to public settings and back, the diffusion of responsibility for economic performance and growth from sponsors to the stakeholders they engage, and the diffusion of surveillance and accountability technologies to and from other industries. Focusing on the wide variety of contexts in which public engagement is used may limit our understanding of the extent to which heterogeneity and standardization are patterned in a tiered system, with communities and organizations that can afford customization typically receiving far more flexible, boutique engagement processes associated with the characteristics of high-quality deliberation than those that cannot.

But across both more limited and more extensive processes, it is critical to note the elements held in common across the diverse contexts in which deliberation is used. Scholarship documenting civic empowerment of the sort found in chapter 5 and scholarship noting political legitimacy and commercial imperatives as factors in deliberative processes are not necessarily contradictory. This chapter describes how, across sectors, practitioners facilitate on similar issue framings of social problems in communities and organizations facing dramatically straitened circumstances. In practice, these standard framings produce predictable outcomes, emphasizing positivity rather than grievance construction, encouraging empathy for decision-makers, and foregrounding powerful stakeholders in all three sectors as collaborators in community-level change. More substantive and engaging than other forms of subsidized participation, deliberation may prompt participant action and shift perspectives.

Nevertheless, that action is likely to focus on local cultural and behavioral changes aligned with sponsor interests. In a two-step process, deliberation empowers citizens as decision-makers while emphasizing the difficulties of administrative decision-making. As a result, structured deliberation events, even those that deal with large-scale social problems, tend to encourage small-scale actions on the part of individuals and communities, and foreground a companion role on the part of public and private sponsors in assisting these local actions through social marketing. An emphasis on results-oriented action may lead to quiescence, and democratization of decision-making may reinforce existing inequalities. The political awareness developed in deliberative processes may include subtle but far-reaching effects, restricting the types of discourse thought to be appropriate in civic problem-solving and reshaping lay perceptions of powerful sponsors.

The shared features of deliberative processes involve the downsizing of public expectations for administrative problem-solving from governments and organizations, and the promotion of behavioral alignment and positive thinking as the route to economic growth. The culture change these similarities have produced is, I argue, not simply culture change within a company or city, but also a change in terms of how growth is painted as the paramount collective good and how accountability through public engagement—really the accountability of the public for their own survival—is framed as the morally responsible path for a financially strapped landscape. The promotion of public engagement as a universal solution across contexts, and framings emphasizing economic development as a requirement for social justice, reveal the kinds of diverse institutional agendas deliberation can serve. This is not simply a matter of market-oriented practitioners administering deliberation in corporate settings or unwittingly allowing sponsors to co-opt deliberation. In fact, the progressive, noncommercial, pro-community connotations of deliberation may be especially useful for and eagerly embraced by sponsors, inasmuch as they demonstrate the compatibility of administrative authority and grassroots empowerment.

The extent to which civic and fiscal outcomes are truly complementary is addressed in the next chapter, which moves from considering the shared outcomes advertised across processes to the reactions of participants to the unintended consequences, unheralded cultural changes, and clear preference for sponsor priorities that deliberation has produced, even when it has also created citizen action and resistance to those developments. How, in an atmosphere that celebrates individual action and empathy for decision-makers, can citizens mobilize together to make change that decision-makers have not envisioned or do not seek?

# PART IV

## THE SPIRIT OF DELIBERATIVE CAPITALISM

## 7

# Sharing the Pain

## The Lessons Deliberation Teaches

To change the world, one has to change the ways of world-making, that is, the vision of the world and the practical operations by which groups are produced and reproduced.

Pierre Bourdieu, "Social Space and Symbolic Power" (1989: 23)

AS WE BEGIN PART IV of the book, we shift perspectives again: from considering the peculiar positioning of public engagement professionals, with their intensive reflexivity and self-criticism described in part II, and from the ways that they produce demonstrably authentic, artistic, and accountable processes for clients seeking particular outcomes from their participants in part III, to considering the ways in which those participants respond to the invocations described in the previous chapter to make tough choices and share the pain of cutbacks, while fulfilling their true selves. What kinds of satisfaction are possible in deliberation? What kinds of displeasure and resistance are possible? What do people make of these confusing, contradictory injunctions in actual practice? We start by considering the possibilities in a best case scenario for deliberative mobilization.

### Bigger, Better, All Together?

Denver is gorgeous in June, and the sparkling, glass-faced convention center was full of promise for conventioneers gathering for the

National Performing Arts Convention (NPAC) 2008, a four-day extravaganza of discussion about reinvigorating the arts in this country. Facing a changing and increasingly competitive environment for arts support and development, leaders of the major performing arts national service organizations, organizations that serve as central advocates for their arts discipline (such as Chorus America, Dance/USA, League of American Orchestras, OPERA America, and Theatre Communications Group) decided to address that challenge directly by co-convening their memberships. With a rallying theme of "Bigger, Better, All Together," the Denver conference was designed to bring together arts leaders across disciplines to learn from each other, identify common goals, and advance a broad arts-based agenda.

A hulking blue bear sculpture peered over the thousands of participants buzzing about, while the harmonies of choirs warming up and actors rehearsing their lines for dramatic performances enlivened the cavernous center. The winsome bear and the recently expanded 2-million-square-foot conference facility were powerful symbols of Mayor John Hickenlooper's stewardship of Denver, a shining example of corporate partnerships in urban economic redevelopment and a winner in the battle that many attendees' cities were losing to hold on to jobs, urban infrastructure, and people, let alone to their symphony orchestras and opera companies.[1] Denver's performing arts would be showcased at the conference to demonstrate the potential to retain creativity in an era of economic downturn, and Hickenlooper would give an inspiring keynote to this effect in the opening plenary. Attendees were only too aware of Richard Florida's theories about the creative class—and many saw their best hope of saving the local arts as making claims about the necessity of cities keeping their arts in order to attract mobile corporations with white-collar workforces.[2]

I was in Denver as part of a multidisciplinary research team of three researchers and ten graduate students, charged with observing and reporting on the conference proceedings as part of a $100,000 effort to evaluate the outcomes of the process for the service organization sponsors. We also conducted a presurvey and postsurvey of a random sample of conference participants to gauge the success of the convention in mobilizing arts leaders. I was on board because AmericaSpeaks was here to facilitate the group's discussions about shared interests in the field

*wishful thinking*

in a four-day deliberative process.[3] Through a series of daily caucuses during the conference and a final 21st Century Town Meeting, conference attendees were asked to participate in developing an "action blueprint" for the performing arts community in America.[4]

These cross-disciplinary discussions focused on a vision for the performing arts, on opportunities and challenges for the future, and on strategies for the three "opportunities/challenges" that eventually emerged from these discussions: arts advocacy, arts education, and diversity. At the 21st Century Town Meeting that capped off the conference, 1,235 conference participants discussed action items and voted by electronic keypads for priority actions at the national, local, and "individual/organizational" levels. The gathering in Denver of thousands of performing arts stakeholders was itself an impressive collective action requiring extensive capacity and resources, and it attracted the attention of the national press and political leaders. But the meeting was seen by its organizers and its participants as a first step in a more ambitious process to define and focus the collective needs and interests of the community to "take action together." As an explicit attempt to galvanize mobilization within a compressed time frame, this effort epitomized the potential of deliberation to inspire collective action.

The context for such collaboration was ripe. The sheer scale of the NPAC conference dramatically illustrated the dense, interconnecting networks of individuals and organizations that contribute to producing arts performances. Not least, the initiative was designed to focus on the contemporary centrality of art and cultural change to contentious politics. Association leaders emphasized artistic expression as key to political efficacy, and caucus discussions invoked the need to "make the case that the arts are a core competency for an educated person and good citizen." Organizers from the national service organizations repeatedly expressed a belief in artistic expression as constitutive of a healthy, well-functioning public sphere.

For scholars of deliberation, the NPAC conference represented an ideal context for exploring common ground and empowering collaborative action. This process was in stark contrast to the " 'hardest case' environment" represented by Community Congress III, where participants in "postdisaster crisis mode" were asked to think about complex details of zoning policy for one exhausting day. These arts professionals had the time and resources to come from around the country to confront shared challenges over four days. The multiday design of the process enabled the group to go into greater depth on issues they knew well, to process results over time in informal conversations and daily caucus newsletters summarizing what had occurred, and to cast their votes at Saturday's town meeting having slept on their evolving concerns and discussions with different groups at each Wednesday, Thursday, and Friday caucus.

Not least, sponsor aims for this process could not have been more of a contrast with the power dynamics described in the prior chapter. The sponsors did not use deliberation to seek legitimacy goals and small-scale actions oriented to individual responsibility in the service of cost-cutting. The service organizations that had come together to form NPAC were literally in service to their memberships and seeking guidance and direction for ambitious multilevel actions, from the individual and organizational level to regional collaborations to national-level policy influence. Rather than creating a feeling of ownership without substantive capacity to shape budgets or make decisions, NPAC leaders *wanted* participants to take ownership of the ambitious actions on the table.

Nevertheless, as our team observed the AmericaSpeaks discussions and conference proceedings, it became increasingly clear to observers, NPAC leaders, and AmericaSpeaks staffers that collaborative action was unlikely to happen. Grad students reported a lack of common language in their reflective memos:

> It was fascinating and frustrating to watch the group struggle with basic terms and concepts, often unable to coalesce around a common understanding. There was clearly little to no sense of a national community in the performing arts, but rather small pockets of peers and colleagues primarily clustered by geographic region or sub-discipline.

Grad student observers also commented about the diffuse nature of conference session conversations: "People were really interested in telling their stories and airing their grievances with the field, and there was no clear time or way for them to do that." Despite their investment in the conference, participants were having difficulty defining the actions necessary to advance the arts.[5]

The AmericaSpeaks process, intended to focus these conversations more explicitly on outcomes and action strategies to achieve them, did not catalyze collective understanding of where and how action in the performing arts should be targeted. Similar comments obtained in the grad student memos of the table discussions they had observed:

> It seemed to me that there was a lot of talk but not a lot of real discussion. People never contradicted one another and always agreed with the person who spoke before them, but would then often continue on to obliviously contradict their agreement and subsequently bring up a different subject.

> Participants seemed to really want it to work well. . . I was also surprised at how little the people at my table took advantage of their regional seating. Although they were all from the Midwest, none of their conversations reflected that fact. They seemed interested in collaboration, but at no point did they talk practically about a collaboration among themselves.

Grad students noted a reticence to think in broader terms about how people could influence policy or change systemic problems:

> I felt something was going UNsaid. . . . We keep talking about our failures and obstacles within the systems in which we function, but it seems it's hard for people (besides the theater people from my morning session) to consider the possibility that the failure is actually the system itself and not entirely our actions within the system.

Another reported, "Even though this caucus was about setting new policies and a common agenda for collective action, nobody said the word 'policy.'" The caucus sessions were creating lots of discussion, but there was concern from participants that the issues addressed were broad and vague.

As the conference went on, our research team noted that "people thought the suggested actions were at the wrong level," and another table participant remarked that the priorities (arts education, advocacy, and diversity) were "such a crappy set of issues." Frustration developed as emerging caucus themes were watered down in their presentation: the theme team rephrased the arts as a "core competency for an educated person and good citizen" to "the potential of arts education and life-long learning in the arts is under-realized." In part, this was because AmericaSpeaks staff instructed the arts organization staff consolidating each session's input that they should "filter out" strategies that weren't feasible: "These will not trickle up if they can't be done."

Conveying a feeling of possibility was paramount, and tended to be enacted by showing participants how much of an impact they were making in the process. An AmericaSpeaks staffer informed me that the public presentation on day two of critiques of the vision statement, which was explicitly not up for debate in the process, were mainly for "affirmation"—for the group to see that they were being heard. An arts leader asserted that the participants were "needy of affirmation." One grad student described this result at his table: "Hearing their problem spoken aloud to the whole room gave them a sense of excitement. Voices were heard." Similarly, one of the conference organizers described the decision to emphasize "strategies" rather than "actions" in the final process: "The reason for the last-minute decision to pull away from action is not overpromising what we have to do to feel successful. This is a baby step in terms of community building, so we are pushing more towards strategy." The theme of "greater collaboration" had by far the most energy behind it by a count of its frequency in table discussions, but AmericaSpeaks staff asserted that it shouldn't be one of the three priorities of focus for the final meeting because "it is more like a strategy that could be applied to all the opportunities."

Conference organizers and observers expressed their own frustrations about getting participants talking beyond short-term survival and breaking out of their "jaded" thinking. One national arts leader said, "Again and again, we are inviting people to imagine something—to think in terms of 2028. ... They are so marinated in survival thinking and problem solving. You could feel rust on those muscles. How entrained they are, how hard it is for them to think beyond that." He concluded that his colleagues were "so underfed and hungry for recognition" that it was "heartbreaking," but that recognizing their pain could go "on and on" without moving the field forward.

These disconnects between field-level collaboration and individual hardship, between what was thought of as feasible or doable as a collective and what was required to make it day to day, drove participants' reluctance to see the "strategies" produced as theirs for the taking. Even though organizers had wanted to hedge to make it seem like progress had been made, they also wanted to show that "accountability is part of the game." To this end, they broke out the discussions for action at three different scales, had a call-out section at the end of the town meeting where audience members announced what actions they would be taking, sat participants in round tables by region to spark connections for collaboration, and had the national organizations' leadership announce their own slate of action commitments in light of the feedback from the meeting.

Nevertheless, participants at NPAC had trouble agreeing on what the role of the artistic pursuits they represented should be in a collective action effort. Participants often saw their projects as divorced from or secondary to the work they would have to do to advocate for their importance. One participant described the expected trade-offs: "We have a lot of passionate and highly productive people that all tend to over-extend themselves as it is 'for the love of their art.' I think it is difficult for many of these same people then to prioritize what they may have to stop doing in order to thoughtfully and actively participate in this 'national dialogue.'" Despite being explicitly invited to help build a collective action agenda, the world of organizing to advance the arts was perceived to be very distant from the everyday concerns of performing arts leaders.

When we compared the results of the preconference survey of participants and the postconference survey, we discovered that participants evinced less interest in or confidence in their capacity for action following the conference than they had prior to it. While the AmericaSpeaks process identified clear majorities for selected action items, presurveys and postsurveys gave hard evidence of the differences in assumptions and perspectives we had observed. In terms of galvanizing participants for change, 48% of postsurvey respondents wanted to be involved in leading efforts for collective action—an exciting result, except that it represented a decline from 64% of presurvey respondents.[6]

Where action could best be focused and how individuals could play a role weren't clear to participants engaged in this national effort. A majority, 75%, thought the most important problems facing the field were local, not national, and 77% believed that the most important problems facing the performing arts could be best addressed at the regional or city level (only 23% preferred the national level).[7] On whether respondents favored collective action or individual solutions, 57% favored individual solutions, despite the fact that the process was designed to foreground collaborative solutions ("Bigger, Better, All Together") and that collaboration was by far the most popular strategy suggestion in the caucus discussions.

When it came to a larger, national-level collective agenda, desire for a clear course of top-down, state-centered action was palpable. Participants believed promotion of the arts should come from institutional elites, not from the grassroots. They agreed that effective advocacy efforts must focus on a unified, strong, "right" public service announcement along the lines of a "Got Milk?" campaign for the arts. A "Got Art?" social marketing campaign was the top priority in the electronic voting for national-level advocacy items, even though a similar campaign has been sponsored by Americans for the Arts and the Ad Council since 2002.[8] The second priority was a national-level Department of Culture or cabinet-level position for arts policy. Participants' conviction in the importance of state-centered, national-level action, despite their sense of the difficulty of accomplishing political change in a climate of contracting government budgets and devolution, indicated that these arts actors maintained a belief in traditional political mobilization strategies (such as lobbying) as primary, even when they were engaged in a nontraditional deliberative effort that was intended to mobilize them for action.

Whereas most deliberative democratic theorists believe that participatory processes like that used in the AmericaSpeaks sessions should spark participants into action, our research suggested that, even in an easiest case scenario, intentional efforts to activate grassroots participation from the top-down may foster more reliance of individuals on the institutions (in this case, the professional service organizations) that support such actions, or more faith in individual-level efforts over collective ones.[9] On the sponsor side, the overall impression was that the service organizations had received endorsements for the strategies they were already using, such as national-level advocacy, but whether they were going to maintain this momentum was hard to gauge. One survey respondent suggests the ways in which the process may have been simultaneously energizing and demobilizing:

> I was amazed and inspired by the numbers of people in attendance, by the organizations represented, and by the commitment of all to the arts. For myself, I'm working so hard in my organization and my discipline, that I don't have energy left over to act to bring issues to the national or regional scene. But, I did feel that there were those who DO have the time and space to make the arts an integral part of American life for all of us, and I was just thrilled. Someday, those of us working in the local trenches will be able to come out from under and help more, and what a day that will be!

At the time, 2008 seemed like an auspicious moment for a grand convening like NPAC—on the eve of a nonincumbent presidential election that would reshape the balance of power. The fiscal crisis that would play out in August and September would, of course, be at a scale that challenged even participants well versed in the hand-to-mouth day-to-day of life in the arts.

But the convening was unable to convey the critical urgency of "if not mobilization now, then when?"—in part because the evidence of collective action offered by the process (that there were people out there who "DO have the time and space to make the arts an integral part of American life for all of us") was sufficiently inspiring to assuage participants' anxieties about their own futures. The lessons of the AmericaSpeaks process seemed to be that for those stuck in the trenches, collective action to get out of those trenches was possible for four days but unrealistic as a long-term commitment.[10]

## Participatory Satisfaction: The Difference Deliberation Makes

> One of the things we found (and there is an interesting link to a study) is that participants always rated the quality of the meeting very high, though

their perceptions of whether it would make a difference varied. This is interesting in light of a finding that facilitators and other practitioners of deliberation place a high value on the quality of the experience—whether it was safe, fun, etc. I have found at our town meetings in Vermont, the opposite is true: there is very little attention to the design (a "pragmatic" approach?) yet there is high efficacy.

Practitioner, NCDD listserv discussion, 2007

Despite the frustrations and tensions NPAC 2008 revealed for a multidisciplinary field that was more a metaphorical than a cohesive community, participants generally agreed that the AmericaSpeaks caucus process was a positive and even transformative experience. In our postconference survey, only 14% of participants disagreed with the statement that their voice was heard in the AmericaSpeaks process, and only one of five disagreed with the statement that a participant from another discipline said something that changed their thinking.[11] We discovered these feelings as well in our participant observation. One student described the reaction at her table: "I spoke to a few of the people at my table before the session started and asked them how they felt about the AmericaSpeaks sessions so far. They were all very pleased with the process so far, and one said that she liked having disagreements during the caucuses because it helped her see things from a different point of view." In our grad students' observations, there seemed to be consensus that, despite the difficulties experienced in the process, overall impressions of the AmericaSpeaks process were positive:

> She said that she liked the process, but that her group had an incredibly hard time with the vision statement.

> This session's deliverable was difficult for people to grasp, and instead of truly identifying opportunities and challenges they simply added to yesterday's list of what the field has done well and poorly. I noticed that even during the call outs, most groups had not actually answered the question at hand. At the end the facilitator asked some of the people at the table how they felt about the AmericaSpeaks process in general, and they all thought that it was a good process and that they would continue to attend the sessions.

In the final analysis, the AmericaSpeaks process and the convention overall garnered many rave reviews in our survey a month later for being impressive, valuable, and inspiring: "All-in-all this was a successful gathering." "A superb experience." "Loved it." "Great conference. I wish more conferences would adopt the America Speaks Caucus idea." "It was an impressive effort to pull the arts together." "America Speaks did an outstanding job. BRAVO to all that went without sleep to compile and print the detail sheets each evening. It was impressive." "The AmericaSpeaks sessions were a great idea. I found this convention much more meaningful and inspiring than the [2004] Pittsburgh convention." "I felt it was a very valuable conference for me. . . . I thought during the town hall sessions I was able to connect and learn from others." "I found it worthwhile and am implementing some of the ideas shared at this event." Intensively designed deliberative events like NPAC are nearly always extraordinarily successful in garnering immediate satisfaction and positive feelings of empowered engagement in participants, even in tough cases like Community Congress III, where a whopping 93% of participants committed to staying engaged.

This book has not dwelled extensively on outcomes at the level of individual processes or on the experiences of participants in deliberative processes because the deliberation literature focuses so heavily on process case studies and measurements of participant perceptions and civic capacity. As a study of the practice of professional facilitation of deliberation, this book has tried to shine a light on the less-noticed struggles and shared discourses of the field, on the kinds of uses to which deliberation is put, and the richly textured cultural influences on the processes that result. Because of this focus, the ways in which practitioners work to resolve tensions and maintain the authenticity of deliberation within larger economic and political contexts of retrenchment and reform have been much more central than the question of short-term effects of processes, which tend to be relatively stable across deliberative case studies in the existing scholarly literature. Deliberation does work as intended, or else it would not be as popular and ubiquitous as it is. Processes produce substantial participant satisfaction and exciting civic capacity building in the short term, but—scholars ruefully admit—seem insufficiently articulated with substantive policy outcomes to alter the larger political landscape.[12] "The difference deliberation makes"[13] on actual policy or power structures is, unfortunately, not very much—and this is generally assumed to be because the larger political context is hostile to the empowering, destabilizing, progressive bent of deliberative solutions.

I argue that, in fact, the difference deliberation makes is quite substantial, insofar as it has altered the cultural resources and practical routines of administrative life and organizational belonging. The analysis in this book has generally assumed the positive short-term and individual-level results suggested as outcomes of contemporary, high-quality deliberation processes. Processes can be positively energizing and capacity building, and they can also lead to nowhere in particular. This is true both when minimizing contention is exactly what clients want to happen, as described in chapter 6, *and* when action is exactly what sponsors and facilitators want, as in the NPAC deliberations described in this chapter. As one participant at the NPAC Conference reported just a month after the meeting,

> To me, it was an exciting and intellectually stimulating experience. Very intense but valuable. Although when I got home that energy dissipated which I'm sure was true for most. So the challenge is to keep that focus and build on the energy. ... The dialog needs to continue. It must continue for something to happen. ... Not that it merited intense journalistic scrutiny but it's almost like it never happened. And to the nation, to individual people—the people we want to bring to the arts—it really didn't.

In the temporary spaces of itinerant America, the windowless convention halls and multipurpose rooms, exciting, intense, even frustrating conversations take place, promising action that never sees the light of day in the cold reality of daily routines.

That intoxicating rush of creative, impassioned energy and the cycle of dispersal and dilution that follows are very real effects, with substantial long-term impact on the shared sense of what is possible in today's climate. I have argued throughout the book that the larger political economic context in which engagement has become a routine administrative solution is not a frustrating limitation to the exciting potential of deliberative interventions. It is not an accident that deliberation has been popularized and spread across sectors in an era of neoliberal governance, nor are the limitations of deliberation evidence of a thwarted bottom-up backlash against the strictures of the existing political structure. Facilitated public engagement itself incorporates and manages stakeholder critiques of the system, quite actively and intentionally.

But deliberators routinely contest reductionist process framings and canned solutions, many scholars point out. Couldn't this be grounds for contesting deliberation when it is intended to be manipulative? Isn't allowing this potential in deliberation better than the alternative of no deliberation at all? Many scholars emphasize that deliberation is complementary with protest and an important space for negotiating power shifts, even if they sometimes fail or don't happen in every case.[14] I take on these questions in the following analysis, which confronts the potential for resistance in deliberation and its frequent occurrence. Certainly, public engagement practitioners themselves—and many participants— have apprehended the limited scope of the empowerment opportunities offered in deliberation, and vigorously contested them.[15]

This chapter investigates why this resistance, even when it is successful at challenging the management of particular engagement processes, is unlikely to pose a significant challenge to the status quo. In this final section of the book, I investigate the relationship between the demobilization that deliberation produces and its contestation, even in settings not designed to produce consent. Systemic critique, energetic enthusiasm, Zen-like acceptance and withdrawal, and grudging, conflicted cynicism are all of a piece in contemporary deliberation. Resistance and deliberative empowerment are inextricably linked to each other.

Rather than seeing the embedding of deliberation in contemporary governance as producing the virtuous circle of participation theorists wish for, this chapter investigates why the ad hoc settings of deliberation are slippery for getting traction on collective action when they work as intended, and almost impossible to contest effectively. This is not because of a vicious cycle in which participants once bitten by unsatisfactory engagement are twice shy about participating in other processes. Deliberative window dressing may in extreme circumstances elicit the frustration of the masses, but authentically deliberative processes are generally successful at incorporating critique. The anger produced in unsuccessful deliberation, at the process and at its sponsors, reinforces the resentment and cynicism of participants toward administrative failures. As shown in chapter 6, this sense of administrative inadequacy—whether the idea that administrators should obey the public bidding or the idea that it is patently "ludicrous" that administrators know best what is going on—is one of the lessons deliberation intends to teach.[16]

*Obamacare*

In its most inspirational form, deliberation demonstrates that others are working hard in socially profitable endeavors that can reap culture change if participants are willing to lend a hand, that the process itself represents a successful co-creative action in this vein, and that those in the trenches have done their civic duty by participating and can rest until a future day when the outlook will be brighter. When it incites resistance, deliberation teaches that administrators are incapable of providing basic services or treating the public with fairness and respect, and that the onus lies on individuals to claim that respect by assuming administrative duties and governing themselves. That both of these outcomes inspire increased tolerance of self-sacrifice or increasing willingness to assume small-scale responsibilities of self-governance helps to explain why deliberation can be so appealing to antigovernment, antitax prophets like Grover Norquist.[17]

The NPAC conference is a good place to look for the hoped-for civic impacts of deliberation because it represented the kind of demonstrably authentic, vociferously creative process that deliberative scholars believe will result in an ideal situation; sponsors in this case were clearly trying to spark innovative ideas, empower participants, and galvanize action. The rest of this chapter employs descriptions of satisfaction and resistance in other processes—and in particular, large-scale, well-resourced processes that encountered significant resistance—to explore the commonalities among deliberative processes' long-term outcomes.

## Distrust of Processes, Redeeming Transformations of Civic Faith, and Enduring Cynicism

As much as deliberative processes encourage participants to assume the role of administrators and see what tough choices they have to make, this assertion of administrators' fellow humanity can ring hollow for participants who are not actually being given decision-making power or are angry at administrators' seeming lack of concern for their needs. Not least, the invocation to "share the pain" may—for those who are already experiencing considerable pain—feel like a slap in the face or like the elimination of hope for a more plentiful future. Incorporation of critique and pushback against administrative framings or preferences is a routine and welcome occurrence in deliberation—as when the input from the Listening to the City process was rejection of all of the proposed design plans for the World Trade Center site, or when activists were given airtime to protest the lack of inclusion of a single-payer option in the CaliforniaSpeaks health care process. Because deliberation is often a strategy of last resort when less substantive engagement strategies have failed or backfired, experienced facilitators anticipate sponsor critique and disillusionment among would-be participants.

The public report on Philadelphia's "Tight Times, Tough Choices" dialogues described levels of distrust in the process that had developed over a long history of residents' relationships with city government:

> More than a few participants arrived with a great deal of distrust and skepticism. They didn't believe our numbers or the city's motives. They worried that this was a sham and that the city already knew what it was going to do and was only looking for cover. ... But it also spoke to a long history of feeling lied to and manipulated by the political powers that be.

To the extent that such concerns are respectfully acknowledged and defused by organizers, deliberation may inhibit action to redress grievances in other venues. The report notes, "A few never got past this, but moderators reported that most people were able to put the skepticism aside, at least temporarily, and get to the work at hand." After the event, a facilitator at one of the Community Congress III sites posted this summary on AmericaSpeaks' website: "The day progressed, city councilmen, the mayor, community leaders, all got up and spoke about the great city of New Orleans, about it rising again. I scanned the room during these speeches, thinking I would see hope in the faces of those in the room. Instead I saw frustration, concern, disbelief and dismissal. The government failed these people, at all levels, and they know it. The distrust I saw was overwhelming."[18] Disillusionment among citizens about the meaning and purpose of their participation, even for those engaged enough to attend large-scale deliberations, is perhaps to be expected in the wake of a massive government failure.

But cynicism and perceived manipulation of the process in deliberative events encompass a number of dimensions. Despite the fact that sponsoring foundations and organizations often try to assume a low profile, suspicion of sponsors' intentions is endemic to ambitious deliberative processes. Regarding the "Our Budget, Our Economy" event, progressive blogger Digby contests the very notion of a neutral process funded by well-known deficit hawk Pete Peterson:

> If you can stomach it, you can watch or listen to the Pete Peterson Austerity Pimp Event here, live. ... Everyone involved is either deluded about how politics works or is a cunning liar. This is one of the greatest scams ever perpetrated on the American people by their wealthy owners. ... Now they are all asking for applause for their "funders." LOL.

A "Blue Shield of California customer and a parent of a child with special needs" vents on a Web comment forum about CaliforniaSpeaks, the AmericaSpeaks process on health care reform in California: "I just can't imagine how America Speaks can think these Insurance industry backed foundations are neutral." Another poster, the president of a local interest group for universal health insurance, claims: "Twenty-first century snake oil is sold with Orwellian marketing expertise. Californians see through the coordination of the California Speaks event with the ad campaign run by one of the California Speaks sponsors to rush a bandaid health-care reform bill into law. ... America Speaks compromised its reputation as a neutral broker of public opinion for a $4 million fee and this is one Californian who was happy to see their revival tents folded and leaving our state."

Those who weren't suspicious about the aims of process funders were suspicious about the relationship of processes to real-world policy, particularly when attempts were made to link processes to decision-making. In the case of CaliforniaSpeaks, this ended up restricting the types of choices participants were offered to those Schwarzenegger's administration believed were feasible for legislative passage. A Californian with a disability who attended despite misgivings states: "Although it had been billed as a free ranging discussion on health care issues on California's healthcare system. [It] quickly got manipulated by the Governor and his staff to be more about getting us to sign onto his concept of reform." Even when explicitly nonpartisan processes are not visibly sponsored by particular interest groups, foundations, or partisan administrations, this lack of readability causes process observers' distrust about who is pulling strings behind the scenes, as in the case of the Ontario Citizen's Assembly, where a commenter does not believe the public could have possibly been in charge:

> The flaws in the proposal go on and on, but the biggest one of all was the composition of the Assembly itself. A random selection of one person from each constituency couldn't have developed this proposal in the time available. It was developed by the Secretariat of the Assembly. Who was on that Secretariat? How were they appointed? The Assembly website is silent on those points.

AmericaSpeaks' national Our Budget, Our Economy dialogues were also critiqued for the selection of members of the public susceptible to manipulation: "Put several thousand people in rooms (organizers say 3,500 participated), manipulate them into giving certain answers, and then pretend this tiny group is speaking for *the entire American people*."

Other sources of suspicion involved facilitators' design and administration of processes. The Tight Times, Tough Choices report noted distrust "of numbers, of workshop process, of how the input would be used." Participants suspect dishonesty and manipulation in the electronic voting, as did one participant at Our Budget, Our Economy:

> At first, during the demographic section of the program early on, I suspected them of rigging the votes. It would have been easy to do. ... But after the stats on self-reported ideology (in which the group scored way more liberal than the comparison stats they had posted), I figured they weren't.

One blogger notes: "Participants were forced to meet an arbitrary goal of $1.2 trillion in deficit cuts, they weren't told that Social Security is separately funded, were given limits on how much they could cut defense, were told that the health care system was broken but weren't allowed to consider options like single-payer coverage." Another blogger was suspicious of the digestion entailed in the theming process,

> They presented five or six statements which they claimed "reflected the overall tone" of the comments they received (I'd like to see a random sample before accepting that) and asked the crowd to vote on which ones should be handed in with the group's findings. All of the chosen statements implied that to reject these budget cuts would mean that politicians are giving in to special interests, leaving participants with no real choice of message at all.

The Tight Times, Tough Choices report claimed that such resistance to limited choices was caused by magical thinking on the part of participants: "More than a few participants chafed at the process and at being asked to work within the choices provided. To a degree, this spoke to a refusal to accept just how serious the fiscal crisis has become, or wishful thinking about magic bullets: 'Just use the stimulus money' or 'Just collect all those back taxes and we won't have to cut anything.'" But often such criticisms involve a desire to have more ambitious options on the table for discussion than just those that are doable in a short time frame; the Philadelphia report also noted "frustration" with the limitations of the process: "It also spoke to a desire to delve into other issues—issues important to the city's long-term finances but not helpful to the immediate task of balancing the FY 10 budget."

Suspicion also falls on the affective dimensions of the process and the extent to which deliberation uses marketing techniques and positive psychology, strategies from organizational development and team building, and New Age and therapeutic practices. All of these are, as described in chapter 3, elements self-consciously incorporated in deliberation by consultants. Practitioners are acutely aware of the need to manage such influences so they do not trigger audience sensitivities, but in many cases, these management strategies fail. The commenter on the Ontario Citizens' Assembly rejected the superficial, power-to-the-people feel: "If we go down this road again let's forget the cuddly Citizens' Assembly." An observer of the Our Budget dialogues recounts his shock at the extent to which the process reminded him of "unethical," canned exercises in team building, "having lived through too many of these corporate events":

> What I found in sunny Pasadena was a cross between a corporate "team-building" and "motivational" exercise and one of Stanley Milgram's sinister "obedience to authority" experiments. ... The experiment as it seems to have been conceived was part *1984*, part *Twilight Zone* (remember all those episodes where "ordinary towns-folk" do terrible things?), and part *Truman Show*: Get a group of people that "looks like America" into rooms across the country, manipulate them into regurgitating some pre-packaged responses, and then use those responses—call them, oh, "America speaks"—to push for a preconceived political agenda. Pretty smart, actually. ... The event, at least while I was there, included constant cheerleading for the budget-slashing goals, exhortations about how wonderful "we" are to be doing this, and one false choice after another.

Another commenter described her impressions of the "pretty sophisti-cated, full-scale marketing push" of the event by referring to the famous faith-inspired direct-selling organization and a game show:

> Have any of your friends ever invited you over to his or her house to discuss "a wonderful opportunity," and it turned out they wanted you to sell Amway?... That's what today's AmericaSpeaks event reminded me of. (That, and a game show, with personable hosts with really good teeth, great special effects and Fabulous Prizes!). ...

The same commenter noted that the process had "glossy" materials and had clearly been tested in run-throughs before the process. She specifically resisted the framing in terms of self-sacrifice: "When you arrived, you were given a glossy information packet and asked to fill out a questionnaire about core values. Now, clearly this approach had been focus-grouped, because the common theme seized on by the moderators was our desire to leave a better world for the next generation. (Apparently they thought this would translate to a spirit of self-sacrifice. Hah!)... Obviously, the plan is to wear down our resistance with more clever infomercials like this one." The observations made in this book regarding the resemblance of deliberative processes to these other contexts are not opaque to (at least some) deliberative participants.

But even for commenters furious about perceived manipulation in a resource-intensive process that was carefully designed and funded by partisan sponsors, critics saw hope in the redeeming power of deliberative conversation and the common sense of the collective. The same commenter annoyed about the infomercial-like qualities of the process described her transformed perspective as the event wore on:

> I was dreading it, especially after I saw the materials they had prepared for us, but my table was pretty darn great. We pushed back a lot against their framing. ... It also helped that several people at my table (all three of whom were African-American) expressed a generalized distrust towards glitzy plans to "fix everything" and scare-tactics thinking (I'm paraphrasing). Having a more skeptical mindset around the table certainly helped us avoid getting caught up in the event's pre-planned agenda.

Another woman who participated in the event described a similar revelation:

> For the first time in a long time, I might have some faith in America. Because no matter how many times the facilitators of this event ... tried to steer us toward cutting Social Security and Medicare, the 3500 or so people who took part in this national town hall weren't buying it. ... You know what most of them wanted to do? Soak the rich—and cut defense spending. ... I thought maybe it was just my table, but when they tabulated the results, it was pretty much the same throughout the crowded ballroom of several hundred attendees. (Whew!) And the national tabulation from the 19 cities across the country showed pretty similar results. ... Anyway, there were many, many insidious attempts to reframe the debate. But people were pushing back on just about everything—in the nicest, most polite way. But they definitely pushed back. Despite the little hints from the emcee about "denial" and "making hard choices,"

*[handwritten margin note: Of course, when you put 3500 democrat voters in a room you get this result]*

the attendees held their ground. And politicians did not get the go-ahead signal to go anywhere near Social Security. Frankly, I was surprised. But in a good way!... But I want to tell you: Today, Americans did us proud.

The blogger concerned about "corporate team-building" had a similar revelation:

> Those were the sorts of choices presented to attendees at this event and they fought the premise strenuously. ... That's where the Milgram "Obedience to Authority" experiment comes in. In that exercise, participants were told they were inflicting pain on other human beings—but that they were being instructed to do so by authority figures. A disturbingly high number of people agreed to do so, and kept inflicting what they believed was "pain" on other people. But here's where the experiment broke down: Participants in Saturday's event wouldn't conduct themselves as the organizers expected. They overwhelmingly preferred more progressive options, even when confronted with the artificially imposed goal of $1.2 trillion in cuts. ... As we said earlier, a very smart idea—but what do you do when it doesn't work out as planned?

The transformations described for participants in the process resemble those authentic transformations in deliberative processes that facilitators advertise, in which those who have the experience of participating learn to have faith in the process and their fellow participants, building momentum for future deliberations.

Not least, skeptical participants celebrated the preference changes experienced by participants with "low information" as they learned more about issues and heard others' views—again, a sought-for outcome in deliberation theory. One reports:

> The low-information voters at my table definitely veered toward believing in the framing. One of them was really excited about reforming the whole tax code and making it simple. I kept quoting actual numbers and examples from my life to help us all visualize things. It worked pretty well.

Another notes:

> About the only real non-progressive moment came when a couple of the older participants said they thought they could support raising the age at which you got full Social Security benefits. "Wait a minute," I said. "That's actually a benefit cut. If you paid in for all those years expecting to get that, you can't turn around and take it away." They hadn't thought of that.
>
> The facilitator kept saying things like, "Are you keeping in mind future generations, and the young people who aren't present here today? Are you voting for their interests as well?" Several of us pointed out that a single-payer system was best for their interests—that it would stimulate the economy and generate more jobs.

That deliberation is an occasion for the rebirth of civic faith, even for heavy skeptics, is part of the marketing described in chapter 6 and a well-known feature of deliberative processes. In this case, even when participants perceive that the process is *not* working, they find hope in the transformations of the group.

The flip side of that marketing—that deliberation is cost-effective because it increases participants' empathy for administrators and their willingness to accept retrenchment and participate appreciatively in producing culture change—may not always be as convincing as promised. Participants may question assumptions about the necessity of retrenchment or reject altogether the outcomes of processes perceived to be manipulative. However, this kind of rejection tends to generate cynicism and regret about the ways administrators are impervious to public input, not to galvanize a broader movement to target the issues more effectively. About the CaliforniaSpeaks process, one participant said, "Well, again this is all very sad because a lot of us left that event feeling like America Speaks just doesn't listen." Similar distrust of the massaging of outcomes obtained in the Our Budget dialogues: "Now we'll see just how AmericaSpeaks frames the results. ... I hope [Americans] keep their guards up. Because this is only the beginning" and "Their press release [about the process outcomes] spun gold into straw." Of the Tight Times, Tough Choices dialogues, the official report noted that suspicions remained for participants: "Still, the questions voiced early in forums lingered to the end: Will the mayor really listen to what we have to say? How will we know that he did?" Even in cases where appreciative, empathetic framings do not resonate with participants, this disconnect drives home claims about the inadequacy of administrative governance.

If those who contest deliberative framings are also those who express "generalized distrust towards glitzy plans," their options for mobilization are limited to individual and small-scale actions—one of the reasons deliberation is seen as so effective in gaining consent for retrenchment. Expressions of discontent with process may take precedence and airtime over expressions of discontent with policy, shifting the terms of debate to the type of participation that might be appropriate, not to increasing public optimism about the palette of strategies available to them for redressing social problems. The "damned if we do and damned if we don't" lessons of deliberative retrenchment may not, in some cases, increase empathy for decision-makers like they did in Philadelphia, but that does not mean that resistant participants do not internalize a message quite similar to the one deliberative proponents had hoped for.

This is evident in progressive bloggers' perceptions of moments of triumph and concern for the future in the Our Budget dialogues. One of the bloggers describes "a happy moment": "loud snickers throughout the room when our hosts showed a video starring Kent Conrad and Judd Gregg." Distrust of Congress was a common theme for the Our Budget dialogues: "Even more heartening, though, was how carefully people looked at the questions. You know what else they said? They'd rather see no cuts at all in any social programs than give Congress the go-ahead to slash them. They don't trust them to look out for the interests of the vulnerable over the corporate interests." Another noted, "We talked about personal responsibility vs. government care, but agreed we just didn't trust Congress to make those decisions." Congress is, of course, the body that does or does not make those decisions, based on the political will, interest advocacy, and pressure expressed by the American public, civic organizations, and corporations. Although progressive bloggers in these cases see distrust of Congress as a positive outcome of rejection of deliberative process framings, this wariness, and the accompanying sense that the best solution is no solution, is similar to that articulated by the antigovernment right as well, as represented by the actions of Tea Party adherents in Congress.

## When Civic Action Means Heavy Equipment, Knives, and Bats

In some cases, however, rejection of public engagement does lead to more substantive action, and in others, public engagement is insufficient to stem public outrage. As deliberative processes have become more common for retrenchment exercises, and as the new normal sets in, anger like that expressed in the Tea Party mobilization against Congressional town halls in 2008 and in the 2010 student riots in England over cuts to higher education have also become more common. Pete Peterson of the Davenport Institute (formerly Common Sense California), the conservative deliberation advocate—no relation to the billionaire conservative funder of the Our Budget dialogues—describes on a deliberation listserv the exciting result of a "**FAILED** attempt at 'civic engagement'" by Hawaii's Department of Land and Natural Resources in the case of roads and bridges washed out in a state park:

> Again, without much of a hint of Party or ideological affiliation, the governing institution convened the public to talk about how they (the government) would fix this problem. The results of this veritable melt-down were, while anomalous, a startling study of what happens when government-convened deliberations over policy fail to grapple with fundamental questions like: are we the only solution here? How can residents be involved? How can civil society at large be involved?... In February/March, representatives from the State's Dept of Land and Natural Resources came out to Kauai to rally residents around proposed legislation, which would have garnered more state monies for the DLNR, and, consequently, Kauai. Missed was an opportunity to solve the actual problem, rather than helping the state government with its predetermined solution.

Peterson recounts for *City Journal*, the conservative Manhattan Institute's quarterly magazine, a story that "brings a reflexive smile to everyone who hears it"—a tale of a "plucky group of Hawaiians" capable of "amazing resourcefulness and sacrifice":

> The go-slow approach did not sit well with area residents, who depend on the park for their livelihoods. Ivan Slack, owner of Na Pali Kayaks,

which operates from the beach in Polihale, summed up the community's frustration: "We can wait around for the state or federal government to make this move, or we can go out and do our part. Just like everyone's sitting around waiting for a stimulus check, we were waiting for this but decided we couldn't wait anymore." Beginning in late March, business leaders and local residents organized together to take the situation into their own hands.

From food donated by area restaurants to heavy machinery offered by local construction companies, a project originally forecast to cost millions and take months (if not years) to complete has been finished in a matter of weeks with donated funds, manpower, and equipment. As Troy Martin from Martin Steel, which provided machinery and five tons of steel at no charge, put it: "We shouldn't have to do this, but when it gets to a state level, it just gets so bureaucratic, something that took us eight days would have taken them years. So we got together—the community—and we got it done." Cleaning up the park was a major undertaking involving bridge-building, reconstructing bathroom facilities, and use of heavy equipment to clear miles of flood-damaged roadways.

... When government does not perform up to expectations, the usual response, running across the ideological spectrum, is either to decry its wastefulness or acquiesce to higher taxes. The story in Kauai, and others bubbling up around the country, demonstrate that there is a "third way": gather some friends and pick up a shovel when the government can't or won't. ... It's doubtful that the Kauai effort would have occurred at all without the dire financial consequences looming for many of the residents and businesses involved.[19]

While this story powerfully represents the larger scale of participatory action of which public engagement stakeholders are capable, it is also hard to miss the ways in which this apparently nonpartisan story is also a tale of the compatibility of civic action and collaboration with neoliberal priorities—a paean to the ability of well-meaning, socially profitable business enterprises to provide for community needs, a condemnation of the ridiculous waste and costly expense of government red tape in the environmental regulation and permitting processes for road building in, of all places where environmental care might be expected, a state park. What is missing here, of course, is a sense of the extent to which these businesses also depend on the largesse of the government in the form of the state park itself—and the ways in which they profit from the regulation and environmental protection that has made the park an attractive destination for tourists.

Other narratives of exit and outrage are less productive or crowd-pleasing. Forms of dissent that disrupt or prevent any substantive dialogue from occurring—shouting, refusal to participate or let others speak, for instance—are becoming more common in public engagement and are areas in which deliberation consultants believe more effective deliberation is the solution. In response to the disruption of Congressional town hall meetings in summer 2008, conversation on the NCDD listserv focused on how "collectively we can help them"—them being the administrators, not the members of the public who were expressing their outrage in unproductive ways. Deliberation consultants could offer public officials a "better way," and particular consultants had uniquely valuable experience that could be hired for such a situation. One practitioner reports that handling outrage is a sophisticated skill: "Dealing with this kind of outrage and public anger is very common to the public engagement business and it's not easy to manage effectively. Most of my consulting work has been around these low trust/high emotion issues." Another practitioner agreed that the town hall meeting format cried out to be remade into deliberative sessions focused on listening and small groups:

> You're right in saying that the technique in this case—Town Hall Meetings—is not an effective way to manage this particular conversation. It's a setup for failure and perfectly designed for someone who wants to disrupt the meeting. In most cases typical public meetings are not effective ways of conducting public engagement, particularly when emotions are high. There are dozens of other tools and better techniques to engage citizens in these kinds of conversations, which IAP2 teaches in its Certificate course.

But if standard deliberation does not work as intended, more sophisticated skills for handling deliberation can be learned in a course specifically focused on handling outrage:

We are also rolling out a new IAP2 course in September ... titled Outrage, Emotion and Public Participation. People who take the course will:

- Understand and learn how to predict, identify and minimize outrage in public participation
- Understand how outrage hinders public participation programs, and how to manage that
- Learn the principles, approaches and strategies for dealing with emotion and outrage in public participation
- Practice applying the principles, strategies and approaches and prepare for upcoming challenges

That the IAP2 has developed a stand-alone course on handling outrage speaks to the deep frustrations of administrators with protest tactics and their increasing difficulties handling angry publics.

Better, more intensively deliberative process designs can provide one solution, but a facilitator describes on a listserv how high the stakes can be and how much deliberation facilitators may need to plan for violence:

As many of you know most of my work in public participation is in the threat of violence or about violent conflict. I think there are two issues if not even more that we need to tease out: 1) How design of such public forums can reflect a way to get to the emotional, explosive aspect of this issue? This is something we can certainly offer to government officials who are hosting and designing such events. 2) In general, for any type of process it is important to consider how and what to do when it is being utilized for protest OR if you move into an emergent crisis. ... It is important to think about the venue itself and exit and entry strategies, the facilitators, the balance between safety and openness for participants, the communication component between event planners and facilitators, the need for onsite mediators separate from facilitators for non event related or high intense conflicts that happen and might detract from other participants, the methodologies employed for how and when security personnel will be engaged, the leadership of who makes decisions at these actual events on the day, chain of command for decision making, crisis management plan and pre-event engagement strategies to ensure that the voices of those who might protest are at least addressed and their leaders are sought out BEFORE a crisis happens.

Fascinatingly, of course, these kinds of top-down solutions to bottom-up outrage and coordinated activism demonstrate the complex technical roles and competency of government agencies in carrying out or assisting with public engagement events.

Occasionally, public engagement consultants question whether they might better serve the public in ways that don't involve deliberation at all. One facilitator asks whether it is appropriate in some instances to have a "convening or intervention":

> Is it enough to bring together members of the public to let them do the things that citizens need to do, or do we need to design processes that enable members of the public to do things with each other that they could not otherwise do? That is, do we need to "help" them, through meeting design and/or facilitation?
>
> My answer is that sometimes we need to be intervention agents, and particularly when 1) the stakes are high; 2) passions are high; and 3) the public discourse has already deteriorated (from full stories to anecdotes and then again to hurling slogans at each other).

He suggested that listserv readers might be interested in the use of mediators to communicate between protestors and the police, "an example of how protests are being handled in a creative manner in the UK" following a commission report on the handling of the G20 protests in 2009. Given that mass rioting in 2011 caused deaths and significant property damage throughout England, the use of mediators was clearly insufficient to the level of civil disobedience and violence provoked by generalized unrest over years of fiscal austerity programs.

Sociologists Richard Sennett and Saskia Sassen note the hopelessness that motivated citizens to arm themselves against rioters:

> In attempting to carry out reform, the government appears incompetent; it has lost legitimacy. This has prompted some people living on Kingsland Road to become vigilantes. "We have to do things for

ourselves," a 16-year-old in Hackney told The Guardian, convinced that the authorities did not care about, or know how to protect, communities like his.

A street of shuttered shops, locked playgrounds and closed clinics, a street patrolled by citizens armed with knives and bats, is not a place to build a life.[20] *baloney. good for them.*

In the face of explosive, misdirected rage at market injustices and overwhelming cynicism about the capacity of state authority in a time of fiscal crisis, the types of civic action available to protect local businesses and communities are not so different in scope, if they are vastly different in scale, from those of the Kauai residents who reluctantly started up their earthmoving equipment. Vigilantism may not elicit "reflexive smiles," but it certainly bespeaks the "plucky" determination of frustrated citizens so activated in the face of government failure that they decide to govern themselves until further notice.

In concluding this section, I return to the rage triggered by the ways contemporary public engagement resembles corporate team building. Public engagement consultants on facilitation listservs traded war stories about facilitating or participating in such sessions. One recounted processes that attempted to activate employees' survival skills by metaphorically replicating their straitened circumstances in precarious companies: "I actually had a boss who had a few ideas for team development including skydiving and having us stranded in a boat in Chesapeake Bay and having us find our way back." In a debate over whether workforce engagement activities can ever be considered truly voluntary, one consultant argued that, in uncertain workplace environments, "No one wants to 'fail the test' of participating," even in a physically demanding, dangerous, or patently futile activity for older employees with preexisting health conditions:

Everyone in this group were seasoned managers who managed large groups of people. We didn't need this activity to learn about teamwork or group dynamics. We didn't learn anything from it. But we all demonstrated to our boss our willingness to participate in a stupid game. Most remarks about this were—well we did it—I wonder what will be next.

Such experiences shift empathy to participants and away from administrative sponsors, even when the participants are white-collar managers. Another facilitator claims that the best experience a workplace engagement practitioner "could have is to be fired":

> I've been through takeovers, mergers, reorgs, and I've been downsized several times. Each one was bruising, and a few left scars. ... The lessons of change are critical. If you are going to plan organizational change, you need to appreciate, in a deeply personal way, what it might mean (and feel like) to the folks who will be affected.

While little sympathy is reserved in deliberations for those "usual suspects" who try to dominate the process, the consequence of exiting engagement processes is often invisibility. Trainees in the deliberation certificate course were warned not to measure deliberative success by the number of stakeholders who show up because, in many cases, huge turnouts meant participation by those who were anxious about being left out and distrustful of the convening authority. For those bad apples who contemplate refusal (or exit, once they see the direction deliberations are headed), the decision to forgo participation, while an option, is often not a palatable one, even when the administering authority is not a private employer.[21]

For community groups and concerned citizens in the Community Congress for New Orleans rebuilding, not participating might mean potential exclusion from any role in decision-making or from participation in future processes.[22] Despite having already committed considerable resources and energy in prior processes, they saw themselves as forced to participate in ongoing engagement efforts that drained their energies for little in return. The eventual exit of even the most engaged participants in progressively draining processes over the course of years, a phenomenon I studied in the environmental planning research I conducted prior to this project,[23] is merely the long-term version of the short-term dissipation of energy described by the NPAC participant who came home activated but had trouble maintaining her focus.

A well-meaning desire on the part of public engagement professionals to help those not empowered by their interventions may, in certain circumstances, mean refusing a role as "intervention agents" at all; one facilitator suggests that practitioners might "need to give up their worldly belongings (i.e. their messiah model), put on their sandals and take up their bed-roll, go out amongst the people, and let that experience teach them how to 'help.'" This final step of authentic engagement facilitation—instead of defending processes from corruption and manipulation, and instead of becoming intervention agents when processes are co-opted by sponsors or participants, public engagement professionals reject their existing hybrid models of individual empowerment and culture change to learn from the experience of participants themselves—would make public engagement facilitation resemble the participatory and collaborative strategies of the 1960s far more than it currently does. Certainly, if the organizers of the NPAC conference had sought out the painstaking, lengthy, messy processes of traditional social movements—of framing, community building, and organizing collective action throughout their memberships—they might have had more effective results than they did using AmericaSpeaks' alternately energizing and demobilizing model. But this deeper level of empathy and participant empowerment would also defeat the concept of professional engagement consulting—of high-quality facilitated engagement with clear outcomes in a defined time frame—altogether.

In such a light, the disempowering outcomes of public deliberation in the present day can be placed in the context of all of the other small-scale participatory victories, large-scale disillusionments, and misdirected anger of life in contemporary institutions in an era that claims to have moved beyond conflict. That deliberative theorists believe in public engagement participants' ability to hand-paddle their oarless ships of state back to shore all by themselves, when those ships are adrift in a sea of similarly beleaguered craft, speaks not to their hope for the future, but their sense that collective action in the present day must be limited to the smallest of gestures. When the civil actions of participants frustrated with this micro-empowerment end up resulting in refusal to participate—or at their most ambitious, in a seaside toilet rebuilt or an urban street corner defended—we should not necessarily be encouraged or surprised.

## Downsizing Dreams: Connecting Democratic Reforms to Disempowerment

Even though you may want to launch a large-scale public dialogue effort, you may also feel overwhelmed or that you want to start creating change right away. You may feel discouraged by the fact that the kinds of changes you're hoping for may be realized too far into the future. Or you may desire to get your feet wet on this approach but you're not sure how to begin walking down this path. Have no fear! Here are some things you could do right now, which will soothe your anxieties because you will be doing something to address the issue you deeply care about. But also because the pressure isn't on your shoulders (yet) to organize a large effort or produce systemic community changes.

From the Everyday Democracy website, 2010

In terms of whether deliberative processes may prompt mobilization, the topics of deliberative dialogues, the structure of their problem framings, and their hoped-for outcomes suggest that deliberation contains more potential for social control than liberation, even in cases where collective action is an explicit goal and processes are generally found to be satisfactory. Far from being a consequence of manipulation of individual processes, this occurs despite the fact that participants do come together in deliberative dialogue to put their individual experiences in collective perspective—traditionally a starting point for the shared grievance construction and transformations of political consciousness that lead to mobilization.[24] For collective sharing of perspectives to result in particular forms of mobilization and not others requires considerable political skill—a nuanced attention to balancing the emotional register of such processes to recognize hurts, defuse anger, and ameliorate frustration without seeming condescending or superficial—exactly the services refined to an art by public engagement consultants. How is it that satisfactory processes and unsatisfactory processes may produce essentially the same results?

To understand deliberation in context, we need to understand how stakeholder discussion and action are subtly managed in contemporary public engagement. First, deliberative process forces empathetic identification with the difficulties of others—that speaking should be accompanied by active listening. Processes begin with expressions of individual interests but use small-group methods to assemble these individual expressions into collective realization of the multisided nature of problems. Following expressions of their own perspectives, those with individual-level interests and agendas are asked to understand the tough choices decision-makers face through role-playing as hypothetical or actual decision-makers. Second, by putting citizen voice at the center, processes move sponsors and powerful actors to roles as collaborative stakeholders who are equivalent contributing members of the democratic polity: supportive, respectful witnesses standing by to make their own unique contributions and to subsidize the individual actions stakeholders are ready to undertake in reciprocal processes of co-creation. Faced with complex challenges, citizens are asked to assume the burden of problem-solving at the community level, while decision-makers and market actors are flattened to the position of claimants, incapable of producing change without the assistance of the public. As such, the empowerment and political action produced by deliberative dialogue are real but small scale in scope, more likely to contain unrest than to challenge inequalities.

Events that emphasize constructive solution generation even in dire circumstances may limit more substantive political action by providing opportunities for small-scale change and allowing stakeholders to vent. Citizens are encouraged to govern themselves as a way of enacting civic virtue: by eating responsibly and staying healthy, by caring for their spouses and parents, and by making sure that their children are educated, productive members of society. The grassroots action encouraged in deliberation typically reinforces institutional authority—whether of agribusiness companies to manage commodity and consumer product supply chains, of governments to impose taxation on citizens, or of companies to reduce health benefits. That these administrative decisions are ostensibly beneficent and aimed toward social profit and community betterment through economic growth is cold comfort when those small-scale actions become back-breaking—when an underinsured person becomes sick, when an aging breadwinner is laid off, or when caring for a partner or parent with dementia interferes with her loved ones' ability to contribute to that economy. Such eventualities—where deliberators have been told that their virtue depends on their civic pride and lack of entitlement, but then are faced with the reality that they are useless to or can't participate in the market—reveal the nonpartisan win-win spirit of deliberation as a cruel joke for some.

As this chapter has shown, even when that authority or those framings of civic virtue are questioned or rejected by participants, or when the articulation of dissent is explicitly welcomed as part of the process,[25] such resistance may not offer much more hope for change than the engagement processes it contests. In an environment of tough choices and shared pain, participants are confronted with unpalatable choices and, if they reject them, forced to deal with the bad choices others have chosen on their behalf. The cynicism engagement occasionally engenders in participants—the sense that administrators are incompetent—is the same criticism that deliberative framings so often encourage; the only difference is that in one case, participants have believed that these critiques are part of the authenticity of the process, and in the other, they perceive such critiques as challenging a sham. That deliberative populaces are capable of such critiques, but essentially unmobilizable, speaks to their desperate positioning in a landscape of extreme capitalism. When such desperation does lead to more ambitious action, it is not necessarily action we want to celebrate, inasmuch as self-governance is not a model for a functioning, complex society of stark inequalities— some people will self-govern with their baseball bats and others with their construction equipment. The unintended consequences—bridges that collapse, vigilante justice, a corporate-sponsored version of Shirley Jackson's lottery[26]—are unpleasant to contemplate.

# CONCLUSION

## Down Market Democracy and the Politics of Hope

There is soul to neoliberalism, and a refusal to accord it respectful attention not only makes caricatures of its many sincere adherents but also
leaves no terrain for engaging them.

Bethany Moreton, "The Soul of Neoliberalism" (2007: 117)

The world of progressive reform not only eludes ethnographic objectifica-
tion, it specifically resists critical analysis because it is morally prized. . . .
As the moral code goes: critique equals pessimism which equals paralysis.

Amanda Lashaw, "How Progressive Culture Resists Critique: The Impasse of
NGO Studies" (2013: 517–518)

IN CLOSING THIS BOOK, WE return to the impressive scene at the
Community Congress in Dallas to understand what deliberation can do
well and what that tells us about our contemporary capacities for social
change. The message in deliberation is usually that administrators can't
fix long-term social problems without the public pitching in—but those
same administrators are able to carry off stunningly well-coordinated
events with the help of public engagement consultants. Running a one-
time event with high tech and a warm touch is not proof positive of
competency or political will for longer-term problem-solving, any more
than the sight of everyday folks coming together once indicates that
they may wield some larger power in the polity. But it should speak to
our leaders' and decision-makers' ability to carry out basic functions of
governance for which publics are increasingly distrustful—the ability

to plan for and respond to natural disasters like Katrina, for instance. The conclusion of this book investigates the larger significance of public engagement and the possibilities for constructing a more powerful politics. Deliberative democracy as practiced today offers us a unique window into the soul of an era characterized by both neoliberalism *and* progressivism.    leftism + more leftism

## Democracy in Our Own Image: The Substance of Public Engagement Expertise

Deliberative scholars often call the participants assembled for events like Community Congress III minipublics, and they are often accompanied by a ministate of public, private, and nonprofit services: private and public security, health and child care, entertainment, sustenance, videography and recording, simultaneous translation for those speaking other languages, accommodation for those with disabilities and those who can't read, and social science researchers and journalists documenting the event for posterity. Despite the frustrations of participants (described in the preceding chapter) with the limited change public engagement produces, we should not overlook the fact that public engagement as it is now practiced is indeed extraordinarily sophisticated and takes considerable skill and expertise. The craft of designing and executing engagement entails complex management work, and dismissing public engagement as mere political theater paints its participants as dupes and overlooks the real labor—the long-term effort, both social and emotional—that public engagement consultants do.

As described in chapters 3 and 4, public engagement practitioners take great care to produce authentic opportunities for laypersons to have real input in decision-making. The long, complicated history of populist rhetoric and expert remedies in American life makes producing a top-down grassroots process—one that hits just the right blend of notes for skeptical audiences and partisan critics—less simple than it seems. Facilitating public engagement requires a nuanced navigation of New Age and social justice discourses, of meditative peace and missionary zeal, of progressive critiques of power and neoliberal critiques of bureaucracy. Facing pressure from publics and sponsors as they try to democratize organizations, public engagement practitioners are ruth-lessly self-critical, carefully policing the authenticity of their processes and struggling with the power they hold. At the same time, they spread their practices as widely as possible through a process I call *selfing*, in which all organizations and people, including themselves, are judged to be universally alike in their need for liberatory interventions. When public engagement is done well, facilitators and sponsors recede into the background, and the front-stage process of deliberation—of a democracy in miniature, with stakeholders sharing their stories, listening to others, and growing together—looks very simple indeed.

What is going on here is clearly not a standard case of the disem-powering effects of experts on public life. But as we are wowed by the success of public engagement—by the incorporation of its practices into all kinds of organizations and for all kinds of purposes—chapters 5 and 6 argue that we should pay more attention to the moral assumptions and shared discourses of public engagement as a method of reforming organizations. Public engagement processes are held up as shining exam-ples of what the people can achieve when they work together, but if we look at them as testaments to political authenticity, we may miss the way their civicness is deeply embedded in market contexts. The very particular forms of social profits that are celebrated in this unique type of civil society are not just evocative adaptations of a simpler form of political life, but draw deeply on the latest trends in corporate culture and labor management.

These aesthetic, social, and community-oriented discourses speak an empathic language of expressive art and soulful connection, critique out-of-touch administrators and hidebound traditions, and celebrate social change, cultural transformation, and individual enlightenment. At a time of pervasive fiscal crisis and increasingly contentious politics, when stakeholders demand more and governments have less to give, public engagement has become a repository of moral virtue. It offers to turn passive consumers into active citizens accountable for their own fates. Engagement has become a popular organizational strategy across sectors because of its ability to reap these transformations, whether its subjects are needy youth whose obesity weighs on economic growth, downsized employees, or residents of communities and states with massive debt burdens. Empowerment is on offer in deliberation, but

Detroit,
Illinois, Philadelphia.'

if we analyze the contexts in which it is produced, we find that the activism it offers is small in scope and aligned with sponsors' goals. Political equality—the chance to be decision-makers for a day—is not worth much when making decisions means budget cuts as far as the eye can see. Ironically, the services participants are offered in the settings of public engagement events show that, with appropriate resources and capacity, hope for a better world is both practical and possible. The real profits of extreme capitalism remain hopelessly out of reach, even as participants are encouraged by the notion that social profits are tantalizingly within their grasp with a little elbow grease and a neighbor's helping hand.

What happens when public engagement outcomes are less than promised? As I argue in chapter 7, the results are ultimately disappointing—both in cases where deliberation is successful and in those where it isn't. Whether it is designed to spark activism or explicitly intended to produce consent, public engagement has surprisingly consistent effects, focusing action on "strength-based" approaches at the individual or local level, while authority and coordinated advocacy at larger scales is ceded to elite sponsors and organizations. Rightly, participants recognize that more complex, long-term issues are just too big to be solved by appreciative citizens, neighborly care, and social marketing, no matter how dedicated Americans are to changing their behavior today. Why, then, with such dispiriting results, does the public invest hope in these uniquely blended civic contexts of politics and drumming, best practices and budget calculators? What makes engagement so appealing, even when participants suspect that do-it-yourself democracy is not all it's cracked up to be?

### Crafting Authentic Community: The Larger Meanings of Deliberative Reform

Despite claims that specific content is irrelevant to the larger civic lessons on offer, the content of deliberation matters. Scholars to this point have concerned themselves with deliberative content in terms of both the qualities of reason-giving conversations in actual deliberations and participants' own reports of empowerment and satisfaction. This book has focused closely on the content of deliberative discourse in terms of the topics of engagement events and their methods. The topics of deliberation are not exclusively about empowerment but also about slashing benefits and jobs while keeping up morale, about youth development, urban growth, and personal social responsibility. The methods of deliberation are not just different formats for civic discussion, but also entail positivity and appreciation, a few hours' worth of generous social services and New Age visioning, serious invocations of patriotism and sacrifice, irreverent celebration of arena rock and soul anthems, edgy slam poetry, and quirky, colorful art.

To this point, analyses of the cultural resonance of public engagement have understood deliberation in terms of "motherhood and apple pie": chicken soup for the soul in a cynical age. In fact, as sections II and III of this book have described, deliberation is both deeply nostalgic and technocratically future oriented. But the nostalgia evoked is not for the reassuring touchstones of 1950s domestic life, but a blend of modern social justice and nineteenth-century virtues—for a burnished Yankee past of centuries-tested town meetings (evoking localism, communitarianism, and humble nonpartisanship) and for the heady romance of 1960s and 1970s activism (evoking racial and ethnic diversity, gender equality, personal growth, environmental awareness, and radical critique). There is political substance to our hopes.

That the turbulent, unfinished changes of those times are now viewed by an unsettled nation through rose-colored glasses might be a painful surprise to grizzled veterans of the Left. But we should take heart that those critiques, and the methods used to express them, are still powerful and so very appealing to the workers, citizens, and stakeholders who remake them, again and again—real, all-consuming, authentically challenging. Empowerment that is reassuringly traditional, at the same time that it acknowledges the complex social problems of our time, can help us to feel powerful and grounded in an environment of systemic cascading failures, insecure employment, and grim visions of a post-carbon future.

In this sense, the deep political authenticity sold in public engagement is just one version of other forms of deep authenticity that have become emotional touchstones for audiences raised on Like buttons and other forms of shallow affective commitment. A new generation has found economical fun in the latest version of the back-to-the-land movement, hoping that canning fruit and gardening on urban rooftops will lead to a way of life based on older, slower models waiting to be rediscovered. When those rooftop farms are funded through crowdsourced micro-lending websites like Kickstarter and provide vegetables to poor people and upscale restaurants alike, so much the better. These dreams have power not because they are illusory, but because they involve real skill and real collaborative effort. That individuals can have it both ways—social profit and social capital, joy and justice, duty and play—is the alluring promise of a multi-institutional world of hybrid public-private-nonprofit enterprise, no less elusive because it seems so easy to achieve when it is done well. Deliberation entails a promise of fractal self-realization, where the part is the crystal-perfect image of the whole, constantly reinventing and reintegrating an authentic self into an authentic community.

## Slow Politics: Always Transforming, Never Transformed

Public engagement incarnates this promise of concurrent, endlessly reflective change because it contains the unrest of the last two decades so effectively while offering new visions of further change and synchrony to come. Comparing its ideologies to those that have come before and those that coexist with it reveals how new amalgamations can solve capitalism's evolving problems, even as they are "co-created" by workers and managers, publics and public figures. Just as Max Weber theorized the Protestant ethic as the spirit of industrial capitalism, historian Bethany Moreton describes the "new animating spirit" developed in Walmart stores for a "feminized post-Fordist workplace" more likely to look like a grocery store than a factory:

> As they trained smalltown Protestants to manage the service economy, managers and business professors found a way for men to retain their authority even as they took on a work environment demanding skills they coded female—patience, humility, communicativeness, eagerness to please. ... In response to the new work environment, a Christian-inflected management theory of servant leadership made a virtue of necessity.[1]

It is hard not to read such a description and compare it with our own time, when a new generation of management consultants has blended *left and left*

a set of seemingly contradictory progressive and neoliberal logics into a philosophy of participatory governance that resonates so deeply because it resolves so many anxieties in a time of vanishing white-collar jobs and dizzying financialization.[2] No longer explicitly Christian, the Zen-inflected management doctrines of being authentic and letting go in the moment resolve anxieties by allowing today's workers not to strive in a losing game, not to do anything more than be and share and hold space in anticipation of transformation, partaking in ritualistic performances of reflexive engagement and deep, heart-based connection.

The endless replication of transformation sought by practitioners in deliberation is also refracted throughout global institutions, as other markets for different kinds of products—advertising, lobbying, philanthropy—are remade in the shape of civic empowerment. As paid canvassers solicit signatures outside, shoppers browse the shelves of Whole Foods for products advertising participatory contests to leverage the rage for engagement, and the cashiers and employees of natural foods companies acquired by multinational corporations are also asked to participate in deliberative events to produce more empowering corporate cultures and better cope with cost-cutting and layoffs. The *process of engagement* is a method for managing and slowing the breakneck pace of social change in our organizational lives.

As "slow" politics on a short time frame,[3] deliberation ends up producing the ad hoc ideas, ephemeral social connections, and short-term successes of empowerment projects everywhere, documented on butcher paper in artistic renderings connecting cartoon figures and colorful words with arrows representing the transformations of a better future. This state of constant renewal, of becoming and never arriving, is ideal for itinerant workers asked to invest themselves in initiatives dropped after six months and in never-ending engagement processes to design future engagement processes, nested within each other like Russian dolls. While planned obsolescence of consumer goods enabled the Walmarts of an earlier era to thrive, the products being produced by a knowledge-based, financialized economy are not products at all but processes—processes intended to produce the involvement of everyone, so we can all have a hand in creating a commons of civic good and social change.

Such kind, respectful invitations and red carpet treatment in forums for storytelling and decision-making go a long way toward soothing the submissive humiliations of life as economy-class travelers, shoppers checking out our own groceries, and workers trying to beat the traffic congestion separating our insecure jobs from our underwater houses. The sights and sounds of a small-town, low-tech, walkable America; of a creative, screen-free childhood; and of a power rock adolescence in gas-guzzling cars made in Detroit are alluring indeed—no matter that they are reinvented in air-conditioned conference rooms at tables decorated with plastic orchids and iPads in struggling center cities.

As anthropologist Amanda Lashaw points out with respect to social reform-oriented NGOs and cultural historian Trysh Travis notes with respect to the politics of transcendence in New Thought (the "if you dream it, it will happen" philosophy that permeates Appreciative Inquiry), it has been hard for critics to see alternate agendas in the good intentions of contemporary neoliberal and progressive discourses because those discourses are already critical and relentlessly civic and public-oriented. What has been sold in the Zen and New Thought and positive psychology–rich settings of deliberation is not religion but social change—political mobilization, speaking truth to organizational power, and collective action—as not just congruent with capitalism, but transcending it entirely for a space that is not only business but also family and center square. Because these blendings of settings, sectors, and logics are so common, it may seem odd that the power of deliberative discourses (and their commercial value for sponsors) rests in the integrity of their political authenticity.

This is not the commodification of revolution within capitalism, but the integration of progressivism's insurgent capacities and its empathetic language of social struggle and salvation of the oppressed in the scarred hearts and aging bodies of individual citizens. Their awareness of the limits of the political consumerism they are routinely sold makes the raw political speech and promise of greater action in public engagement that much more powerful. Just as "servant leadership" lifted floor polishing and shelf stocking into a higher register of virtue as customer care, deliberating about public priorities and community hopes in precious free time is appealing not because publics fall for the social consciousness and environmental friendliness sold with the energy drinks they need to make it through the day, but because they fear it is not enough. Authentic self-sacrifice is the spirit and soul of deliberative capitalism.

In this sense, social scientists' responsibilities as observers of contemporary organizational life are not to assuage those fears in better-realized engagement processes, but to identify those incipient discomforts and nagging suspicions without losing sight of the enduring promise, and very real perils, of change itself. To do this, we must challenge the reassuring notion of self-sameness promoted in public engagement: that families and companies and countries are similarly dysfunctional and similarly amenable to identical remedies. The idea that context matters—institutional and historical and social differences really do influence whether sacrifices that make sense in one setting can be radically inappropriate in another—is critical to understanding where and when engagement might be a useful or empowering remedy. Just envisioning change is not change enough. That Americans have persistently struggled with how to collaborate, for what purpose, and with whose help can provide reassurance that our own ideals, and our failures to achieve them in exactly the ways we want, are perennial risks of believing in a better future.

# POSTSCRIPT

## Notes on Data and Methods

SCHOLARS AND THOSE CURIOUS ABOUT the process of studying a highly mobile group of predominantly progressive reformers may be interested in more information about the methodological strategy. The intent of the methodology described in this postscript was to explore the expanding field of public engagement facilitation and the tensions it produces among practitioner, public, and client interests. In summer 2006, I began the initial stages of fieldwork on a qualitative, ethnographic project that would take up the next five years of my life and take me all over the continental United States and beyond. At first, as I joined the professional associations for engagement consultants and interviewed the founders of the National Coalition for Dialogue and Deliberation, I was captivated by the apparent paradox that these individuals were experts in empowering laypersons. As I went to professional conferences, listened in on conference calls and webinars, and pored over the listserv messages deluging my inbox, I learned how these sophisticated professionals shared their passion with others and managed the tensions they faced in their work. As a professor at a small liberal arts college, I got the chance to test out on my very patient students the techniques I was learning in dialogue and deliberation training courses and a weeklong public participation certification course. Whenever I could, I attended major public deliberation events sponsored by governments and by private organizations as a volunteer or facilitator. The opportunity arose to take part in a research team studying a process for performing arts professionals to develop a collective action agenda. With my collaborators and graduate students, we could study the process from all sides, sitting in on backstage meetings and surveying participants before and after the process to see how it had affected their perspectives.

I continued to interview key people in the field, and when I believed that I had a good sense of the frameworks that dialogue and deliberation professionals used to understand their work, I conducted an online survey in September and October 2009 with Francesca Polletta, another sociologist who was interested in how facilitators understood the gender dynamics she had observed in the Listening to the City deliberations. Francesca and I were committed to sharing this work with the larger field, and I developed an interactive website with survey results and presented my findings at dialogue and deliberation conferences and for professional organizations on international conference calls and in person. As I conducted the project over an extended period of time, I had the chance to see how the field responded to disasters such as Katrina, the election of Barack Obama, the contentious town hall meetings on health care, and other historic opportunities and challenges for the field. We lived through these events, and many meals and late night bar sessions to make sense of them, together.

It was not just in the classroom that my researcher-observer and academic hats blurred. I was amazed at how many of my academic colleagues attended dialogue and deliberation conferences and were heavily invested in the field, as well as how often I was approached after presenting at an academic conference by an audience member who identified herself or himself as a former or current engagement facilitator. In sum, while qualitative scholars often talk about sharing their research with their subjects, my multimethod ethnographic work was unusually dialogic because of the specific subject matter I was studying. Given that academics are so heavily invested in the field and have so much shared idealism about the power of informed conversation, I often did not have to go very far to share my research or to become a subject of deliberative interventions myself.

Nevertheless, my unique viewpoint on the subject as an ethnographer was a continuing challenge, in part because of the involvement of the academic world in deliberative initiatives, and in part because of the moral passions and active participation that deliberation inspires. Such challenges are part and parcel of what ethnographer Amanda Lashaw calls "the ethical and methodological challenges that arise" when "turning progressive phenomena into objects of critical analysis": "studying a milieu that is too familiar to the researcher, among NGO professionals who already analyze themselves, and in a field of advocacy that is morally prized."[1] As I scrupulously tried to maintain a distance between my research and my academic life, I found the boundaries between these increasingly breaking down in practice. With so many academics around at deliberation professionals' conferences, it took extra effort to make sure that my subjects were aware of my study and my role as an outside observer rather than a full-fledged member of their community. For a group committed to public access and transparency, I still wanted to respect participants' right to privacy. On the other hand, I also had to become a subject of my own subjects, as many of the settings in which I was observing insisted on full participation of everyone in the room, sometimes to my discomfort. To allow participants to see behind the curtain of my own research process, I insert in the book extensive first-person descriptions of field settings like the one that starts chapter 1, even though each chapter draws on multiple forms of evidence—field notes, organizational documents, survey data—to support its argument. The more research I conducted, the more I became convinced that despite the small army of deliberation researchers, the story of people like Susan was not being told by other scholars.

As a multimethod field study supported with survey data, analysis involved cross-referencing the many different forms of data collected to confirm that inductive findings from one source were also surfacing in other sources and among different kinds of actors. Ethnographic research of this sort is ideal for "identifying the mechanisms through which governance is accomplished and the strategies through which governance is attempted, experienced, resisted and revised, taken in historical depth and cultural context."[2] The following sections describe data collection and citation practices for each method.

## Fieldwork

I conducted fieldwork from 2006 through 2009 at a variety of sites in the United States and Canada. To get a closer perspective on business practices in the public deliberation industry, I conducted extensive participant observation in various training and certification venues and professional conferences: a weeklong public participation facilitation certification course, three more specialized training sessions, two national and two international professional association conferences, a deliberation methods conference, monthly webinars and teleconferences, and "in-world" meetings, trainings, and lectures in Second Life. These field experiences provide an ideal perspective on the concerns of deliberation professionals regarding marketing of firms and projects, public, client, and volunteer relations, project management, professional development, and field advancement.

In addition, I sought to understand stakeholder, volunteer, and client perspectives on professional deliberation facilitation through the lens of major national-scale public and nonprofit sector deliberation projects. Having been certified in deliberation facilitation, I served as a volunteer table facilitator at Community Congress III, a national deliberative meeting on New Orleans redevelopment and recovery. I also served as a volunteer (performing duties like trash collection and handing out documents) at Our Budget, Our Economy, a national deliberative meeting on strategies for trimming the budget deficit by 2025. As part of a larger research collaborative, I had full access to the National Performing Arts Convention 2008, a national meeting with four separate deliberative events, allowing observation of facilitator training, table dialogues, coding meetings, and interactions between the deliberation consultants and their clients. I also conducted presurveys and postsurveys of a random sample of conference participants and intensive interviews with the clients and the chief process facilitator regarding process outcomes. When I reference data from observations, the specific fieldwork setting (a training course, conference, etc.) is described in the text.

## Informal Interviews

I conducted informal interviews and follow-up communications with more than fifty individuals over the course of the fieldwork. These were conducted over the phone and in person and lasted from thirty minutes to multiple hours over the course of months and years. Interviewees were selected for their diversity and their ability to reveal reflections and backstage discussions on the activities observed, and they represented all corners of the field and beyond. The sample included founders and leaders of professional associations; directors, professional facilitators, and staff members of deliberation facilitation and funding organizations; themers (people who collect "gems" and digest the content of deliberative sessions into themes); process recorders and an internal process "journalist"; former practitioners; current independent practitioners within large and small deliberation consultancies in the United States, the European Union, Canada, and Australia; practitioners within full-service consultancies such as engineering firms; public administrators and internal agency facilitators; stakeholder management and deliberation software developers and entrepreneurs; academics; pracademics; civic engagement institute founders; amateur table facilitators; facilitation trainers; facilitation trainees; and attendees of facilitation certificate programs. Because the currency of the field is nonhierarchical and reciprocal discussion, these conversations were intensive and open-ended, commonly occurring in offices and at deliberative events and conferences, but also in informal settings in airports, hotel common spaces, and cars and over meals in bars and restaurants.

I have also been interviewed by former interviewees and have shared preliminary findings from the research (at deliberation and public administration conferences and on a public website) with practitioners in an ongoing dialogue. In cases when interviews were not recorded and transcribed, questions and answers were reconstructed from field jottings as quickly as possible after the conversation took place in electronic document files, with notation for exact phrasing or paraphrasing. Electronic communications were imported from e-mail software to the interview file database. Subsequent to data collection, electronic files were coded inductively in the manner previously described. To protect confidentiality, some individuals and organizations are identified with pseudonyms or within brackets indicating organizational category, and some minor identifying details have been changed. The desire to protect confidentiality has been balanced with bibliographic citation and identification of publicly promoted methods, public figures, and organizations with historical importance in the field to provide proper crediting of authorial sources and where recognition of historic contributions and publicity are reasonable or expected.

## Archival Research

Analysis of deliberation practitioners' listservs, organization and process websites, blogs, and social networking sites; field handbooks; and unique data sources supplements the information gathered through participant observation. Listserv postings were collected, coded by source, and stored in a full-text, searchable database containing more than 8,400 documents representing three and a half years of electronic conversations on the field. Other electronic documents, including formal publications, electronic slide shows, and webpages, in addition to digital images, datafiles, and screen captures of websites and online meetings, and digital photographs documenting conference activities,[3] were categorized, coded, and stored in full-text, searchable databases by organizational source, using image library and indexing software. Additional files for brochures and other ephemera collected during fieldwork, including handbooks, CDs, and DVDs, were maintained for each organization. My research assistants and I conducted content analyses using inductive coding of text files, major guidebooks in the field, and unique data sources. We developed separate coding schemes for each document type. According to standard practices in content analysis,[4] we refined codes over the course of the coding process and then continued to test codes by applying them independently on texts used in the analysis to confirm intercoder reliability, which was above 85% in all cases and typically above 90%. We reconciled all coding differences prior to analysis.[5] The source of data from archival research, including publicly available documents, is described in the text rather than cited in the bibliography to protect the identities of informants. Excerpts provided in the text have been corrected for minor spelling, grammar, and punctuation errors that might prove distracting to readers.

## Practitioner Survey

As a supplement to the fieldwork, informal interviews, and archival research, a nonrandom online survey of dialogue and deliberation practitioners, distributed through more than twenty online listservs and Web-based community networks in the field, was conducted in September and October 2009 in collaboration with Francesca Polletta of University of California, Irvine, to solicit a broader perspective on the dominant tensions and shared beliefs surfacing in the qualitative research. The survey, whose target population was volunteer and professional deliberation practitioners in the United States, yielded 433 completed responses, 345 of which were from respondents based in the United States. For a variety of reasons, I chose to focus on surveying individual deliberation practitioners connected to the field through e-mail listservs rather than conducting a random mail survey of deliberation organizations and consultancies.

A number of issues drove this choice. A simple random sample of membership rolls of the NCDD or IAP2 would not yield a sample that represented the population of deliberation practitioners. My awareness that many practitioners were not members of either organization, and that many deliberation practitioners belong to professional associations as "organizational members" while some members are neither volunteer nor professional practitioners, led to an expanded approach that attempted to sample the full range and diversity of practitioners. Based on the ethnographic research, this survey focused on all self-identified deliberation practitioners, including those running independent, privately owned deliberation consultancies and those working within full-service consultancies and public agencies not exclusively dedicated to deliberation. There is, given their diversity (engineering firms, public relations firms, and urban planning firms, to name a few, in addition to natural resource agencies, urban planning agencies, redevelopment corporations, etc.), no comprehensive listing of such organizations comparable to those used by Kreiss and Walker, nor any reporting requirements for subsidizing public deliberation that would allow for random sampling.[6] Even consultants that specialize in facilitation projects for public agencies are typically not preapproved in contracting databases.

Although nonrandom sampling is not appropriate for a developed field in which organizations or practitioners are readily identified in available sampling frames, this method is appropriate in a case in which the population of organizations remains undefined. Not only is the field of actors involved in deliberative democracy "so complex, diffuse, and diverse"[7] that it is extremely difficult to isolate as a distinct field, but also there is, despite the developing professional associations described here, still no common qualification that would make identification of deliberation practitioners possible. It is in part this amorphous character that makes elaboration of influences on the field worth studying, inasmuch as it constitutes an interstitial field that draws legitimacy from a variety of related fields.[8] I concluded that the self-selection of those who identified themselves as deliberation practitioners, and the bias in such a sample toward those most invested in the field and most connected to electronic networks through existing institutional structures and organizational communities, was acceptable, given my research interest in industry promotion and development, and preferable to designing my own nonrandom sampling frame, as in the case of the Jacobs, Cook, and Delli Carpini survey of sponsoring organizations.[9] I took a number of measures to address and account for problems of sampling bias through self-selection in the survey. I included questions on survey recruitment, level of survey engagement, organizational affiliation, and demographics to gauge representativeness for particular subgroups and response rates for particular listservs. Comparison of the demographics of subsamples of our survey to data on subsamples of the target population collected in my research (existing surveys of association members or attendees at professional conferences, for example) typically revealed differences of a few percentage points on average on both demographic questions and substantive questions, such as distribution of client types.

Regarding response rates, the Jacobs, Cook, and Delli Carpini study used a purposive sampling frame of organizations involved in sponsoring deliberation and had an overall response rate of 23%. Based on our analysis of individual listserv response rates, we had much lower response rates than the Jacobs, Cook, and Delli Carpini survey, which used mail surveys and telephone follow-ups of a purposive sampling frame of organizations involved in sponsoring deliberation.[10] Listserv invitations in our survey had comparable click-through rates of, for example, 24%, but a completion rate for the same list of 14.4%. Because many individuals belonged to multiple lists and thus received the survey solicitation multiple times, the response rate for any particular list can be presumed to be slightly lower than the actual response rate. Given the length of the survey (forty-five questions), overlapping list memberships, and the fact that some individuals on the lists were not in the target population (not from the United States, for example, or not involved in dialogue and deliberation as a practitioner), these response rates are in line with typical response rates for Internet surveying, which vary quite a bit but are on average about 10% less than typical mail response rates.[11] See the public survey website (http://sites.lafayette.edu/ddps/) for survey results and for a larger discussion of survey design, sampling, and limitations.

While the survey sample was nonrandom and therefore cannot be generalized to all deliberation practitioners in the United States, it is an important first step in understanding those areas of broad agreement and tension within the field and a valuable supplement to the extensive field research and archival analysis described earlier. These data are described in the text as survey results; the N given in the footnote reflects the total number of valid responses.

# NOTES

## Introduction

1. Obama (2009a: 4685–4686).
2. All quotes are from the National Coalition for Dialogue and Deliberation's list-serv. Sources of ethnographic material in this book are described in the text.
3. As Morone points out, this insight about the ambiguity of the public good goes as far back as Madison: "consensus about (or 'unperplexed pursuit' of) the public good is 'more ardently to be wished for than seriously to be expected'; even if 'the people commonly intend it,' they often fail 'to reason right about the means of promoting it'" (1998: 8–9).
4. Selznick (1949); Morone (1998).
5. Della Porta (2013).
6. Eliasoph (2009, 2011) discusses similar failed lessons in the case of empowerment projects. Hibbing and Theiss-Morse assert that public proximity to the decision-making process in deliberation breeds discontent and disgust because the public wants "stealth democracy" (2002). The explanation I offer focuses instead on the relationship between the types of activism and attitudes deliberation practitioners try to produce and why these are not empowering in the ways scholars have theorized—both when they are successful and when they are not.

## Chapter 1

1. UNOP (2007: 1).
2. Lukensmeyer (2007: 13).
3. Lukensmeyer (2007: 11).

4. Williamson (2007: 23–24).
5. Williamson (2007: 24).
6. Lukensmeyer (2007: 9).
7. Lukensmeyer (2007: 11).
8. Lukensmeyer (2007: 9).
9. Baiocchi (2005).
10. Lang (2007); Warren and Pearse (2008b).
11. Delli Carpini, Huddy, and Shapiro (2002); Fung (2004); Kadlec and Friedman (2007); Mansbridge (1980); Sanders (1997); Wilson (2008); Young (2000).
12. Rarely is it noted that demonstration projects might have the reverse effect if they are unsuccessful.
13. Bingham, Nabatchi, and O'Leary (2005); Hendriks (2006b); Ryfe (2007b).
14. Hendriks and Carson (2008); Leighninger (2006); Ryfe (2002).
15. Carson and Lewanski (2008); Fischer (2004); Levine, Fung, and Gastil (2005: 3).
16. Beierle and Cayford (2003); Glock-Grueneich and Ross (2008); Hendriks (2008).
17. For more information on the survey of public participation practitioners and other research strategies, interested readers can refer to the postscript to this book on data and methods.
18. These questions differentiate this book from the work of other scholars who claim, based on experimental or empirical cases, that deliberation is not effective (Hibbing and Theiss-Morse 2002, for example). Given the accumulating evidence of the limited impact of deliberative interventions, why does the new public engagement look the way it does and remain so powerful for so many people? I argue that answering these questions requires understanding its use in context, and taking scholars', practitioners', and participants' enthusiasm and reservations seriously—as part of a longstanding, ongoing dialogue on what engagement can and should mean in America.
19. Pacewicz (Forthcoming).
20. Pacewicz (Forthcoming).
21. Pacewicz (Forthcoming).
22. Lukensmeyer (2012).
23. Levine (2014).
24. Conversely, it also demonstrates the virtues of studying professionals like Lukensmeyer who remain central to the field, even as the organizational dynamics of the field change.

## Chapter 2

1. Ganuza and Baiocchi (2012: 1, 10).
2. Obama (2009b).
3. Listserv database.
4. Ryfe (2005: 43); Sirianni and Friedland (2001).

5. Button and Ryfe (2005: 10).
6. Pateman (1970); Walker, McQuarrie, and Lee (2015).
7. Leighninger (2010: 2).
8. Snow (2004); Staggenborg and Taylor (2005).
9. Armstrong and Bernstein (2008); Polletta (2006); Zald and McCarthy (1980).
10. Armstrong and Bernstein (2008).
11. This activity is different in scope, but not in kind, from the grassroots lobbying described later in this chapter and is a reality with which facilitators are extremely familiar. Those members of "the public" who participate in any process are likely to be members of organized groups.
12. Lukensmeyer (2009).
13. Polletta (2002).
14. On "what killed civic engagement," see Putnam (2000: 283–284). For a different take, see Wuthnow (1998).
15. Putnam (1995: 65–78).
16. Leighninger describes this rising citizen entitlement and the "psychological toll" it takes on public administrators (2006: 2).
17. Pacewicz (Forthcoming).
18. Many former activists had already changed strategies by the end of the 1980s, in line with increasing public intolerance for contentious tactics. On activists' life courses and the cultural changes that accompanied the decline of the left and the radical politics of the 1960s, see Whalen and Flacks (1989) and Sirianni and Friedland (2001).
19. For a retrospective look at the movement, its critics, and the enduring changes it has produced in the justice system, see Olson and Dzur (2004: 139–176). For contemporary assessments, see Abel (1982) and Harrington (1985).
20. On the evolution of collaborative environmental institutions, see Wondolleck and Yaffee (2000), Cortner and Moote (1999), Kraft and Mazmanian (2009), and National Research Council (1999).
21. For comparative analysis of these efforts, see Fung (2004); also see Leighninger (2006).
22. Martin (Forthcoming).
23. Pacewicz (Forthcoming).
24. McQuarrie (2007).
25. Terhune (1998).
26. Bradley, in Leighninger (2006: xiii).
27. Public Conversations Project (2010); Fowler et al. (2001).
28. See Sirianni (2009) for a number of initiatives supported by the Kettering Foundation, Philanthropy for Active Civic Engagement, the Industrial Areas Foundation, the National Civic League, the Paul Aicher Foundation, the Northwest Area Foundation, and others. On the promotion of civic engagement within academia, see Ostrander and Portney (2007).

29. On harnessing popular support for deliberation, see Gastil (2000). In the United States, David Osborne was the prophet of these reforms (Osborne 1988; Osborne and Gaebler 1992). Handler (1996) discusses the quality of the empowerment that resulted.

30. Scholars of neoliberalism such as Mudge (2008) point out that, far from being an agenda of the center-right, neoliberal governance reforms in Europe and the United States were pushed by politicians of the center-left just as forcefully. President Clinton and his Interior Secretary Bruce Babbitt promoted multi-stakeholder governance in environmental decision-making at the federal level. On the intersection of new public management and deliberative democracy, see Parkinson (2004; 2006).

31. Espeland (2000) gives a detailed account of the process of democratization since 1969 in the Bureau of Reclamation. Three federal administrators, Roger Bernier of the Centers for Disease Control and Prevention (CDC) and Pat Bonner and Leanne Nurse at the Environmental Protection Agency (EPA), are respected leaders in the deliberative democracy movement. Despite the excitement over the initiative to listen to ideas about how to listen, the EPA conducted just such an online process, "The National Dialogue on Public Involvement in EPA Decisions," under the Bush administration in July 2001. See also Beierle (2001).

32. Adams (2007) provides a useful guide to the varieties of participation available to everyday citizens.

33. Sirianni (2009).

34. Wyman and Shulman (2002: 6).

35. Armstrong and Bernstein argue that a "multi-institutional politics" model of society recognizes "that society is composed of multiple and often contradictory institutions ... [and] views institutions as overlapping and nested" (2008: 82).

36. Clemens (1997); Davis and Zald (2005).

37. Michels (1962 [1911]); for more recent examples of the argument, see Piven and Cloward (1977) and Bosso (2005).

38. On "blended" social action, see Sampson, McAdam, MacIndoe, and Weffer-Elizondo (2005).

39. Skocpol (2003).

40. Chaskin, Brown, Venkatesh, and Vidal (2001).

41. Fisher (2006); Walker (2014).

42. These studies are, respectively, Goss (2006), Hindman (2008), and Caplan (2008). The most famous version of the argument that voters do not vote in their best interests is made by Frank (2004). For an earlier analysis of "un-politics," see Crenson (1971).

43. On the wisdom of crowds, see Surowiecki (2004). Regarding the phenomenon of limited attendance, see Irvin and Stansbury (2004). On the avoidance of political talk, see Eliasoph (1998); on scripted participation, see Walker (2014).

44. Sirianni (2009); Adams (2007); Briggs (2008).

45. Jacobs, Cook, and Delli Carpini (2009).

46. Barnes, Newman, and Sullivan (2007); Hendriks and Carson (2008); Lee (2007).

47. Pateman (1970).

48. Senger (2003); O'Leary and Bingham (2003).

49. Jacobs, Cook, and Delli Carpini (2009:136).

50. Figures are from Kyriss (2006) and McCallum (2009). Total training revenue in 2008 was $338,000. More than 3,100 training days were projected by IAP2 for 2009.

51. See this book's Postscript for more information on the design of the 2009 Dialogue and Deliberation Practitioners Survey, which yielded a nonrandom sample of 345 volunteer and professional deliberation practitioners in the United States. All results are available online at the public survey results website: (http://sites.lafayette.edu/ddps/).

52. Formative training programs cited by practitioners in the survey include "Stanford T-group training," "IBM Jam," "Plowshares," "Encounter Programs," "federal mediation training," "Transactional Analysis training," "AT&T University," "Quality Circle," "Community Dispute Resolution Training," "activist trainings," "advanced facilitation for Covey 7 Habits of Highly Effective People," "Gestalt Intervener Certificate," "Environmental Stakeholder dialogue," and "extensive in-house government and corporate facilitator training," in addition to common trainings on specific deliberative facilitation methods.

53. Interview transcript.

54. N = 222.

55. For more on the effects of financialization, see Krippner (2005). For popular sources on corporations adopting counterculture and movement garb beginning in mid-century, see Frank (1997); for contemporary versions of the same phenomenon, see Harold (2007); for a survey of the adoption of social movement critiques within business management, see Boltanski and Chiapello (2007), and for an analysis of the collective interests of business associations, see Spillman (2012).

56. Elliott (2006).

57. Zukin, Keeter, Andolina, Jenkins, and Delli Carpini (2006).

58. For critiques of digital mythologies of democratization, see Turner (2006) and Mosco (2004). Some examples of this literature include Surowiecki (2004), Tapscott and Williams (2006), Weinberger (2007), Shirky (2008), and Benkler (2006).

59. Yankelovich (2007). Interest organizations and social movement groups have vigorously contested this framing. For examples of their arguments against the "equality" imposed in collaborative management, see Whelan (2007) and McCloskey (1996). For academic treatments, see Kenney (2000) and Hibbard and Madsen (2003).

60. Armstrong and Bernstein (2008); King and Pearce (2010).

61. Cashore, Auld, and Newsom (2004); Bartley and Smith (2010). On community investment, see Boyle and Silver (2005).

62. Abramowicz (2008); Halvorsen (2001); Hodge and Bowman (2006); Papadopoulos and Warin (2007). An example of this belief in practice is the use of public design and naming contests by government agencies.

63. Frank (2000); Boltanski and Chiapello (2007).

64. Jacobs, Cook, and Delli Carpini (2009: 144).

65. N = 660.

66. Jacobs, Cook, and Delli Carpini (2009).

67. N = 167.

68. Jacobs, Cook, and Delli Carpini (2009: 147).

69. Molotch (1976).

70. N = 334.

71. Hendriks and Carson (2008).

72. Habermas (1989); Crenson and Ginsberg (2002); Vogel (1989); Wolin (2008).

73. Mosse (2003: 57).

74. Kashefi and Mort (2004: 300).

75. Ryfe (2007a).

76. Swyngedouw (2005: 1991).

77. Somers (2005: 220).

78. Button and Ryfe (2005: 21).

79. Birnbaum (2006).

80. Field notes, as quoted by a project manager for the firm.

81. N = 222.

82. Jacobs, Cook, and Delli Carpini (2009).

83. N = 220. This figure excludes one project reported at $360 million and one project reported at $125 million, which were discarded from the total as outliers—although these figures are certainly not outside the realm of possibility on large-scale projects. The $36 million total does not likely represent inflation through duplicate reporting of the same large projects using many facilitators; when professionals' budget reports are compared with those of volunteer respondents, only two volunteers reported the most recent project in which they had participated as over $100,000. Nonresponse on this question was high (36%), presumably because respondents were either not familiar with the budget size of the last project in which they engaged or chose not to disclose this information. As stated later, commercial aspects of the industry are often avoided and even rejected as immaterial in conversation among field members. To my knowledge, none of the member surveys conducted by the professional associations has asked questions about budget or even organization size, despite asking about sector of clients and other relevant details of practice. As such, it is not likely that respondents overestimated the budget size of projects because of social desirability.

84. Howard (2006); Kreiss (2012); Walker (2014).
85. Jacobs, Cook, and Delli Carpini (2009).
86. As evidenced by the interest of international NGOs and transnational governance organizations, international interest in deliberation is frequently tied to civil society and democracy promotion efforts in the developing world. The Kettering Foundation has sponsored the International Civil Society Consortium for Public Deliberation, and other organizations based in the United States and Commonwealth countries have sponsored similar efforts aimed at developing an international movement for deliberation.
87. Edelman (2010); Martin (2009).
88. Walker (2014).
89. Travis (2009: 6–7).
90. Boltanski and Chiapello (2007); Medvetz (2012).
91. In *Think Tanks in America*, Medvetz points out that conservative think tanks were so successful because they used forms of authority in alien contexts—ambiguity was essential to their power (2012).
92. Leighninger (2009: 5).
93. Briggs (2008); Jacobs, Cook, and Delli Carpini (2009).
94. Sampson, McAdam, MacIndoe, and Weffer-Elizondo (2005); Armstrong and Bernstein (2008).
95. See Medvetz (2012) on the analytical limitations of definitions for "interstitial fields."
96. Briggs asserts that instead of asking "how might we improve the relationship between citizens and their government?" a more germane question for the current era is "how might we improve the relationships among citizens, government, and private parties...?" (2008: 297).
97. Field notes.
98. Examples include Holman, Devane, and Cady (2007), Chambers (2002), and Creighton (2005). The Deliberative Democracy Consortium hosts a resource database on their website for public officials and others (2012).
99. See Silver (2006) for a critique of this activity. One example of democratized grant-making is the Case Foundation's 2009 "Make It Your Own" competition.
100. Jacobs, Cook, and Delli Carpini argue that the deliberation movement is progressive, populist, communitarian, republican, and democratic all at once (2009: 151). Morone (1998) would be likely to assert that the assemblage of so many incompatible values is evidence of an "antipolitical" democratic wish.

## Chapter 3

1. I was so busy participating that it was impossible to get precise fieldnotes on the exact dialogue used for this quote. This is taken from two sets of notes on the reflective panel recorded in the conference blog.
2. Travis (2007: 1019).

3. Bourdieu (1990 [1980]); Desmond (2006). This chapter and the next explore the ways in which the specific habitus of deliberative practice has developed rapidly into a cohesive set of shared debates and embodied rituals.

4. Vaisey (2009: 1683).

5. Trysh Travis, in a study of Oprah's Book Club, critiques the scholarship on Oprah's Book Club in ways that are strikingly similar regarding exclusively political readings of education and empowerment. Scholarship on Oprah's Book Club "has been almost exclusively laudatory, and… has praised the club as a triumph of what we might call the cultural politics of progressive multiculturalism." In contrast, Travis focuses on two elements scholars have ignored in their celebrations of the literate dialogue sparked by the club: how the "commercial dimension" is "fundamental, not incidental, to its workings" and how "New Thought principles—mysticism, universalism, idealism, and the belief in the power of thought to alter material reality—feature prominently" (Travis 2007: 1017–1018).

6. Eliasoph (2009: 307).

7. Thornton and Ocasio (2008: 101); Eliasoph (2009: 294).

8. Fung and Wright (2003).

9. Reitman (2009) [based on Walter Kirn's book of the same name]; Lodge (1995).

10. Ehrenreich (2009).

11. Illouz (2008); Cain (1991: 3).

12. McAdam (1982).

13. N = 341.

14. NCDD conference blog.

15. NCDD conference blog.

16. Interview transcript.

17. See, for example, the survey data on practitioners who prefer promoting D&D by "emphasizing useful outcomes," as described in chapter 6.

18. Young (2000); Sanders (1997); Fung (2004); Hendriks (2009); Kadlec and Friedman (2007).

19. NCDD et al. (2009: 7).

20. Demographic information that might be construed as polarizing or an invasion of privacy, such as sexual or political orientation, is collected much less often.

21. Ryfe (2005); Walsh (2007).

22. As compared with the demographics of deliberative practitioners as a whole. Note that this subset of practitioners includes many prominent field leaders.

23. Thomas and Leighninger (2010).

24. N = 339.

25. Advanced degrees are those beyond baccalaureate. N = 344; N = 340, respectively.

26. Leighninger (2010: 3).

27. N = 344.

28. DDC (2008: 22).

29. DDC (2008: 23).

30. Disproportionate participation by women can be even higher than the disproportionate representation of women in the practitioner corps, with some rates as high as 79% (Northwest Local Health Integration Network 2009).

31. Discussion page, survey website.

32. Hendriks and Carson (2008: 308).

33. In AmericaSpeaks' "Our Budget, Our Economy" deliberations, Esterling, Fung, and Lee find slight underrepresentation of whites, overrepresentation of African Americans, and underrepresentation of Latinos compared with census data on the larger population in the six cities studied (2010).

34. Fieldnotes.

35. Eliasoph (2011).

36. N = 331.

37. Unwilling clients might also include reluctant public officials or organizations whose processes were being sponsored by foundations, as in the case of Community Congress III.

38. Interview transcript.

39. The "our corporate culture" phrase indicates the extent to which the IAP2 training is oriented toward employees of larger firms. This phrase was clarified by the trainer as meaning either "Sponsor's culture, agency's culture. If you are a consultant, the culture of your client or your consultancy."

40. Chambers (2002).

41. Interview transcript.

42. Compare to Krause (2014) on humanitarian relief agencies' focus on the "good" project as a product.

## Chapter 4

1. Arnstein (1969).

2. Ehrenreich (2009: 4).

3. Hochschild (1983).

4. Mansbridge (1980: 278).

5. Barley and Kunda (1992); Jermier (1998). Of course, managerial reforms encouraging workplace participation have borrowed heavily from participatory social movements, beginning in the Progressive era (Graham 1995; Rothschild and Whitt 1986; Sirianni 1987). The issue here is not who borrowed first, but which borrowings are publicly recognized.

6. 31%; N = 341.

7. Boltanski and Chiapello (2007).

8. This is precisely the objection launched by some activists who resisted the restricted focus of Participatory Budgeting (PB), according to Ganuza and Baiocchi: "For some radical activists within UAMPA, the PB meant imbuing participation with a different logic, focused on resolving the specific issues of life in the city, 'which prevented us from attacking the core problems: how the city was financed,

what state model was desired.' The UAMPA decided to remain outside 'because it seemed a contradiction to be discussing how to share out a scant municipal resource, fighting for a piece of the budget, instead of debating the financing of the cities.'" (2012:7).

9. Eliasoph (2011: xvii).
10. N = 341.
11. Emphasis mine.
12. Eliasoph (2011).
13. Sanders (1997); Young (2000).
14. Hochschild (1983).
15. Johnson, Prashantham, Floyd, and Bourque (2010); Polletta (2002); Staggenborg and Lang (2007).
16. Creed, DeJordy, and Lok (2010); Alexander (2004).
17. Eliasoph catalogues similar disconnects in efforts to empower teens *because* they are defined as needy (2011).

## Chapter 5

1. *Sic.* The exact quote is: "The last temptation is the greatest treason: / To do the right deed for the wrong reason," from *Murder in the Cathedral* (1935).
2. Bidwell (2005).
3. N = 333.
4. Boltanski and Chiapello (2007); Thrift (2005).
5. Frank (1997); Thrift (2005).
6. Frank (1997).
7. White (2011); see also Woden and Teachout on "slow" democracy (2012).
8. Hendriks and Carson (2008: 304).
9. Cox (2005); Thrift (2005); Vann and Bowker (2001); Wenger (1998). Nigel Thrift (2005: 10) refers to these new managerial discourses of caring and sharing as part of the "mass moral engineering" of "soft capitalism."
10. N = 324.
11. Involve (2005).
12. Fourcade and Healy (2007: 286).
13. Kelty (2008).
14. Owen (1997).
15. Chambers (2002: xvi).
16. N = 245; N = 342.
17. N = 329.
18. Baiocchi (2003).
19. Eliasoph (2009: 295).
20. Hendriks and Carson (2008: 305).
21. N = 339.
22. N = 246.

23. Rutte (2007).

24. Center for Advances in Public Engagement (2008).

25. AmericaSpeaks' mission was "to reinvigorate American Democracy by engaging citizens in the public decision-making that most impacts their lives."

26. Lukensmeyer, Yao, and Brown (2013: 503).

27. Examples from graphic facilitation photos and database files.

28. See Thrift (2005) for an extensive analysis of "learning" as a managerialist discourse.

29. The question of whether deliberation as practiced meets normative ideals as developed in political theory has preoccupied deliberation researchers (Thompson 2008), to the exclusion of research on how real deliberation practiced with scrupulous attention to remedying inequality and challenging authority might be useful in particular historical and institutional settings in managing or marginalizing the challenges it produces. Not incidentally, deliberative democratic theory can be a useful validation tool in these efforts (Mutz 2008).

30. Snider (2010).

31. Mills (2007).

32. Interview transcript.

33. Center for Advances in Public Engagement (2008).

34. Mills (2007: 12).

35. Field notes. One practitioner at an event sponsored by a major foundation reported this sentiment as "They [her organization] are the Volkswagen, we [the foundation] are the Cadillac."

36. Dietz and Stern (2008).

37. For this reason, "high-quality" deliberative processes actually move stakeholder grievances out of public view; most, but by no means all, stakeholders are willing to trade increased decision-making power for less access to public claims making (Lee 2007). This relocation of politicized negotiation is accompanied by an increase in creative expression, as described in the next paragraph.

38. Girard and Stark (2007: 147).

39. British Columbia (2004).

40. Holman, Devane, and Cady (2007).

41. Goldman and Torres (2004).

42. Mills (2007).

43. Dietz and Stern (2008).

44. NCDD et al. (2009: 6).

45. Lukensmeyer (2007: 13).

46. Mills (2007).

47. Evidence for such a turn is supplied by discussions within cultural sociology and sociology of culture (Perrin 2009; Wagner-Pacifici 2008), within social movement research (Reger and Taylor 2009), and in the discipline as a whole (Collins 2009).

48. Crimp (1988); Lippard (1984); Marsh (1985); Reed (2005); Reger and Story (2005); Roman (1988); Roth (1983); Sawchuk (2006).

49. Eyerman (2002); Eyerman and Jamison (1998); Spencer (1989).

50. Scholars disagree regarding whether the liberatory power of art can be fully realized within contemporary mass culture (Carducci 2006; Chen 2009; Harold 2007; Kozinetz 2002).

51. Stamatov (2002: 345); Roy (2010: 3).

52. Korczynski (2011); Roy and Dowd (2010).

53. Roy (2010); Whittier (2009).

54. Polletta and Lee (2006).

## Chapter 6

1. Klein (2010).

2. The *Economist* (2010).

3. In April 2010, Fishkin reported to the NCDD listserv that his Center for Deliberative Democracy had won an award from the University of Chicago's "New Science of Virtues" project. He wrote to the listserv with his plans: "Our idea is to investigate whether deliberation fosters the virtues of democratic citizenship ... deliberation may make citizens more open to different points of view, more participatory, more concerned with the public interest."

4. Martin (2015).

5. Elyachar (2002; 2005); Krause (2014).

6. See, for example, Batliwala (2007) and Berkovitch and Kemp (2010).

7. Wetzel (2014).

8. Eliasoph (2011).

9. Mizruchi and Fein (1999); Powell and DiMaggio (1991).

10. CIPE (2008).

11. Schuman (2005). This normative isomorphism may be typical of developing fields in general, but it is also mimetic insofar as it draws on the logics of best practices and accountability used in the corporate world (Mizruchi and Fein 1999).

12. Ganuza and Baiocchi (2012: 1–2).

13. NCDD et al. (2009).

14. OGP (2011). Governmental and nongovernmental actors alike, including AccountAbility, Canadian International Development Agency, the Co-Intelligence Institute, the Community Development Society, the Harwood Institute, the Government of Canada, International Association for Impact Assessment, IAP2, International IDEA, Involve, the Organization of American States (OAS), Public Agenda, and the United Nations Development Programme, have also developed largely similar guidelines, standards, and best practices for public deliberation and democratic engagement.

15. Ganuza and Baiocchi (2012).

16. This tension accounts for the split in the survey between deliberation practitioners who favored deliberation as an end in itself and those who saw it as useful for other things.

17. Due to extensive crossover with the fields of management consulting and organizational development, this familiarity may extend beyond veterans of other deliberative processes to veterans of any facilitated workshop for adults—team-building retreats, leadership development seminars, quarterly strategic planning meetings, and so on.

18. Stavros and Hinrichs (2007).

19. See, for example, Gasdaska (2010). Pacewicz describes the diffusion of Envision processes in his study of "River City" (2013).

20. Deliberation practitioners are generally familiar with this "Kaufman paradox": "Although participation in democracies helps people increase their capacities, those who have not yet had the experience of participation will sometimes not have sufficient capacity to bring off a successful democracy. What they need is precisely what, because of their need, they cannot get" (Mansbridge 2003: 177).

21. N = 327.

22. Baiocchi (2003: 69).

23. Peterson (2009).

24. Emphasis mine.

25. Zacharzewski (2010), emphasis mine.

26. N = 334; Klatch (1999); McAdam (1990).

27. Briggs (2008: 221).

28. Lawrence (2002).

29. Eliasoph (2009: 299).

30. Shaping America's Youth (2007).

31. Participant guide, emphasis mine.

32. N = 1,726.

33. N = 334.

34. Resistance to increased taxation may account for the finding by Simonsen and Robbins (1999) that increased citizen engagement in resource allocation increased their desire to cut services. Public preferences for increased taxation may seem like an obvious case of deliberation producing progressive outcomes directed against the antitax, antistatist conservative movement of recent decades. Martin argues that the redistributive politics of tax reform are complex, and the tax revolt began as "a progressive movement for social protection from the market" (2008: 22).

35. N = 334.

36. Emphasis mine.

37. Atkinson (1999); Barnes, Newman, and Sullivan (2007); Head (2007).

38. Logan and Molotch (1987).

39. Zacharzewski (2010: 5).

40. Tepper (2009); see also Earl (2003).
41. Lee (2007).
42. Emphasis mine.
43. Zacharzewski (2010: 7).
44. Zacharzewski (2010: 3–4).
45. Martin (2015).
46. Polletta (2015).
47. Ganuza and Baiocchi (2012: 3).
48. See Delli Carpini, Huddy, and Shapiro (2002); Gastil and Levine (2005); Jacobs, Cook, and Delli Carpini (2009); and Gastil (2008) for reviews on the promise of deliberation.
49. Emphasis mine.
50. Zacharzewski (2010: 2–3).
51. Zacharzewski (2010: 5). The homebound and institutionalized elderly are, of course, generally underrepresented in public engagement, although those older than sixty-five are typically overrepresented.
52. In cases where issues are highly contentious and resistance is already organized, processes are advantageous in providing administrators with evidence of support for administrative goals from a substantial portion of "unaffiliated" citizens.
53. Zacharzewski (2010: 8).
54. N = 332.
55. Bonnemann (2010); Levine (2009); Snider (2010).
56. Kreiss (2012: 128).
57. Kreiss (2012: 164).
58. Field notes, conference session, and teleconference.
59. N = 8,473.
60. Walker (2014).
61. Fung and Lee (2009). Such comparisons overestimate the efficacy even of the limited forms of activation produced by postcard distribution following deliberative dialogue, since the control group of nonparticipants did not receive postcards.
62. McCamish (2008). Three of three facilitators in an online conference call on enhancing participation through technology had participated in the Tolle webinar series. Facilitators on the call proposed the "Oprah" model as one of a variety they were considering for "scaling up" their public engagement methods.
63. Edelman (2010).
64. Karpf (2012); Kreiss (2012); Nielsen (2012); Scholz (2009); Zittrain (2008).

## Chapter 7
1. Duffy, Binder, and Skrentny (2010).
2. Florida (2002).
3. Lingo, Taylor, and Lee (2008).

4. For more information on NPAC 2008, including the daily caucus newsletters, the final reports of the I-DOC team and NPAC organizers, lists of sponsors and donors, and town hall results, see the National Performing Arts Convention website: www.performingartsconvention.org/about/archive.php.

5. This might not be surprising in a competitive environment, but participants shared interests on concrete, actionable issues ranging from public support for arts education and arts resources in local communities to artists' economic needs, including social insurance and copyright protection, to favorable immigration and trade policies for international performances and artists' raw materials.

6. N = 66. Respondents changed opinions in both directions following the conference (some had indeed wanted passive roles before and leadership roles following their participation), but those who had wanted to be leaders previously were more likely to change their opinions.

7. N = 100 (total number of valid responses in the postsurvey) on all of the statistics in this paragraph.

8. Americans for the Arts (2009).

9. Vallas (2006); Walker (2014).

10. This is a different outcome from that described by Hibbing and Theiss-Morse (2002), who assert that deliberation is unsuccessful because Americans are already uninterested in being involved in decision-making. The actual practice of deliberation as described in this book includes many of the "other pursuits"—sports fandom, therapy, music, art—that they find Americans prefer to "politics."

11. N = 100.

12. Deliberative Democracy Consortium (2008); Delli Carpini, Cook, and Jacobs (2004); Dryzek (2012); Ryfe (2005).

13. Esterling, Fung, and Lee (2010).

14. Fung, Young, and Mansbridge (2004); Pellow (1999); Thomas (2003).

15. Eliasoph (2009: 292).

16. Beth Simone Noveck of the Obama administration has described participatory reforms as "a shift in how we conceive of government itself ... that we're involved in the co-creation of public decision-making where we make decisions together, solve problems together, and work on issues together that we hold in common." Noveck goes on to argue that federal administration is incompetent and out of touch compared with individuals at the community level: "The notion that central management sitting in Washington is going to know best how to solve a problem that's occurring out across the country in dealing with people on a day-to-day basis is just ludicrous. It's the people who are actually in the front lines of dealing with those problems who will know."

17. Such support might still seem surprising, given the extent to which deliberation is offered in exchange for greater extraction, as Martin argues. The kinds of tax morale deliberation can produce, however, are the kinds that predominantly fall on little guys. Indeed, as described in chapter 6, deliberation often enacts a drama

where little guys are entrusted with sharing the pain of corporate America to spare businesses supposedly debilitating taxes.

18. Rodriguez (2007).
19. Peterson (2009).
20. Sennett and Sassen (2011).
21. Tronti (1980).
22. Lee (2007).
23. Lee (2007).
24. Levitsky (2008); Polletta (2000).
25. Hendriks (2009).
26. The American version of the television show *The Office* has an episode where employees have to specify anonymously the conditions for which they will need health care, to dark comic effect.

## Conclusion

1. Moreton (2007: 108).
2. Krippner (2005).
3. Clark and Teachout (2012).

## Postscript

1. Lashaw (2013: 503).
2. Scheppele (2004: 391).
3. Digital photo tagging and liveblogging is common at professional conferences and events in the field. I shared the digital photos I took at field conferences with other practitioners and conference sponsors in online photo databases.
4. Roberts (1997); Weber (1990).
5. Since text files varied enormously in length and context, only documents of similar origin and source have been analyzed in comparative terms to provide quantitative support in this book, such as in figure 6.1., the comparison of process outcomes described in *The Change Handbook*.
6. Kreiss (2009); Walker (2009).
7. Leighninger (2009: 3).
8. Medvetz (2012).
9. Jacobs, Cook, and Delli Carpini (2009).
10. Jacobs, Cook, and Delli Carpini (2009: 143).
11. Shih and Fan (2008).

# REFERENCES

Abbott, Andrew. 1988. *The System of Professions: An Essay on the Division of Expert Labor.* Chicago: University of Chicago Press.

Abel, Richard L., ed. 1982. *The Politics of Informal Justice, Vols. 1 and 2.* New York: Academic Press.

Abramowicz, Michael. 2008. *Predictocracy: Market Mechanisms for Public and Private Decision Making.* New Haven, CT: Yale University Press.

Adams, Brian E. 2007. *Citizen Lobbyists: Local Efforts to Influence Public Policy.* Philadelphia: Temple University Press.

Alexander, Jeffrey. 2004. "Cultural Pragmatics: Social Performance between Ritual and Strategy." *Sociological Theory* 22:527–573.

Americans for the Arts. 2009. "The Arts: Ask for More: National Arts Education Public Awareness Campaign." (http://artsaskformore.artsusa.org/).

André, Pierre, Bert Enserink, Desmond Connor, and Peter Croal. 2006. *Public Participation International Best Practice Principles. Special Publication Series No. 4.* Fargo, ND: International Association for Impact Assessment.

Armstrong, Elizabeth A., and Mary Bernstein. 2008. "Culture, Power, and Institutions: A Multi-Institutional Politics Approach to Social Movements." *Sociological Theory* 26:74–99.

Arnstein, Sherry R. 1969. "A Ladder of Citizen Participation." *Journal of the American Planning Association* 35:216–224.

Atkinson, Rob. 1999. "Discourses of Partnership and Empowerment in Contemporary British Urban Regeneration." *Urban Studies* 36:59–72.

Baiocchi, Gianpaolo. 2003. "Emergent Public Spheres: Talking Politics in Participatory Governance." *American Sociological Review* 68:52–74.

————. 2005. *Militants and Citizens: The Politics of Participatory Democracy in Porto Alegre*. Palo Alto, CA: Stanford University Press.

Barley, Stephen R., and Gideon Kunda. 1992. "Design and Devotion: Surges of Rational and Normative Ideologies of Control in Managerial Discourse." *Administrative Science Quarterly* 37:363–399.

Barnes, Marian, Janet Newman, and Helen Sullivan. 2007. *Power, Participation and Political Renewal: Case Studies in Public Participation*. Bristol, UK: Policy Press.

Bartley, Tim. 2007. "Institutional Emergence in an Era of Globalization: The Rise of Transnational Private Regulation of Labor and Environmental Conditions." *American Journal of Sociology* 113:297–351.

Bartley, Tim, and Shawna N. Smith. 2010. "Communities of Practice as Cause and Consequence of Transnational Governance: The Evolution of Social and Environmental Certification." Pp. 347–374 in *Transnational Communities: Shaping Global Economic Governance*, edited by Marie-Laure Djelic and Sigrid Quack. Cambridge, UK: Cambridge University Press.

Bastian, Sunil, Nicola Bastian, and Duryog Nivaran. 1996. *Assessing Participation: A Debate from South Asia*. Delhi, India: Konark.

Batliwala, Srilatha. 2007. "Taking the Power Out of Empowerment: An Experiential Account." *Development in Practice* 17:557–565.

Beierle, Thomas C. 2001. "Democracy Online: An Evaluation of the National Dialogue on Public Involvement in EPA Decisions." Washington, DC: Resources for the Future.

Beierle, Thomas C., and Jerry Cayford. 2003. "Dispute Resolution as a Method of Public Participation." Pp. 53–68 in *The Promise and Performance of Environmental Conflict Resolution*, edited by Rosemary O'Leary and Lisa Bingham. Washington, DC: Resources for the Future.

Benhabib, Seyla. 1996. *Democracy and Difference: Contesting Boundaries of the Political*. Princeton, NJ: Princeton University Press.

Benkler, Yochai. 2006. *The Wealth of Networks: How Social Production Transforms Markets and Freedom*. New Haven, CT: Yale University Press.

Berkovitch, Nitza, and Adriana Kemp. 2010. "Economic Empowerment of Women as a Global Project: Economic Rights in the Neo-Liberal Era.'" Pp. 158–179 in *Confronting Global Gender Justice: Women's Lives, Human Rights*, edited by Debra Bergoffen, Paula Ruth Gilbert, Tamara Harvey, and Connie L. McNeely. Oxford: Routledge.

Bidwell, David. 2005. "Exception Proves the Rule." *Participation Quarterly*: February.

Binder, Amy. 2007. "For Love and Money: Organizations' Creative Responses to Multiple Environmental Logics." *Theory and Society* 36:547–571.

Bingham, Lisa Blomgren, Tina Nabatchi, and Rosemary O'Leary. 2005. "The New Governance: Practices and Processes for Stakeholder and Citizen Participation in the Work of Government." *Public Administration Review* 65:547–558.

Birnbaum, Jeffrey H. 2006. "Targeting Likely Advocates with Web Ads." *Washington Post*. August 21, D1.

Boltanski, Luc, and Eve Chiapello. 2007. *The New Spirit of Capitalism.* New York: Verso.

Bonnemann, Tim. 2010. "Does the Budget Puzzle Qualify as 'Deliberative Choice Work'?" Blog post: November 16. (http://www.intellitics.com/blog/2010/11/16/does-the-budget-puzzle-qualify-as-deliberative-choice-work/).

Bosso, Christopher J. 2005. *Environment, Inc.: From Grassroots to Beltway.* Lawrence: University Press of Kansas.

Bourdieu, Pierre. 1989. "Social Space and Symbolic Power." *Sociological Theory* 7:14–25.

———. 1990 [1980]. *The Logic of Practice.* Stanford, CA: Stanford University Press.

Boyle, Mary-Ellen, and Ira Silver. 2005. "Poverty, Partnerships, and Privilege: Elite Institutions and Community Empowerment." *City and Community* 4:233–253.

Bradley, Bill. 2006. "Foreword." Pp. xiii–xv in *The Next Form of Democracy: How Expert Rule Is Giving Way to Shared Governance and Why Politics Will Never Be the Same,* by Matt Leighninger. Nashville, TN: Vanderbilt University Press.

Briggs, Xavier de Souza. 2008. *Democracy as Problem-Solving: Civic Capacity in Communities across the Globe.* Cambridge, MA: MIT Press.

British Columbia Citizens' Assembly on Electoral Reform. 2004. "Final Report: Making Every Vote Count: The Case for Electoral Reform in British Columbia." (www.citizensassembly.bc.ca).

Button, Mark, and David Michael Ryfe. 2005. "What Can We Learn from the Practice of Deliberative Democracy?" Pp. 20–33 in *The Deliberative Democracy Handbook: Strategies for Effective Civic Engagement in the Twenty-First Century,* edited by John Gastil and Peter Levine. San Francisco: Jossey Bass.

Cain, Carole. 1991. "Personal Stories: Identity Acquisition and Self-Understanding in Alcoholics Anonymous." *Ethos* 19:210–253.

Canadian Institute for Public Engagement. 2008. "Who We Are." Ottawa: Canadian Institute for Public Engagement. (http://www.instituteforpublicengagement.org/home_e.html).

Caplan, Bryan. 2008. *The Myth of the Rational Voter.* Princeton, NJ: Princeton University Press.

Carcasson, Martín. 2009. *Occasional Paper 2: Beginning with the End in Mind: A Call for Goal-Driven Deliberative Practice.* New York: Public Agenda/Center for Advances in Public Engagement.

Carducci, Vince. 2006. "Culture Jamming: A Sociological Perspective." *Journal of Consumer Culture* 6:116–138.

Carson, Lyn, and Rodolfo Lewanski. 2008. "Fostering Citizen Participation Top-Down." *International Journal of Public Participation* 2:72–83.

Cashore, Benjamin William, Graeme Auld, and Deanna Newsom. 2004. *Governing through Markets: Forest Certification and the Emergence of Non-State Authority.* New Haven: Yale University Press.

Cazenave, Noel A. 2007. *Impossible Democracy: The Unlikely Success of the War on Poverty Community Action Programs.* Albany: State University of New York Press.

Center for Advances in Public Engagement. 2008. "Public Engagement: A Primer from Public Agenda." New York: Public Agenda. (www.publicagenda.org/files/public_engagement_primer.pdf).

Chambers, Robert. 2002. *Participatory Workshops: A Sourcebook of 21 Sets of Ideas and Activities*. London: Earthscan.

Charmaz, Kathy. 2006. *Constructing Grounded Theory: A Practical Guide through Qualitative Analysis*. London: SAGE.

Chaskin, Robert J., Prudence Brown, Sudhir Venkatesh, and Avis Vidal. 2001. *Building Community Capacity*. New York: Aldine de Gruyter.

Chen, Katherine. 2009. *Enabling Creative Chaos: The Organization behind the Burning Man Event*. Chicago: University of Chicago Press.

Chen, Katherine, and Siobhan O'Mahony. 2009. "Differentiating Organizational Boundaries." *Research in the Sociology of Organizations* 26:183–220.

CIPE. See Canadian Institute for Public Engagement.

Clark, Susan, and Woden Teachout. 2012. *Slow Democracy: Rediscovering Community, Bringing Decision Making Back Home*. White River Junction, VT: Chelsea Green.

Clemens, Elisabeth S. 1997. *The People's Lobby: Organizational Innovation and the Rise of Interest Group Politics in the United States, 1890–1925*. Chicago: University of Chicago Press.

———. 2004. "The Alchemy of Organization: From Participation to Preferences." *Sociological Forum* 19:323–338.

———. 2006. "Lineages of the Rube Goldberg State: Building and Blurring Public Programs, 1900–1940." Pp. 187–215 in *The Art of the State: Rethinking Political Institutions*, edited by Ian Shapiro, Stephen Skowronek, and Daniel Galvin. New York: New York University Press.

Collins, Patricia Hill, session organizer. 2009. "How Communities Matter: Perspectives of Artists, Academics and Activists." Opening Plenary Session of the American Sociological Association Annual Meeting, San Francisco, CA. August 7.

Cortner, Hanna J., and Margaret A. Moote. 1999. *The Politics of Ecosystem Management*. Washington, DC: Island Press.

Cox, Andrew. 2005. "What Are Communities of Practice? A Comparative Review of Four Seminal Works." *Journal of Information Science* 31:527–540.

Cox, Geoff. 2010. "Democracy 2.0." *Concept Store* 3:60–64.

Creed, W., E. Douglas, Rich DeJordy, and Jaco Lok. 2010. "Being the Change: Resolving Institutional Contradiction through Identity Work." *Academy of Management Journal* 53:1336–1364.

Creighton, James L. 2005. *The Public Participation Handbook: Making Better Decisions through Citizen Involvement*. San Francisco: Jossey-Bass.

Crenson, Matthew. 1971. *The Un-Politics of Air Pollution: A Study of Non-Decisionmaking in the Cities*. Baltimore, MD: Johns Hopkins University Press.

Crenson, Matthew A., and Benjamin Ginsberg. 2002. *Downsizing Democracy: How America Sidelined Its Citizens and Privatized Its Public*. Baltimore, MD: Johns Hopkins University Press.

Crimp, Douglas, ed. 1988. *AIDS: Cultural Analysis/Cultural Activism*. Cambridge, MA: MIT Press.

Davis, Gerald F., and Doug McAdam. 2000. "Corporations, Classes, and Social Movements after Managerialism." *Research in Organizational Behaviour* 22:195–238.

Davis, Gerald F., and Mayer N. Zald. 2005. "Social Change, Social Theory, and the Convergence of Movements and Organizations." Pp. 335–350 in *Social Movements and Organization Theory*, edited by Gerald F. Davis, Doug McAdam, W. Richard Scott, and Mayer N. Zald. Cambridge, UK: Cambridge University Press.

DDC (see Deliberative Democracy Consortium).

Deliberative Democracy Consortium. 2008. *Where Is Democracy Headed? Research and Practice on Public Deliberation*. Washington, DC: Deliberative Democracy Consortium.

———. 2012. "Resources." Washington, DC: Deliberative Democracy Consortium. (http://www.deliberative-democracy.net/).

Della Porta, Donatella. 2013. *Can Democracy Be Saved?* Cambridge, UK: Polity.

Delli Carpini, Michael X., Fay Lomax Cook, and Lawrence R. Jacobs. 2004. "Public Deliberation, Discursive Participation, and Citizen Engagement: A Review of the Empirical Literature." *Annual Review of Political Science* 7:315–344.

Delli Carpini, Michael X., Leonie Huddy, and Robert Y. Shapiro. 2002. *Political Decision Making, Deliberation, and Participation: Research in Micropolitics*. Oxford: JAI Press.

Desmond, Matthew. 2006. "Becoming a Firefighter." *Ethnography* 7:387–421.

Dewey, John. 1927. *The Public and Its Problems*. New York: H. Holt.

Dietz, Thomas, and Paul C. Stern, eds. 2008. *Public Participation in Environmental Assessment and Decision Making*. Washington, DC: National Research Council.

Dryzek, John S. 1990. *Discursive Democracy: Politics, Policy, and Political Science*. New York: Cambridge University Press.

———. 2012. *Foundations and Frontiers of Deliberative Governance*. Oxford: Oxford University Press.

Duffy, Meghan, Amy Binder, and John Skrentny. 2010. "Elite Status and Social Change: Using Field Analysis to Explain Policy Formation and Implementation." *Social Problems* 57:49–73.

Earl, Jennifer. 2003. "Tanks, Tear Gas and Taxes: Toward a Theory of Movement Repression." *Sociological Theory* 21:44–68.

Eblen, Ruth A., and William Eblen. 1994. *The Encyclopedia of the Environment*. Boston: Houghton Mifflin.

*Economist*. 2010. "Ancient Athens Online." May 6. (http://www.economist.com/node/16056622?story_id=16056622).

Edelman. 2010. *Public Engagement in the Conversation Age: Vol 2*. London: Edelman. (http://edelmaneditions.com/2010/11/public-engagement-in-the-conversation-age-vol-2/).

Ehrenreich, Barbara. 2009. *Bright-Sided: How the Relentless Promotion of Positive Thinking Has Undermined America*. New York: Henry Holt.

Eliasoph, Nina. 1998. *Avoiding Politics: How Americans Produce Apathy in Everyday Life*. New York: Cambridge University Press.

———. 2009. "Top-Down Civic Projects Are Not Grassroots Associations: How the Differences Matter in Everyday Life." *Voluntas* 20:291–308.

———. 2011. *Making Volunteers: Civic Life after Welfare's End*. Princeton, NJ: Princeton University Press.

Eliasoph, Nina, and Paul Lichterman. 2010. "Making Things Political." Pp. 483–493 in *Handbook of Cultural Sociology*, edited by John R. Hall, Laura Grindstaff, and Ming-cheng Lo. New York: Routledge.

Eliasoph, Nina, and Jade Yu-Chieh Lo. 2012. "Broadening Cultural Sociology's Scope: Meaning-Making in Mundane Organizational Life." Pp. 763–787 in *The Oxford Handbook of Cultural Sociology*, edited by Jeffrey C. Alexander, Ronald Jacobs, and Philip Smith. New York: Oxford University Press.

Elliott, Stuart. 2006. "New Rules of Engagement." *New York Times*. March 21. (http://www.nytimes.com/2006/03/21/business/media/21adco.html).

Elyachar, Julia. 2002. "Empowerment Money: The World Bank, Non-Governmental Organizations, and the Value of Culture in Egypt." *Public Culture* 14:493–514.

———. 2005. *Markets of Dispossession: NGOs, Economic Development and the State in Cairo*. Durham, NC: Duke University Press.

Espeland, Wendy Nelson. 1997. "Authority by the Numbers: Porter on Quantification, Discretion, and the Legitimation of Expertise." *Law & Social Inquiry* 22:1107–1133.

———. 2000. "Bureaucratizing Democracy, Democratizing Bureaucracy." *Law and Social Inquiry* 25:1077–1109.

Espeland, Wendy Nelson, and Michael Sauder. 2007. "Rankings and Reactivity: How Public Measures Recreate Social Worlds." *American Journal of Sociology* 113:1–40.

Espeland, Wendy Nelson, and Mitchell L. Stevens. 1998. "Commensuration as a Social Process." *Annual Review of Sociology* 24:313–343.

Esterling, Kevin, Archon Fung, and Taeku Lee. 2010. "The Difference Deliberation Makes: Evaluating the 'Our Budget, Our Economy' Public Deliberation." Washington, DC: AmericaSpeaks.

Eyerman, Ron. 2002. "Music in Movement: Cultural Politics and Old and New Social Movements." *Qualitative Sociology* 25:443–458.

Eyerman, Ron, and Andrew Jamison. 1998. *Music and Social Movements: Mobilizing Traditions in the Twentieth Century*. New York: Cambridge University Press.

Fischer, Frank. 2004. "Professional Expertise in a Deliberative Democracy: Facilitating Participatory Inquiry." *The Good Society* 13:21–27.

Fisher, Dana R. 2006. *Activism, Inc.: How the Outsourcing of Grassroots Campaigns Is Strangling Progressive Politics in America*. Stanford, CA: Stanford University Press.

Fligstein, Neil, and Doug McAdam. 2011. "Toward a General Theory of Strategic Action Fields." *Sociological Theory* 29:1–26.

Florida, Richard. 2002. *The Rise of the Creative Class: And How It's Transforming Work, Leisure, Community and Everyday Life*. New York: Basic Books.

Fourcade, Marion, and Kieran Healy. 2007. "Moral Views of Market Society." *Annual Review of Sociology* 33:285–311.

Fowler, Anne, Nicki Nicholas Gamble, Frances X. Hogan, Melissa Kogut, Madeline McComish, and Barbara Thorp. 2001. "Talking with the Enemy." *Boston Globe*. January 28, F1.

Frank, Thomas. 1997. *The Conquest of Cool: Business Culture, Counterculture, and the Rise of Hip Consumerism*. Chicago: University of Chicago Press.

———. 2000. *One Market under God: Extreme Capitalism, Market Populism, and the End of Economic Democracy*. New York: Doubleday.

———. 2004. *What's the Matter with Kansas? How Conservatives Won the Heart of America*. New York: Holt.

Fung, Archon. 2003. "Deliberative Democracy, Chicago Style: Grass-Roots Governance in Policing and Public Education." Pp. 111–143 in *Deepening Democracy: Institutional Innovations in Empowered Participatory Governance*, edited by Archon Fung and Erik Olin Wright. New York: Verso.

———. 2004. *Empowered Participation: Reinventing Urban Democracy*. Princeton, NJ: Princeton University Press.

Fung, Archon, John Gastil, and Peter Levine. 2005. "Future Directions for Public Deliberation." Pp. 271–288 in *The Deliberative Democracy Handbook: Strategies for Effective Civic Engagement in the 21st Century*, edited by John Gastil and Peter Levine. San Francisco: Jossey Bass.

Fung, Archon, Mary Graham, and David Weil. 2007. *Full Disclosure: The Perils and Promise of Transparency*. New York: Cambridge University Press.

Fung, Archon, and Taeku Lee. 2009. *Public Impacts: Evaluating the Outcomes of the CaliforniaSpeaks Statewide Conversation on Health Care Reform*. Washington, DC: AmericaSpeaks.

Fung, Archon, and Erik Olin Wright. 2003. "Thinking about Empowered Participatory Governance." Pp. 3–41 in *Deepening Democracy: Institutional Innovations in Empowered Participatory Governance*, edited by Archon Fung and Erik Olin Wright. New York: Verso.

Fung, Archon, Iris Marion Young, and Jane Mansbridge. 2004. "Deliberation's Darker Side" [Interview]. *National Civic Review* 93:47–54.

Ganuza, Ernesto, and Gianpaolo Baiocchi. 2012. "The Power of Ambiguity: How Participatory Budgeting Travels the Globe." *Journal of Public Deliberation* 8: Article 8.

Gasdaska, Allyson. 2010. "Imagine Chicago." NCDD Resource Center. (http://ncdd.org/rc/item/3252).

Gastil, John. 2000. *By Popular Demand: Revitalizing Representative Democracy through Deliberative Elections.* Berkeley: University of California Press.

———. 2008. *Political Communication and Deliberation.* Los Angeles: SAGE.

Gastil, John, and William M. Keith. 2005. "A Nation That (Sometimes) Likes to Talk: A Brief History of Deliberation in the United States." Pp. 3–19 in *The Deliberative Democracy Handbook*, edited by John Gastil and Peter Levine. San Francisco: Jossey-Bass.

Gastil, John, and Peter Levine, eds. 2005. *The Deliberative Democracy Handbook: Strategies for Effective Civic Engagement in the 21st Century.* San Francisco: Jossey-Bass.

Girard, Monique, and David Stark. 2007. "Socio-technologies of Assembly: Sense-making and Demonstration in Rebuilding Lower Manhattan." Pp. 145–176 in *Governance and Information Technology: From Electronic Government to Information Government*, edited by David Lazer and Viktor Mayer-Schoenberger. New York: Oxford University Press.

Glaser, Barney G., and Anselm Strauss. 1967. *The Discovery of Grounded Theory: Strategies of Qualitative Research.* Chicago: Aldine.

Glock-Grueneich, Nancy, and Sarah Nora Ross. 2008. "Growing the Field: The Institutional, Theoretical, and Conceptual Maturation of 'Public Participation.'" *International Journal of Public Participation* 2:1–32.

Goldman, Joe, and Lars Hasselblad Torres. 2004. "Inventory of Major Deliberative Methods in the United States." Washington, DC: AmericaSpeaks. (http://www.americaspeaks.org/library/del_methods_matrix_as.pdf).

Goss, Kristin. 2006. *Disarmed: The Missing Movement for Gun Control in America.* Princeton, NJ: Princeton University Press.

Graham, Pauline, ed. 1995. *Mary Parker Follett: Prophet of Management.* Boston: Harvard Business School Press.

Greenwood, Royston, and Roy Suddaby. 2006. "Institutional Entrepreneurship in Mature Fields: The Big Five Accounting Firms." *Academy of Management Journal* 49:27–48.

Habermas, Jürgen. 1989. *The Structural Transformation of the Public Sphere.* Cambridge, MA: MIT Press.

Hallett, Tim, and Marc J. Ventresca. 2006. "Inhabited Institutions: Social Interactions and Organizational Forms in Gouldner's *Patterns of Industrial Bureaucracy.*" *Theory & Society* 35:213–236.

Halvorsen, Kathleen E. 2001. "Assessing Public Participation Techniques for Comfort, Convenience, Satisfaction, and Deliberation." *Environmental Management* 28:179–186.

Handler, Joel F. 1996. *Down from Bureaucracy: The Ambiguity of Privatization and Empowerment.* Princeton, NJ: Princeton University Press.

Harold, Christine. 2007. *OurSpace: Resisting the Corporate Control of Culture.* Minneapolis: University of Minnesota Press.

Harrington, Christine. 1985. *Shadow Justice: The Ideology and Institutionalization of Alternatives to Court.* Westport, CT: Greenwood.

Haveman, Heather A., and Hayagreeva Rao. 1997. "Structuring a Theory of Moral Sentiments: Institutional and Organizational Coevolution in the Early Thrift Industry." *American Journal of Sociology* 102:1606–1651.

Haydu, Jeffrey. 2002. "Business Citizenship at Work: Cultural Transposition and Class Formation in Cincinnati, 1870–1910." *American Journal of Sociology* 107:1424–1467.

Head, Brian W. 2007. "Community Engagement: Participation on Whose Terms?" *Australian Journal of Political Science* 42:441–454.

Hendriks, Carolyn M. 2006a. "Integrated Deliberation: Reconciling Civil Society's Dual Role in Deliberative Democracy." *Political Studies* 54:486–508.

———. 2006b. "When the Forum Meets Interest Politics: Strategic Uses of Public Deliberation." *Politics & Society* 34:571–602.

———. 2008. "The Social Context of Public Deliberation: Letting Practice Shape Theory." *International Journal of Public Participation* 2:87–91.

———. 2009. "Deliberative Governance in the Context of Power." *Policy & Society* 28:173–184.

Hendriks, Carolyn M., and Lyn Carson. 2008. "Can the Market Help the Forum? Negotiating the Commercialization of Deliberative Democracy." *Policy Sciences* 41:293–313.

Hibbard, Michael, and Jeremy Madsen. 2003. "Environmental Resistance to Place-Based Collaboration in the U.S. West." *Society & Natural Resources* 16:703–718.

Hibbing, John R., and Elizabeth Theiss-Morse. 2002. *Stealth Democracy: Americans' Beliefs about How Government Should Work*. Cambridge, UK: Cambridge University Press.

Hindman, Matthew. 2008. *The Myth of Digital Democracy*. Princeton, NJ: Princeton University Press.

Hirsch, Paul M., and Michael Lounsbury. 1997. "Ending the Family Quarrel: Toward a Reconciliation of 'Old' and 'New' Institutionalisms." *American Behavioral Scientist* 40:406–418.

Hochschild, Arlie. 1983. *The Managed Heart*. Berkeley: University of California Press.

———. 2001. *The Time Bind: When Work Becomes Home and Home Becomes Work*. New York: Owl.

Hodge, Graeme A., and Diana Bowman. 2006. "The 'Consultocracy': The Business of Reforming Government." Pp. 97–126 in *Privatization and Market Development: Global Movements in Public Policy Ideas*, edited by Graeme A. Hodge. Northampton, MA: Edward Elgar.

Holman, Peggy, Tom Devane, and Steven Cady. 2007. *The Change Handbook*, 2nd ed. San Francisco: Berrett-Koehler.

Howard, Philip N. 2006. *New Media Campaigns and the Managed Citizen*. New York: Cambridge University Press.

IFC. (See International Finance Corporation).

IISD. (See International Institute for Sustainable Development).

Illouz, Eva. 2008. *Saving the Modern Soul: Therapy, Emotions, and the Culture of Self-Help*. Berkeley: University of California Press.

Innes, Judith, and David Booher. 2000. *Public Participation in Planning: New Strategies for the 21st Century*. Berkeley: University of California, Institute of Urban and Regional Development.

International Finance Corporation (IFC). 1998. *Doing Better Business through Effective Public Consultation and Disclosure: A Good Practice Manual*. Washington, DC: International Finance Corporation.

———. 2007. *Stakeholder Engagement: A Good Practice Handbook for Companies Doing Business in Emerging Markets*. Washington, DC: International Finance Corporation.

International Institute for Sustainable Development (IISD), the International Institute for Environment and Development, IUCN–The World Conservation Union, the African Institute of Corporate Citizenship, Development Alternatives, and Recursos e Investigación para el Desarrollo Sustentable. 2004. *Issue Briefing Note: Stakeholder Engagement, ISO and Corporate Social Responsibility*. Winnipeg, Canada: International Institute for Sustainable Development.

Involve. 2005. *Full Report: The True Costs of Public Participation*. London: Involve. (http://www.involve.org.uk/blog/2005/11/16/the-true-costs-of-public-participation/ ).

Irvin, Renee A., and John Stansbury. 2004. "Citizen Participation in Decision Making: Is It Worth the Effort?" *Public Administration Review* 64:55–65.

Jacobs, Lawrence R., Fay Lomax Cook, and Michael X. Delli Carpini. 2009. *Talking Together: Public Deliberation and Political Participation in America*. Chicago: University of Chicago Press.

Jermier, John M. 1998. "Critical Perspectives on Organizational Control." *Administrative Science Quarterly* 43:235–256.

Johnson, Gerry, Shameen Prashantham, Steven W. Floyd, and Nicole Bourque. 2010. "The Ritualization of Strategy Workshops." *Organization Studies* 31:1589–1618.

Journal of Public Deliberation. 2010. "Aims & Scope." (http://services.bepress.com/jpd/aimsandscope.html).

Kadlec, Allison, and Will Friedman. 2007. "Deliberative Democracy and the Problem of Power." *Journal of Public Deliberation* 3: Article 8. (http://services.bepress.com/jpd/vol3/iss1/art8).

Karpf, David. 2012. *The MoveOn Effect: The Unexpected Transformation of American Political Advocacy*. New York: Oxford University Press.

Kashefi, Elham, and Maggie Mort. 2004. "Grounded Citizens' Juries: A Tool for Health Activism?" *Health Expectations* 7:290–302.

Kaufman, Jason. 2003. *For the Common Good? American Civic Life and the Golden Age of Fraternity*. New York: Oxford University Press.

Kelleher, Christine A., and Susan Webb Yackee. 2008. "A Political Consequence of Contracting: Organized Interests and State Agency Decision Making." *Journal of Public Administration Research and Theory* 19:579–602.

Kelty, Christopher. 2008. *Two Bits: The Cultural Significance of Free Software.* Durham, NC: Duke University Press.

Kenney, Douglas S. 2000. *Arguing about Consensus: Examining the Case against Western Watershed Initiatives and Other Collaborative Groups Active in Natural Resources Management.* Boulder, CO: Natural Resources Law Center.

King, Brayden G., and Nicholas Pearce. 2010. "The Contentiousness of Markets: Politics, Social Movements, and Institutional Change in Markets." *Annual Review of Sociology* 36:249–267.

Klatch, Rebecca E. 1999. *A Generation Divided: The New Left, the New Right, and the 1960s.* Berkeley: University of California Press.

Klein, Joe. 2010. "How Can a Democracy Solve Tough Problems?" *Time.* September 2. (http://www.time.com/time/magazine/article/0,9171,2015790,00.html).

Korczynski, Marek. 2011. "Stayin' Alive on the Factory Floor: An Ethnography of the Dialectics of Music Use in the Routinized Workplace." *Poetics* 39:87–106.

Kozinetz, Robert V. 2002. "Can Consumers Escape the Market? Emancipatory Illuminations from Burning Man." *Journal of Consumer Research* 29:20–38.

Kraft, Michael E., and Daniel A. Mazmanian, eds. 2009. *Toward Sustainable Communities: Transition and Transformations in Environmental Policy.* Cambridge, MA: MIT Press.

Krause, Monika. 2014. *The Good Project: Humanitarian Relief NGOs and the Fragmentation of Reason.* Chicago: University of Chicago Press.

Kreiss, Daniel. 2012. *Taking Our Country Back: The Crafting of Networked Politics from Howard Dean to Barack Obama.* New York: Oxford University Press.

Krippner, Greta R. 2005. "The Financialization of the American Economy." *Socio-Economic Review* 3:173–208.

Kyriss, LaVerne. 2006. "2005 Annual Report." Denver, CO: International Association for Public Participation.

Lampland, Martha, and Susan Leigh Star. 2009. *Standards and Their Stories: How Quantifying, Classifying, and Formalizing Practices Shape Everyday Life.* Ithaca, NY: Cornell University Press.

Lang, Amy. 2007. "But Is It for Real? The British Columbia Citizens' Assembly as a Model of State-Sponsored Citizen Empowerment." *Politics & Society* 35:35–69.

Lashaw, Amanda. 2013. "How Progressive Culture Resists Critique: The Impasse of NGO Studies." *Ethnography* 14:501–522.

Lawrence, Steven. 2002. "Children and Youth Funding Update." New York: Foundation Center.

Lee, Caroline W. 2007. "Is There a Place for Private Conversation in Public Dialogue? Comparing Stakeholder Assessments of Informal Communication in Collaborative Regional Planning." *American Journal of Sociology* 113:41–96.

Lee, Caroline W., Michael McQuarrie, and Edward T. Walker. Forthcoming. *Democratizing Inequalities: Dilemmas of the New Public Participation.*

Leighninger, Matt. 2006. *The Next Form of Democracy.* Nashville, TN: Vanderbilt University Press.

———. 2009. "Funding and Fostering Local Democracy: What Philanthropy Should Know about the Emerging Field of Deliberation and Democratic Governance." Denver, CO: Philanthropy for Active Civic Engagement.

———. 2010. "Creating Spaces for Change: Working toward a 'Story of Now' in Public Engagement." Battle Creek, MI: W. K. Kellogg Foundation.

Levine, Peter. 2009. "Collaborative Problem-Solving: The Fake Corporate Version." Blog post: January 27. (http://peterlevine.ws/?p=5615).

———. 2014. "Reflections on AmericaSpeaks on Its Last Day." Blog post: January 3. (http://peterlevine.ws/?p=13066).

Levine, Peter, Archon Fung, and John Gastil. 2005. "Future Directions for Public Deliberation." *Journal of Public Deliberation* 1: Article 3. (http://services.bepress.com/jpd/vol1/iss1/art3).

Levitsky, Sandra R. 2008. " 'What Rights?' The Construction of Political Claims to American Health Care Entitlements." *Law & Society Review* 42:551–589.

Lingo, Elizabeth Long, and Andrew Taylor, with Caroline Lee. 2008. *National Performing Arts Convention 2008: Assessing the Capacity of the Field for Collective Action: Report of the 2008 I-DOC Team.* Nashville, TN: Vanderbilt University, Curb Center for Art, Enterprise, and Public Policy.

Lippard, Lucy R. 1984. *Get the Message? A Decade of Art for Social Change.* New York: E. P. Dutton.

Lodge, David. 1995. *Small World.* New York: Penguin.

Logan, John R., and Harvey L. Molotch. 1987. *Urban Fortunes: The Political Economy of Place.* Berkeley: University of California Press.

Lukensmeyer, Carolyn J. 2007. "Large-Scale Citizen Engagement and the Rebuilding of New Orleans: A Case Study." *National Civic Review* 182:3–15.

———. 2009. "Top 10—AmericaSpeaks' Best in 2009." E-mail listserv communication, December 22.

———. 2012. "AmericaSpeaks Newsletter: Special Announcement from Carolyn Lukensmeyer." E-mail correspondence, June 19.

Lukensmeyer, Carolyn with Wendy Jacobson. 2013. *Bringing Citizen Voices to the Table: A Guide for Public Managers.* San Francisco, CA: Jossey Bass.

Lukensmeyer, Carolyn J., Margaret Yao, and Theo Brown. 2013. "Fostering Inclusion from the Outside In: Engaging Diverse Citizens in Dialogue and Decision Making." Pp. 482–505 in *Diversity at Work: The Practice of Inclusion*, edited by B. Ferdman. Somerset, NJ: Wiley.

Mansbridge, Jane. 1980. *Beyond Adversary Democracy.* New York: Basic Books.

———. 2003. "Practice-Thought-Practice." Pp. 175–199 in *Deepening Democracy: Institutional Innovations in Empowered Participatory Governance*, edited by Archon Fung and Erik Olin Wright. New York: Verso.

Marcuse, Peter. 2007. "New York after 9/11." *Contemporary Sociology* 36:525–528.

Marquis, Christopher, and Julie Battilana. 2009. "Acting Globally but Thinking Locally? The Enduring Influence of Local Communities on Organizations." *Research in Organizational Behavior* 29:283–302.

Marquis, Christopher, and Michael Lounsbury. 2007. "Vive la Résistance: Competing Logics and the Consolidation of U.S. Community Banking." *Academy of Management Journal* 50:799–820.

Marsh, Dave, ed. 1985. *Sun City*. New York: Penguin.

Martin, Isaac William. 2008. *The Permanent Tax Revolt: How the Property Tax Transformed American Politics*. Stanford, CA: Stanford University Press.

———. 2015. "The Fiscal Sociology of Public Consultation." In *Democratizing Inequalities: Dilemmas of the New Public Participation*, edited by Caroline W. Lee, Michael McQuarrie, and Edward Walker.

Martin, Olivia. 2009. "Tories Offer £1m Prize for Voters' Website." *Guardian*: December 30. (http://www.guardian.co.uk/politics/2009/dec/30/tories-prize-voters-website).

McAdam, Doug. 1982. *Political Process and the Development of Black Insurgency, 1930–1970*. Chicago: University of Chicago Press.

———. 1990. *Freedom Summer*. New York: Oxford University Press.

McCallum, Stephani Roy. 2009. *2008 Annual Report*. Thornton, CO: International Association for Public Participation.

McCamish, Thornton. 2008. "Book Review: Pushing for the Power of Now." *The Age* (Melbourne): July 13.

McCloskey, Michael. 1996. "Opinion: The Skeptic: Collaboration Has Its Limits." *High Country News*: May 13.

McQuarrie, Michael. 2007. "Backyard Revolution to Neoliberalism: Community Development, Civil Society, and the American Third Way." PhD dissertation, New York University.

Medvetz, Thomas M. 2006. "The Strength of Weekly Ties: Relations of Material and Symbolic Exchange in the Conservative Movement." *Politics & Society* 34:343–368.

———. 2012. *Think Tanks in America*. Chicago: University of Chicago Press.

Michels, Robert. 1962 [1911]. *Political Parties: A Sociological Study of the Oligarchical Tendencies of Modern Democracy*. New York: Free Press.

Mills, Joel. 2007. "Designer Democracy and the Future of National Renewal." Paper presented at Global Democracy Conference, Longwood University.

Mizruchi, Mark S., and Lisa C Fein. 1999. "The Social Construction of Organizational Knowledge: A Study of the Uses of Coercive, Mimetic, and Normative Isomorphism." *Administrative Science Quarterly* 44:653–683.

Molotch, Harvey. 1976. "The City as a Growth Machine." *American Journal of Sociology* 82:309–332.

Moreton, Bethany E. 2007. "The Soul of Neoliberalism." *Social Text* 92:103–123.

Morone, James A. 1998. *The Democratic Wish: Popular Participation and the Limits of American Government*. New Haven, CT: Yale University Press.

Mosco, Vincent. 2004. *The Digital Sublime: Myth, Power, and Cyberspace*. Cambridge, MA: MIT Press.

Mosse, David. 2003. "The Making and Marketing of Participatory Development." Pp. 43–75 in *A Moral Critique of Development: In Search of Global Responsibilities*, edited by Philip Quarles van Ufford and Ananta Kumar Giri. London: Routledge.

Moynihan, Daniel Patrick. 1969. *Maximum Feasible Misunderstanding: Community Action in the War on Poverty*. New York: Free Press.

Mudge, Stephanie Lee. 2008. "What Is Neo-liberalism?" *Socio-Economic Review* 6:703–731.

Mutz, Diana. 2008. "Is Deliberative Democracy a Falsifiable Theory?" *Annual Review of Political Science* 11:521–538.

National Coalition for Dialogue & Deliberation (NCDD), the International Association for Public Participation (IAP2), the Co-Intelligence Institute, and others. 2009. "Core Principles for Public Engagement." (http://ncdd.org/rc/item/3643).

National Research Council. 1999. *New Strategies for America's Watersheds.* Washington, DC: National Academies Press.

NCDD. (See National Coalition for Dialogue and Deliberation).

Nielsen, Rasmus Kleis. 2012. *Ground Wars: Personalized Communication in Political Campaigns.* Princeton, NJ: Princeton University Press.

North West Local Health Integration Network. 2009. *Share Your Story, Shape Your Care Community Engagement Initiative: Summary Report.* Thunder Bay, ON: North West Local Health Integration Network.

Obama, Barack. 2009a. "Memorandum of January 21, 2009: Transparency and Open Government." *Presidential Documents* 74(14): January 26.

_____. 2009b. "Open Government: A Progress Report to the American People." Washington, DC: Office of the President. (http://www.slideshare.net/whitehouse/ogi-progress-report-to-the-american-people).

OGP. (See Open Government Partnership).

O'Leary, Rosemary, and Lisa B. Bingham. 2003. *The Promise and Performance of Environmental Conflict Resolution.* Washington, DC: Resources for the Future.

Olson, Susan M., and Albert W. Dzur. 2004. "Revisiting Informal Justice: Restorative Justice and Democratic Professionalism." *Law & Society Review* 38:139–176.

The *Onion.* 2007. "Town Hall Meeting Gives Townspeople Chance to Say Stupid Things in Public." The *Onion* 43:September 8.

Open Government Partnership. 2011. "Secretary Clinton and Brazilian Foreign Minister to Launch Open Government Partnership on July 12." Media note. (http://www.state.gov/r/pa/prs/ps/2011/07/167745.htm).

Osborne, David. 1988. *Laboratories of Democracy.* Cambridge, MA: Harvard Business School Press.

Osborne, David, and Ted Gaebler. 1992. *Reinventing Government: How the Entrepreneurial Spirit Is Transforming the Public Sector.* New York: Plume.

Osterman, Paul. 2006. "Overcoming Oligarchy: Culture and Agency in Social Movement Organizations." *Administrative Science Quarterly* 51:622–649.

Ostrander, Susan A., and Kevin E. Portney, eds. 2007. *Acting Civically: From Urban Neighborhoods to Higher Education.* Lebanon, NH: University Press of New England.

Owen, Harrison. 1997. *Open Space Technology: A User's Guide.* San Francisco: Berrett-Koehler.

Pacewicz, Josh. Forthcoming. *Partisans and Partners: The Politics of the Post-Industrial Economy.* Chicago: University of Chicago Press.

Papadopoulos, Yannis, and Philippe Warin. 2007. "Are Innovative, Participatory, and Deliberative Procedures in Policy Making Democratic and Effective?" *European Journal of Political Research* 46:445–472.

Parkinson, John. 2004. "Why Deliberate? The Encounter between Deliberation and New Public Managers." *Public Administration* 82:377–395.

———. 2006. *Deliberating in the Real World: Problems of Legitimacy in Deliberative Democracy.* Oxford: Oxford University Press.

Pateman, Carol. 1970. *Participation and Democratic Theory.* New York: Cambridge University Press.

Pellow, David N. 1999. "Negotiation and Confrontation: Environmental Policymaking through Consensus." *Society and Natural Resources* 12:189–203.

Perrin, Andrew J. 2006. *Citizen Speak: The Democratic Imagination in American Life.* Chicago: University of Chicago Press.

———. 2009. "The Future of Cultural Sociology." (http://www.ibiblio.org/culture/?q=node/29).

Peterson, Pete. 2009. "Tocqueville Surfs: Lessons in Self-Governance from Obama's Home State." *City Journal*: May 22. (http://www.city-journal.org/2009/eon0522pp.html).

Piven, Frances Fox, and Richard A. Cloward. 1977. *Poor People's Movements: Why They Succeed, How They Fail.* New York: Pantheon.

Polletta, Francesca. 2000. "The Structural Context of Novel Rights Claims: Southern Civil Rights Organizing, 1961–1966." *Law & Society Review* 34:367–406.

———. 2002. *Freedom Is an Endless Meeting: Democracy in American Social Movements.* Chicago: University of Chicago Press.

———. 2006. "Mobilization Forum: Awkward Movements." *Mobilization* 11:475–500.

———. 2015. "Public Deliberation and Political Contention." In *Democratizing Inequalities: Dilemmas of the New Public Participation*, edited by Caroline W. Lee, Michael McQuarrie, and Edward Walker.

Polletta, Francesca, and John Lee. 2006. "Is Telling Stories Good for Democracy? Rhetoric in Public Deliberation after 9/11." *American Sociological Review* 71:699–723.

Porter, Theodore M. 1995. *Trust in Numbers: The Pursuit of Objectivity in Science and Public Life.* Princeton, NJ: Princeton University Press.

Post, Robert C., and Nancy L. Rosenblum. 2002. "Introduction." Pp. 1–25 in *Civil Society and Government*, edited by Robert C. Post. Princeton, NJ: Princeton University Press.

Powell, Walter W., and Paul J. DiMaggio. 1991. "The Iron Cage Revisited: Institutional Isomorphism and Collective Rationality in Organizational Fields." Pp. 63–82 in *The New Institutionalism in Organizational Analysis*, edited by Walter W. Powell and Paul J. DiMaggio. Chicago: University of Chicago Press.

Prasad, Monica. 2006. *The Politics of Free Markets: The Rise of Neoliberal Economic Policies in Britain, France, Germany, and the United States.* Chicago: University of Chicago Press.

Prewitt, Kenneth. 1987. "Public Statistics and Democratic Politics." Pp. 261–274 in *The Politics of Numbers*, edited by William Alonso and Paul Starr. New York: Russell Sage Foundation.

Public Conversations Project. 2010. "Talking with the Enemy." (http://www.publicconversations.org/dialogue/policy/abortion).

Putnam, Robert D. 1993. *Making Democracy Work: Civic Traditions in Modern Italy.* Princeton, NJ: Princeton University Press.

———. 1995. "Bowling Alone: America's Declining Social Capital." *Journal of Democracy* 6:65–78.

———. 2000. *Bowling Alone: The Collapse and Revival of American Community.* New York: Simon & Schuster.

Quinn, Sarah. 2008. "The Transformation of Morals in Markets: Death, Benefits, and the Exchange of Life Insurance Policies." *American Journal of Sociology* 114:738–780.

Reed, T. V. 2005. *The Art of Protest: Culture and Activism from the Civil Rights Movement to the Streets of Seattle.* Minneapolis: University of Minnesota Press.

Reger, Jo, and Lacey Story. 2005. "Talking about My Vagina: Two College Campuses and the Vagina Monologues." Pp. 139–160 in *Different Wavelengths: Studies of the Contemporary Women's Movement*, edited by Jo Reger. New York: Routledge.

Reger, Jo, and Judith K. Taylor, session organizers. 2009. "Social Movements, Culture and Art." Section on Collective Behavior and Social Movements Paper Session, American Sociological Association Annual Meeting, San Francisco, August 8.

Reitman, Jason. 2009. *Up in the Air.* DW Studios and Cold Spring Pictures. (http://www.theupintheairmovie.com/).

Roberts, Carl W., ed. 1997. *Text Analysis for the Social Sciences: Methods for Drawing Statistical Inferences from Texts and Transcripts.* Mahwah, NJ: Erlbaum.

Rodriguez, Marisol. 2007. "Facilitator Perspectives: Community Congress III Houston." *AmericaSpeaks Spotlight: Updates from the Field.* Washington, DC: AmericaSpeaks. Retrieved December 16, 2007. (http://www.america-speaks.org/spotlight/?p=34).

Roman, David. 1988. *Acts of Intervention: Performance, Gay Culture, and AIDS.* Bloomington: Indiana University Press.

Roth, Moira, ed. 1983. *The Amazing Decade: Women and Performance Art in America.* Los Angeles: Astro Artz.

Rothschild, Joyce, and J. Allen Whitt. 1986. *The Cooperative Workplace: Potentials and Dilemmas of Organizational Democracy and Participation.* New York: Cambridge University Press.

Roy, William G. 2010. *Reds, Whites and Blues: Social Movements, Folk Music, and Race in America.* Princeton, NJ: Princeton University Press.

Roy, William G., and Timothy J. Dowd. 2010. "What Is Sociological about Music?" *Annual Review of Sociology* 36:183–203.

Rutte, Martin. 2007. "Martin Rutte Speaker and Consultant." Santa Fe, NM: Livelihood. Retrieved May 12, 2007. (http://www.martinrutte.com/aboutmartin.html).

Ryfe, David M. 2002. "The Practice of Deliberative Democracy: A Study of 16 Deliberative Organizations." *Political Communication* 19:359–377.

———. 2005. "Does Deliberative Democracy Work?" *Annual Review of Political Science* 8:49–71.

———. 2007a. "The Next Form of Democracy" [review]. *Journal of Public Deliberation* 3: Article 2. (http://services.bepress.com/jpd/vol3/iss1/art2).

———. 2007b. "Toward a Sociology of Deliberation." *Journal of Public Deliberation* 3: Article 3. (http://services.bepress.com/jpd/vol3/iss1/art3).

Saint-Martin, Denis. 2004. *Building the New Managerialist State: Consultants and the Politics of Public Sector Reform in Comparative Perspective*. New York: Oxford University Press.

Sampson, Robert J., Doug McAdam, Heather MacIndoe, and Simón Weffer-Elizondo. 2005. "Civil Society Reconsidered: The Durable Nature and Community Structure of Collective Civic Action." *American Journal of Sociology* 111:673–714.

Sanders, Lynn M. 1997. "Against Deliberation." *Political Theory* 25:347–364.

Sawchuk, Peter H. 2006. "Labor Education and Labor Art: The Hidden Potential of Knowing for the Left Hand." *Labor Studies Journal* 31:49–68.

Scheppele, Kim Lane. 2004. "Constitutional Ethnography: An Introduction." *Law & Society Review* 38:389–406.

Schneiderhan, Erik, and Shamus Khan. 2008. "Reasons and Inclusion: The Foundation of Deliberation." *Sociological Theory* 26:1–24.

Scholz, Trebor. 2009. "The Internet as Playground and Factory: A Conference on Digital Labor." (http://digitallabor.org/).

Schudson, Michael. 1999. *The Good Citizen: A History of American Civic Life*. Cambridge, MA: Harvard University Press.

Schuman, Sandor. 2005. *The IAF Handbook of Group Facilitation: Best Practices from the Leading Organization in Facilitation*. San Francisco: Jossey-Bass.

Selznick, Philip. 1949. *TVA and the Grassroots: A Study in the Sociology of Formal Organization*. Berkeley: University of California Press.

Senger, Jeffrey M. 2003. *Federal Dispute Resolution: Using ADR with the United States Government*. San Francisco: Jossey Bass.

Sennett, Richard, and Saskia Sassen. 2011. "Cameron's Broken Windows." *New York Times*: August 10. (http://www.nytimes.com/2011/08/11/opinion/when-budget-cuts-lead-to-broken-windows.html).

Shaping America's Youth. 2007. "About SAY: Our Corporate Partners." Portland, OR: Academic Network, LLC.

Shih, Tse-Hua, and Xitao Fan. 2008. "Comparing Response Rates from Web and Mail Surveys: A Meta-Analysis." *Field Methods* 20:249–271.

Shirky, Clay. 2008. *Here Comes Everybody: The Power of Organizing without Organizations*. New York: Penguin.

Silver, Ira. 2006. *Unequal Partnerships: Beyond the Rhetoric of Philanthropic Collaboration*. New York: Routledge.

Simonsen, William, and Mark Robbins. 1999. *Citizen Participation in Resource Allocation*. Boulder, CO: Westview Press.

Sirianni, Carmen. 2009. *Investing in Democracy: Engaging Citizens in Collaborative Governance*. Washington, DC: Brookings Institution Press.

Sirianni, Carmen, ed. 1987. *Worker Participation and the Politics of Reform*. Philadelphia: Temple University Press.

Sirianni, Carmen, and Lewis Friedland. 2001. *Civic Innovation in America*. Berkeley: University of California Press.

Skocpol, Theda. 2003. *Diminished Democracy: From Membership to Management in American Civic Life*. Norman: University of Oklahoma Press.

Snider, J. H. 2010. "Deterring Fake Public Participation." *International Journal of Public Participation* 4:90–102.

Snow, David A. 2004. "Social Movements as Challenges to Authority: Resistance to an Emerging Conceptual Hegemony." Pp. 3–25 in *Authority in Contention: Research in Social Movements, Conflict, and Change*, edited by Daniel J. Meyers and Daniel M. Cress. New York: Elsevier.

Somers, Margaret R. 2005. "Let Them Eat Social Capital: Socializing the Market versus Marketizing the Social." *Thesis Eleven* 81:5–19.

Soule, Sarah A. 2009. *Contention and Corporate Social Responsibility*. New York: Cambridge University Press.

Spencer, Jon Michael. 1989. *Protest and Praise: Sacred Music and Black Religion*. Minneapolis: Fortress Press.

Spillman, Lyn. 2012. *Solidarity in Strategy: Making Business Meaningful in American Trade Associations*. Chicago: University of Chicago Press.

Staggenborg, Suzanne, and Verta Taylor. 2005. "Whatever Happened to the Women's Movement?" *Mobilization* 10:37–52.

Staggenborg, Suzanne, and Amy Lang. 2007. "Culture and Ritual in the Montreal Women's Movement." *Social Movement Studies* 6:177–194.

Stamatov, Peter. 2002. "Interpretive Activism and the Political Uses of Verdi's Operas in the 1840s." *American Sociological Review* 67:345–366.

Star, Susan Leigh, and James Griesemer. 1989. "Institutional Ecology, Translations, and Boundary Objects: Amateurs and Professionals in Berkeley's Museum of Vertebrate Zoology, 1907–1939." *Social Studies of Science* 19:387–420.

Stavros, Jackie, and Gina Hinrichs. 2007. "SOARing to High and Engaging Performance: An Appreciative Approach to Strategy." *AI Practitioner*, August:1–3.

Surowiecki, James. 2004. *The Wisdom of Crowds: Why the Many Are Smarter Than the Few and How Collective Wisdom Shapes Business, Economies, Societies, and Nations*. New York: Random House.

Swyngedouw, Erik. 2005. "Governance Innovation and the Citizen: The Janus Face of Governance-beyond-the-State." *Urban Studies* 42:1991–2006.

Tapscott, Don, and Anthony D. Williams. 2006. *Wikinomics: How Mass Collaboration Changes Everything*. New York: Penguin.

Tepper, Steven J. 2009. "Stop the Beat: Quiet Regulation and Cultural Conflict." *Sociological Forum* 24:276–306.

Terhune, George. 1998. "The Quincy Library Group Case Study." Paper presented at the "Engaging, Empowering, and Negotiating Community: Strategies for Conservation and Development Conference," West Virginia University. (http://www.qlg.org/pub/miscdoc/casestudy.htm).

Thomas, Craig W. 2003. "Habitat Conservation Planning." Pp. 144–172 in *Deepening Democracy*, edited by Archon Fung and Erik Olin Wright. New York: Verso.

Thomas, Nancy L., and Matt Leighninger. 2010. "No Better Time: A 2010 Report on Opportunities and Challenges for Deliberative Democracy." The Deliberative Democracy Consortium and the Democracy Imperative. (www.deliberative-democracy.net).

Thompson, Dennis F. 2008. "Deliberative Democratic Theory and Empirical Political Science." *Annual Review of Political Science* 11:497–520.

Thornton, Patricia H. 2002. "The Rise of the Corporation in a Craft Industry: Conflict and Conformity in Institutional Logics." *Academy of Management Journal* 45:81–101.

Thornton, Patricia H., Candace Jones, and Kenneth Kury. 2005. "Institutional Logics and Institutional Change in Organizations: Transformation in Accounting, Architecture, and Publishing." *Research in the Sociology of Organizations* 23:125–170.

Thornton, Patricia H., and William Ocasio. 2008. "Institutional Logics." Pp. 99–129 in *The Sage Handbook of Organizational Institutionalism*, edited by R. Greenwood, C. Oliver, R. Suddaby, and K. Sahlin-Andersson. Thousand Oaks, CA: SAGE.

Thrift, Nigel. 2005. *Knowing Capitalism*. Thousand Oaks, CA: SAGE.

Travis, Trysh. 2007. "It Will Change the World If Everybody Reads This Book: New Thought Religion in Oprah's Book Club." *American Quarterly* 59:1017–1041.

———. 2009. *The Language of the Heart: A Cultural History of the Recovery Movement from Alcoholics Anonymous to Oprah Winfrey*. Chapel Hill: University of North Carolina Press.

Tronti, Mario. 1980 [1965]. "The Strategy of Refusal." *Autonomia* 3:28–34.

Turner, Fred. 2006. *From Counterculture to Cyberculture: Stewart Brand, the Whole Earth Network and the Rise of Digital Utopianism*. Chicago: University of Chicago Press.

UNOP [Unified New Orleans Plan]. 2007. *Preliminary Report: Community Congress III*. New Orleans, LA: UNOP.

Vaisey, Stephen. 2009. "Motivation and Justification: A Dual-Process Model of Culture in Action." *American Journal of Sociology* 114:1675–1715.

Vallas, Steven P. 2006. "Empowerment Redux: Structure, Agency, and the Remaking of Managerial Authority." *American Journal of Sociology* 111:1677–1717.

Vann, Katie, and Geoffrey C. Bowker. 2001. "Instrumentalizing the Truth of Practice." *Social Epistemology* 15:247–262.

Vogel, David. 1989. *Fluctuating Fortunes: The Political Power of Business in America*. New York: Basic.

Wagner-Pacifici, Robin. 2008. "The Arts and Humanities." Presented at the Culture Section Mini-Conference. (http://www.ibiblio.org/culture/?q=node/9#comment-1).

Walker, Edward T. 2014. *Grassroots for Hire: Public Affairs Consultants in American Democracy*. New York: Cambridge University Press.

Walker, Edward, Michael McQuarrie, and Caroline W. Lee. 2015. "Rising Participation and Declining Democracy." In *Democratizing Inequalities: Dilemmas of the New Public Participation*, edited by Caroline W. Lee, Michael McQuarrie, and Edward Walker. New York: New York University Press.

Walsh, Katherine Cramer. 2007. *Talking about Race: Community Dialogues and the Politics of Difference*. Chicago: University of Chicago Press.

Warren, Mark E., and Hilary Pearse. 2008a. "Introduction: Democratic Renewal and Deliberative Democracy." Pp 1–19 in *Designing Deliberative Democracy: The British Columbia Citizens' Assembly*, edited by M. Warren and H. Pearse. Cambridge, UK: Cambridge University Press.

———. 2008b. *Designing Deliberative Democracy: The British Columbia Citizens' Assembly*. Cambridge, UK: Cambridge University Press.

Weber, Robert Philip. 1990. *Basic Content Analysis*. Newbury Park, CA: SAGE.

Weinberger, David. 2007. *Everything Is Miscellaneous: The Power of the New Digital Disorder*. New York: Holt.

Wenger, Etienne. 1998. *Communities of Practice: Learning, Meaning, and Identity*. Cambridge, UK: Cambridge University Press.

Wetzel, Christopher. 2014. "The Field of Tribal Leadership Training, Cultures of Expertise, and Native Nations in the United States." In *Restorying Indigenous Leadership*, edited by Cora Voyageur, Laura Brearley, and Brian Calliou. Banff, AB: Banff Centre Press.

Whalen, Jack, and Richard Flacks. 1989. *Beyond the Barricades: The Sixties Generation Grows Up*. Philadelphia: Temple University Press.

Whelan, James. 2007. "Six Reasons Not to Engage: Compromise, Confrontation and the Commons." *COMM-ORG Papers* 13. University of Wisconsin. (http://comm-org.wisc.edu/papers2007/whelan.htm).

White, Damian. 2011. Communication to Environmental Sociology listserv. August 1.

Whittier, Nancy. 2009. *The Politics of Child Sexual Abuse: Emotion, Social Movements, and the State*. New York: Oxford University Press.

Williamson, Abigail. 2007. *Citizen Participation in the Unified New Orleans Plan*. Cambridge MA: Kennedy School of Government.

Wilson, Patricia A. 2008. "Deliberative Planning for Disaster Recovery: Remembering New Orleans." *Journal of Public Deliberation* 5: Article 1.

Wolin, Sheldon S. 2008. *Democracy, Inc.: Managed Democracy and the Specter of Inverted Totalitarianism*. Princeton, NJ: Princeton University Press.

Wondolleck, Julia M., and Steven L. Yaffee. 2000. *Making Collaboration Work: Lessons from Innovation in Natural Resource Management*. Chicago: University of Chicago Press.

Wuthnow, Robert. 1998. *Loose Connections: Joining Together in America's Fragmented Communities*. Cambridge, MA: Harvard University Press.

Wyman, Miriam, and David Shulman. 2002. *From Venting to Inventing: Dispatches from the Frontiers of Participation in Canada*. London: Commonwealth Foundation.

Yankelovich, Daniel. 2007. *Profit with Honor: The New Stage of Market Capitalism*. New Haven, CT: Yale University Press.

Young, Iris Marion. 2000. *Inclusion and Democracy*. New York: Oxford University Press.

Zacharzewski, Anthony. 2010. "Democracy Pays: How Democratic Engagement Can Cut the Cost of Government." Brighton, UK: The Democratic Society and Public-i.

Zald, Mayer N., and Michael Lounsbury. 2010. "The Wizards of Oz: Towards an Institutional Approach to Elites, Expertise, and Command Posts." *Organization Studies* 31:963–996.

Zald, Mayer N., and John D. McCarthy. 1980. "Social Movement Industries: Competition and Cooperation among Movement Organizations." *Research in Social Movements, Conflict, and Change* 3:1–20.

Zittrain, Jonathan. 2008. "Ubiquitous Human Computing." *Philosophical Transactions of the Royal Society* 366:3813–3821.

Zukin, Cliff, Scott Keeter, Molly Andolina, Krista Jenkins, and Michael X. Delli Carpini. 2006. *A New Engagement? Political Participation, Civic Life, and the Changing American Citizen*. New York: Oxford University Press.

# INDEX

"$f$" indicates material in figures. "n." indicates material in notes.

AccountAbility, 252n. 14
activism
  alignment with interests of sponsors,
    226
  art and, 143
  commodification of, 41
  "grasstops," 34
  of 1960s era, 75–77, 219, 227
  in origin stories, 75–79
  of practitioners, 28, 103, 241n.6
  professionalization of, 40–41, 45–46,
    59
  protests. *See* protests
  social, 58, 76, 78, 115
activists
  in CaliforniaSpeaks process, 203
  in deliberative processes, 174
  solidarity of, corporations and, 46
  strategies of, 115, 243n.18
  targeting of businesses by, 47
  of transparency movement, in
    Obama administration, 54
Adams, Brian E., 244n. 32
"adult education," 103
Advertising Research Foundation, 46
African Americans, 85, 208, 249n.33

AIDS activism, 143
Alexander, Christopher, 114
Alinskyite community organizing
    methods, 151
Allianz, 50
alternative dispute resolution, 36, 38,
    42, 243n.19
Altria Group, 52
America Speaking Out, 180
Americans for the Arts, 148, 196
AmericaSpeaks
  advertising by, 162
  Bigger, Better, All Together event,
    27, 51–52, 190–200
  in brainstorming phase for Open
    Government Directive, 35
  CaliforniaSpeaks, 47, 141–42, 170,
    182, 203–5, 210
  Clinton's Dialogue on Race and,
    38–39
  closure of, 27
  Community Congress III by. *See*
    Community Congress III
  critiques of, 210
  efficacy evaluation by, 182, 254n.61
  engagement strategies of, 174

AmericaSpeak (*cont.*)
  mission of, 137, 251n.25
  at NPAC, 190–99, 219
  Our Budget event. *See* Our Budget,
    Our Economy event
  postcards preaddressed to
    participants' lawmakers from, 182,
    254n.61
  SAY, 165–66
  Tough Choices in Health Care, 170
  21st Century Summits, 137
  21st Century Town Meeting, 20,
    38–39, 59, 141–42, 148, 191
Animating Democracy, 148
antiapartheid movement, 143
"anticipatory consultation," 174
Appreciative Inquiry (AI)
  advertising copy for, 176
  for alignment with sponsors'
    interests, 170
  Cooperrider's founding theory for,
    135
  for faith communities, 107
  New Thought in, 230
  positive philosophy of, 133, 159
  warm-up exercises in, 111
Appreciative Inquiry Summits, 135
Armstrong, Elizabeth A., 244n. 35
art, 71–72, 143–49, 190–200, 252n.50,
  255n.5
Asian Americans, 85

Babbitt, Bruce, 244n. 30
Baiocchi, Gianpaolo, 32, 152, 157–58,
  174
banks, 49
Bernier, Roger, 244n. 31
Bernstein, Mary, 244n. 35
Bigger, Better, All Together event, 27,
  51–52, 190–200
"blended" social action, 244n. 38
Bonneman, Tim, 179
Bonner, Pat, 244n. 31
Boston, 39

Bourdieu, Pierre, 65, 189
boutique consultancies, 45, 140
branding of processes, 142
Brazil, Pôrto Alegre, 21, 152
Briggs, Xavier, 165, 247n.96
British Columbia Citizens' Assembly,
  21, 141
Brown, Theo, 137
Buddhism, 107, 109, 114–15. *See also*
  Zen
Bureau of Reclamation, 244n. 31
Bush, George W. (GWB), 39
Bush administration (GWB), 244n. 31
Bush-Clinton Katrina Fund, 12
business associations, 245n. 55
businesses and corporations
  "caring, sharing" approach of, 128–
    29, 250n.9
  as change agents, 47, 166
  counterculture and, 129, 245n.55
  democracy and, 50
  dialogue in, 102–3
  facilitation for, 46–51, 134–39, 169–171
  interest groups and, 47, 245n.59
  marketing to, 163
  outcomes of processes for, 169
  psychological assessment of, 104
  rebel stance of, 128–29
  social capital of, 46
  social marketing by, 166
  social movements and, 245n. 55,
    245n.59
  sponsoring deliberations, 48*f*, 49,
    53, 135
  taxes, resistance to, 168, 256n.17
  youth project underwriting by, 165
Button, Mark, 31, 34–35, 51
buycotting, 46

Cadbury Schweppes, 165–66
Cain, Carole, 75
California
  D&D Practitioners Survey
    respondents in, 85

facilitator demand in, 150–51
health care processes in, 47, 141–42, 170, 182, 203–5, 210
Los Angeles, 39, 178–79
Schwarzenegger's administration in, 204–5
CaliforniaSpeaks, 47, 141–42, 170, 182, 203–5, 210
campaigning, 36, 180
Campbell Soup Company, 165–66
Canada
British Columbia Citizens' Assembly, 21, 141
electoral reform in, 52
guidelines, standards, and best practices from government of, 252n. 14
Ontario Citizen's Assembly, 205, 206
participatory budgeting in Toronto, 116
Canadian Coalition on Dialogue and Deliberation (C2D2) conference, 115–17
Canadian International Development Agency, 252n. 14
canvassing organizations, 41
capitalism
civic participation and, 38, 153
extreme, profits of, 226
participants' critiques and, 222
social change and, 230
social critiques of, 127–28
"soft," 250n. 9
solutions for problems of, 228
spirit of, 228, 231
"cardstorming," 91
Carnegie Corporation of New York, 12
Carson, Lyn, 87, 130, 134
Case Foundation, 12, 247n.99
census data, 180
Center for Deliberative Democracy, 252n. 3
Centers for Disease Control and Prevention (CDC), 244n. 31
chambers of commerce, 48f, 49, 135

Champions of Participation conferences, 35
Change Handbook, The, 141, 163, 169, 256n.5
ChoiceDialogues for Health Viewpoints, 168, 170
choicework, 175
Christianity, 106–7, 115
CIGNA, 165–66
circle sharing, 20, 33–34, 79–82
City Journal, 212
civic engagement institutes, 39
civic partnerships, 24–25, 38. See also public engagement
civil rights movement, 143
class, socioeconomic, 13–14, 16, 83
clients
alignment with interests of, 181–82
authority of, 103
credibility of, 92
culture of, 249n. 39
definition of, 57, 89
demographic data collection for, 181
homogeneity of, 101–2
IAP2 survey of, 49
marketing to, 155, 177
outcomes of processes for, 163–64
"positive core" of, 133
selling of deliberation to, 53
social change by, 7, 47, 133
sponsors and, 49
strategies for management of, 89–93, 103, 125–26
types of, 49
unwilling, 91, 249n.37
value of processes for, 178, 254n.52
Clinton, Bill, 38, 39, 244n.30
Coffee Party, 180
Co-Intelligence Institute, 252n. 14
"collaborative decision-making," 55
collaborative governance, 38. See also public engagement
colleges and universities, 48f, 49, 58, 157
Common Sense California, 150–51

communitarian, 58, 227, 247n.100
Community Congress I, 14
Community Congress II, 11, 18
Community Congress III
  AmericaSpeaks report on, 14, 142
  customization for, 142
  description of, 11–21
  frequently-used practices in, 25, 158
  future engagement efforts and, 88
  vs. NPAC, 191
  participation in, 218
  purpose of, 235
  response to, 199
  satisfaction rates for, 59
  summary of, 203
  unwilling clients of, 249n. 37
community development corporations
  (CDCs), 48–49
Community Development Society,
  252n. 14
community mediation movement, 42
community policing, 38
comprehensive community planning,
  49–50, 164, 167–68
ConAgra Foods, 165–66
conferences. *See also specific events*
  addicted to, 68
  critique of, 50
  demographics of attendees, 85
  free marketplace ethic of, 130–33
  functions of, 112
  objectives of, 68
Congressional town halls, 212, 214
Conrad, Kent, 211
conservatism, 78–79
conservatives
  antitax, antistatist, 253n. 34
  on government responsiveness, 36
  language/terminology and, 79, 82,
    83*f,* 117–18, 180
  marketing to, 94
  vituperative comments of, 54–55
consultants. *See* public engagement
  practitioners
consumerism, 230

Conversation Cafés, 145
Cook, Fay Lomax, 47–49, 239,
  247n.100
Cooperrider, David, 135
corporations. *See* businesses and
  corporations
Cox, Geoff, 143
crowds, wisdom of, 41, 244n.43
crowdsourcing, 32–33, 228
culture, 28, 142, 243n.18

D&D Practitioners Survey
  on "adult education," 103
  on age, 44, 75–76
  on budgets/cost of projects, 52
  on business projects, 134
  on career path, 44, 76
  on challenges, 127, 135
  on "community of practice," 130
  conducting, 233, 237–240
  on deliberation, 253n. 16
  demographic data collection by, 85
  N, definition of, 240
  on online deliberative methods, 179
  on organizational positions, 45
  results of, 245n. 51
  on roles, 45
  on sponsors, 48–49, 135
  on tools access, 160
  on topics, 49–50, 164, 167, 169
  on training, 156
  on transformative power of
    processes, 106
  on voluntarism, 133
DaimlerChrysler, 12, 49
Davenport Institute, 150–51
"decide-announce-defend" model, 37
decreased resistance, 174
"deep acting," 100
deep democracy, 32, 38, 67
deliberation movement, 247n. 86,
  247n.100
deliberative democracy, 3, 57
Deliberative Democracy Consortium,
  54, 247n.98

Deliberative Poll, 54, 152
Delli Carpini, Michael, 47–49, 239, 247n.100
democracy
  "Baskin-Robbins," 142
  businesses and, 50
  for common vs. conflicted interests, 102
  deep, 32, 38, 67
  designer, 139–142
  digital, 41
  "diminished," 41
  "down market," 28
  in formal institutions, 40
  "Kaufman paradox" in, 253n. 20
  production of, in America, 3
  public engagement and, 28, 37
  ROI and, 162–63
  "slow," 250n. 7
  "stealth," 241n. 6
Democracy Imperative, 54
Democracy Pays report, 162, 173
democratic, 58, 247n.100
Democratic Society, 171
democratization process, 244n. 31
Department of Housing and Urban Development, 15
designer democracy, 139–142
Dewey, John, 40, 137
dialogue and deliberation (D&D), 3. *See also* public engagement
Digby (blogger), 163, 204
digital campaigning, 52, 180, 182
digital media platforms, 180
"digital utopian" narratives, 47
dispute resolution, 36, 38, 42, 44, 243n.19
Dove forums, 46

economic development
  civic partnerships for, 38
  in comprehensive community planning, 167
  conference programs and, 99
  grassroots civic action and, 154

public engagement on problems of, 153
  social justice and, 184
  topic framing and, 171
  youth development and, 165, 167
*Economist, The*, 152
economy
  ability to contribute to, 221
  knowledge-based, 229
  lobbying and, 151
  public engagement and, 26, 28, 38, 153–55
Edelman, 53
"education and youth" topic, 164–67
Ehrenreich, Barbara, 74, 99
Eliasoph, Nina, 66–67, 88, 103, 108, 134, 137, 154, 165, 241n.6, 250n.17
Eliot, T. S., 123, 250n.1
empowered participation, 38. *See also* public engagement
empowerment
  bureaucrats and, 108
  contexts for, 225–26
  from crowdsourcing, 33
  diversity and, 88
  economic profitability and, 154
  frustration with micro, 7, 26, 219
  OD methods and, 102–3
  in origin stories, 75
  quality of, 244n. 29
  of teens, 250n. 17
  topic choice and, 226–27
  through youth organization projects, 165–67
Endangered Species Act, 38
environmental planning, 38–39, 141, 218, 243n.20, 244n.30
Environmental Protection Agency (EPA), 244n. 31
Envision processes, 159, 253n.19
equality, 155
Espeland, Wendy Nelson, 244n. 31
ethnicity, 84
evangelicalism, 106–7

Everyday Democracy, 31–32, 55, 159–160, 219–220
expert mindset, 108

facilitators. *See* public engagement practitioners
facipulation, 93, 100, 114–15
family systems research, 106
FedEx Corporation, 165–66
field, 57–58
Fielding Graduate University, 138*f*
financialization, 245n. 55
fishbowl method, 117
Fishkin, James, 54, 152, 252n.3
Florida, Richard, 190
Fluke, Andy, 68, 117–18
focus groups, 175
Ford Foundation, 12, 52
forum movement, 33
foundations
    best practices study grants from, 156–57
    "Cadillac" processes of, 140, 251n.35
    neutrality of, 204
    sponsorship by, 48*f*, 49
    youth project underwriting by, 165
Frank, Thomas, 128–29
Fung, Archon, 32, 109

Ganuza, Ernesto, 32, 157–58, 174
Gastil, John, 32, 109
gender, 15, 84–87, 95, 97, 227, 233. *See also* men; women
Giffords, Gabrielle, 27
Girard, Monique, 141
Goldman, Joe, 31, 33, 141
government agencies
    businesses in decision-making process of, 47, 246n.62
    economic benefit of engagement with, 173
    information management of participants by, 181
    preapproval of practitioners in

contracting databases, 238
    sponsoring deliberations, 48–49, 135
    TQM and, 161
    "vending machine" model for, 162
government officials
    as change agents, 166
    citizen entitlement and, 243n. 16
    decision-making model of, 37
    worries and fears of, 173
grants, 59, 165, 247n.99
graphic recording, 144–45
grassroots lobbying, 41, 51, 52, 182
grassroots lobbying industry, 243n. 11
Great Consultation, 153
Greater New Orleans Foundation, 12
Gregg, Judd, 211

Habermas, Jürgen, 50
Hard Times, Hard Choices poll, 168
Harwood Institute, 252n. 14
Hawaiian state park maintenance, 212–14
health care processes
    CaliforniaSpeaks, 47, 141–42, 170, 182, 203–5, 210
    Choicebook use in, 168
    ChoiceDialogues for Health Viewpoints, 168, 170
    *The Office* on, 256n.26
    options given during, 203, 206
    protests during, 203
    sponsors' neutrality in, 204
    Tough Choices in Health Care, 170
Heierbacher, Sandy, 2, 68, 78, 91, 93, 117–18, 123, 130, 156
Hendriks, Carolyn, 87, 130, 134
Hibbing, John R., 241n. 6, 242n.18, 255n.10
Hickenlooper, John, 190
Hispanics, 85, 181, 249n.33
Hochschild, Arlie, 100, 111
"holding space," 113, 115, 118, 229
human relations movement, 102
humanitarian relief agencies, 249n. 42

icebreaker techniques, 111
idealism, 78
Illouz, Eva, 75
Imagine processes, 159
Industrial Areas Foundation,
    243n. 28
industry trade groups, 48f, 49, 135
"inhabited institutions" approach,
    23–24
instrumentalism, 133
interest groups
    businesses and, 47, 245n.59
    disempowering, 39
    lobbying for, 41
    manipulation by, 2
    national, 40
    progressive movements and, 40
    scripted participation by, 41
    social movements and, 245n. 59
International Association for Impact
    Assessment, 252n. 14
International Association of Public
    Participation (IAP2)
    best practices, guidelines, and
        standards from, 252n. 14
    client survey by, 49
    conferences, 96–99, 104–6, 115
    founding of, 43
    membership in, 43, 238
    "our corporate culture," 249n. 39
    training from, 43, 117, 123–26,
        139–140, 214–15, 245n.50
International Civil Society Consortium
    for Public Deliberation, 247n. 86
International IDEA, 252n. 14
International Monetary Fund (IMF),
    52
international trade policies, 50
interstitial field, 239, 247n.95
interventions, 216
Involve, 252n. 14
Iowa Citizens' Summit on Childhood
    Obesity, 166
isomorphism, 156

Jacobs, Larry, 47–49, 239, 247n.100
Jefferson, Thomas, 36

Kashefi, Elham, 50
"Kaufman paradox," 253n. 20
Kettering Foundation, 52, 156, 179,
    243n.28, 247n.86
keypad polling, 148, 181
King, Rodney, 39
Klein, Joe, 152
Kodak, 138
Kraft, 52
Kreiss, Daniel, 180

labor movement, 143
Lashaw, Amanda, 223, 230, 234
Latinas/Latinos, 85, 181, 249n.33
Lee, John, 147
Leighninger, Matt, 34, 55, 57, 85,
    243n.16
Levine, Peter, 109
limited attendance, 244n. 43
listening, 43, 160, 175, 220
Listening to the City process, 12, 141,
    203, 233
lobbying
    belief in, 196
    deliberative democracy and, 36
    economy and, 151
    grassroots, 41, 51, 52, 182
    grassroots lobbying industry, 243n.11
    regulating, 41
    social organizations and, 41
local nonprofit organizations, 48–49, 56
Logan, John R., 171
logics, 24, 67
Los Angeles, 39, 178–79
Louisiana Recovery Fund, 12
Lukensmeyer, Carolyn, 15, 18, 19, 21,
    25, 27, 31, 33, 54, 123, 137,
    242n.24
Maine "Tough Choices in Health
    Care" process, 170
Make It Your Own competition, 247n. 99

management consulting, 253n. 17
managerialist discourse, 251n. 28
Manhattan Institute, 212
Mansbridge, Jane, 102
Martin, Isaac, 38, 153, 174, 253n.34, 255n.17
Mary Reynolds Babcock Foundation, 12
McCoy, Martha, 31–32, 33, 54
McNeil Nutritionals, 165–66
mediation, 38, 42, 76–77, 243n.19
Medvetz, Thomas M., 247n. 91, 247n.95
Meeting in a Box Community Dialogues, 159
Memorandum on Transparency and Open Government, 1–2, 33, 35, 54
men
    at IAP2 vs. NCDD conferences, 97
    participation by, 15
    in practitioner corps, 86
    recruiting, 88, 181
    retention of authority of, 228
    topic choice and participation of, 88
Michigan "Hard Times, Hard Choices" poll, 168
Milgram, Stanley, 207, 209
Mills, Joel, 139, 141, 142
Molotch, Harvey L., 171
Moreton, Bethany, 223, 228
Morone, James A., 31, 35, 241n.3, 247n.100
Mort, Maggie, 50
mortgage lenders, 49
Mosse, David, 50
Mudge, Stephanie Lee, 244n. 30
"multi-institutional politics" model, 40, 244n.35
music, 142, 143
Nagin, Ray, 11–12
name, unique project, 142
national chapter groups, 41, 48f
National Civic League, 243n. 28

National Coalition for Dialogue and Deliberation (NCDD)
    conferences. See NCDD conferences
    founding of, 43
    guidelines from, 157
    listserv, 1–2, 214
    membership in, 238
    philosophy of, 130
    Public Engagement Principles Project, 84, 157
National Environmental Policy Act, 42
National Institute of Civil Discourse
national interest groups, 40
National Issues Forums Moderator Training, 156
National Performing Arts Convention (NPAC), 190–200, 202, 219, 235, 255nn.4-6
National Research Council, 141
National Youth Administration, 165
NCDD conferences
    description of, 68–79, 82
    on empathy, 136
    journey wall exercise at, 104, 105f
    participatory art projects at, 71–72, 146, 147f
    "walking the talk" at, 111–12
neighborhood schools councils, 38
Neighborhood Youth Corps, 165
neoliberalism, 39, 176, 213, 223, 244n.30
New Age spirituality, 36, 66, 78–82, 107
New Age terminology, 117–18
New Age whole-body exercises, 63
New Earth, A (Tolle), 182
New Orleans
    Community Congress I on, 14
    Community Congress II on, 11, 18
    Community Congress III on. See Community Congress III
New Orleans Saints, 13
new public management, 39, 244n.30
New Thought, 66, 230, 248n.5

New York City "Listening to the City" process, 12, 141, 203, 233
*New York Times*, 178
newspapers, 49
NIKE, 165–66
*1984* (Orwell), 207
No Better Time Conference, 54–56
Norquist, Grover, 79, 151, 202
Northwest Area Foundation, 243n. 28
not-for-profit civic associations, 47. *See also* local nonprofit organizations
Noveck, Beth Simone, 255n. 16
Nurse, Leanne, 244n. 31

Obama, Barack, 1
Obama administration
    on democratic renaissance, 39
    engagement strategies of, 32
    idea-ranking website of, 35
    Open Government Directive, 1–2, 33, 35, 54
    on participatory reforms, 255n. 16
    transparency movement activists in, 54
Obama campaign, 180
*Office, The*, 256n.26
Office of Public Engagement, 54
Office of Social Innovation and Civic Participation, 54
Ontario Citizen's Assembly, 205, 206
Open Government Directive, 1–2, 33, 35, 54
Open Government online process, 45
Open Government Partnership, 157
Open Space (OS)
    agenda for, 43
    circle sharing in, 82
    events using, 43
    "holding space" in, 113
    "invitation" approach of, 177
    "magic" of, 174
    markets and, 135–36
    New Age practices in, 79–81
    Owen's promotion of

Open Space Technology (OST), 132–34, 177
Oprah's Book Club, 248n. 5
Organization of American States (OAS), 252n. 14
"organizational development and human resources" topic, 164, 169–170
organizational development (OD), 80–81, 102–3, 108, 206, 253n.17
Osborne, David, 244n. 29
Our Budget, Our Economy event
    demographics of attendees, 249n. 33
    Digby's blogs
    NCDD listserv chat
    participants' reactions to, 204–11
    purpose of, 235
    responsibilities from, 7
    sponsor of, 212
Owen, Harrison, 132–36

Pacewicz, Josh, 24–26, 38, 96, 253n.19
participants
    accountability of, 176
    age of, 254n. 51
    attitude and mood of, 169–170
    demographics of, 84, 180–81
    empathy of, 170, 175, 210, 220–21
    framing of, 172
    homebound or institutionalized, 254n. 51
    magical thinking by, 206
    management software for, 181–82
    with past experiences with unsuccessful processes, 127, 201
    privacy of, 181
    profiling of, 181
    recruiting, 43, 84, 181
    resistance by, 82, 176
    selection of, 158, 205
    statistics on, 42, 52
    suspicions of, 7, 82, 201–11, 222
participatory art, 71–72, 143–45

participatory budgeting
    activists on focus of, 249–250n. 8
    diffusion of, 157–58, 174
    online processes for, 178–79
    in Philadelphia "City Budget"
        workshops, 167–68, 203, 205–6,
        210–11
    in Pôrto Alegre, 21, 152
    scholarly analysis of, 21, 152
    in Toronto, 116
Patillo, Anne, 97
Paul Aicher Foundation, 243n. 28
Peace Tiles, 75, 144, 146, 147f
Peterson, Pete, 54, 150–51, 161, 179,
    204, 212
petitioning, 41
Philadelphia "City Budget" workshops,
    167–68, 203, 205–6, 210–11
Philanthropy for Active Civic
    Engagement, 243n. 28
playacting, 111
Playback Theatre, 147
poetry, 146–47
political orientation, 248n. 20
political theory, 251n. 29
Polletta, Francesca, 44, 147, 233, 238
populist, 247n.100
Portwood, Jack, 91
pracademic, 58
profession, 57
progressive movements, 40, 78–79,
    230, 247n.100, 249n.5, 253n.34
Protestants, 106, 228
protests
    decline of, in late 20th century, 37
    deliberation and, 201, 214–16
    during health care processes, 203
    tactics for, 243n. 18
Public Agenda, 252n. 14
Public Conversations Project, 104,
    159–160
public engagement. See also deep
    democracy
    academia and, 243n. 28
    accountability through, 89, 176, 184

    aids for discussions in, 158–59
    authenticity of, 140, 172, 174–75,
        177–78, 227, 230
    authority in, 3, 38, 221, 226
    backlash against, 92
    benefits of, 53–54, 174, 176
    capitalism and, 38
    challenges facing, 135
    commodification of, 50–51
    compulsory, 177
    concept of, 219
    consequences of, 7
    content of, 226
    contexts for, 101–2, 141, 200,
        225, 231
    cost-effectiveness of, 210
    critiques during, 201, 203, 222
    crowdsourcing and, 33
    culture and, 28, 171–72, 174–75, 184
    decline of, in late 20th century,
        37–38, 243n.14
    defining, 55–57
    democracy and, 28, 37
    design of, 139–142, 149, 155, 205
    dialogue in, 102–3
    discontent and disgust
    discussion management in, 220–21
    disruption of, 214–16
    economic evaluations of, 131
    economy and, 26, 28, 38, 153–55
    effectiveness of, 173, 242n.18
    facilitators. See public engagement
        practitioners
    family systems research on, 106
    Fishkin model of, 152
    format for, 158
    fundamental principles of, 3
    government officials in, 244n. 31
    grievances in, 201–11, 221–22, 251n.37
    impact of, 199–200, 242n.18
    individual vs. collective action in, 74
    individualization and, 6
    institutionalization of, 77
    language/terminology in, 55, 79–82,
        83f, 117–18, 180

levels of, 137
marginalization and, 86
message in, 223
methods for, 43, 159, 227
mission of, 34
new public management and, 244n.
    30
normative vs. rational understanding
    of, 79
outcomes of, 79, 163–64, 169, 220,
    226, 248n.17
past/future orientation of, 227
performance measures for, 218
as political movement, 33–36
political theory and, 251n. 29
politicizing/depoliticizing, 115–18
popular support for, 244n. 29
practices, strategies, and techniques
    used in, 33–34, 89, 174, 206
promise of, 228
public relations and, 53
resistance in, 201–3, 208
rhetoric against, 2
rules for, 40
security for, 215
services for events, 224
settings for, 22, 127
social value of, 130
studying, methodology for, 232–37
subsidizing, 84
taxes and, 38
tiered system of, 183
as unique spaces, 6
unsuccessful, 127, 201, 242n.12,
    255n.10
uses for, 153
public engagement industry
    best practices, guidelines, and
        standards for, 156–58, 252n.11,
        252n.14
    budgets for, 52, 246n.83
    commercial aspects of, 246n. 83
    as "community of practice," 130,
        145f
    core values of, 157

costs and expenses of, 51–52
definition of, 57
demographic data collection by, 84,
    248n.20
heterogeneity in, 45
market for, 128–131, 153
measurement tools for, 157
organizations in, 44–45
standardization in, 155–59
public engagement practitioners
    activism and attitudes produced by,
        28, 241n.6
    age of, 75
    attributes of, 28, 67
    authenticity of, 100, 108–9, 118–19
    background of, 44
    behavior of, 126
    bureaucratization and, 32
    commercialization and, 59, 153
    commodification by, 53, 123, 153
    compensation for, 89
    co-optation of, 32, 103
    credibility of, 90
    definition of, 2–3
    democratization activities of, 224–25
    demographics of, 85, 248n.22,
        249n.30
    on disruptions, 214–16
    eco-chic products bought by, 129
    education level of, 85, 248n.25
    empathy of, 107–8, 218–19
    employment of, 44–45
    expertise, fair market value of, 88
    on failure, 93
    habitus of, 64–65, 119, 248n.3
    identification of, 239
    identity construction by, 66–67, 112,
        123
    individuality of, 104
    as institutional insiders, 35
    as intervention agents, 218–19
    in journey wall exercise, 104, 105f
public engagement practitioners (cont.)
    licensed trainers of, 43
    local decision-making and, 45–46

market-oriented, 50–51, 130–31, 184
membership in professional
    organizations, 238, 243n.11
methodology for studying, 232–37
need for, 41–42, 94
neutrality of, 92
origin stories of, 75–79
pressure on, sources of, 90
professionalization of, 42–46, 59, 109
projects of, annual, 52
reflexivity of, 118
roles and responsibilities of, 4,
    43–44, 114, 224
self-actualization by, 106
selfing by, 107, 114, 119, 225
volunteer work by, 133
"walking the talk," 109–16, 118
workload of, 46
Public Engagement Principles Project,
    84, 157
public relations, 53, 140
public speaking strategies, 98–99
Putnam, Robert, 37, 39

R. J. Reynolds Tobacco Company, 136
race
    Clinton's national dialogue on, 38
    Community Congress participation
        and, 13–15
    D&D Practitioners Survey on, 85
    diversity at events, 83–85, 88,
        249n.33
    of practitioners, 85–87
    talking and, 21
rational voter myth, 41, 244n.42
real estate developers, 38, 49
reinventing government, 39. See also
    neoliberalism
republican, 56, 58, 247n.100
return on investment (ROI), 162
Robbins, Mark, 253n. 34
Rockefeller Brothers Fund, 12
Rockefeller Foundation, 12
Ryfe, David M., 31, 34–35, 50–51

Sassen, Saskia, 216–17
scripted participation, 41, 244n.43
self-actualization, 106
selfing, 107, 114, 119, 225
Sennett, Richard, 216–17
sexual orientation, 248n. 20
Shaping America's Youth (SAY),
    165–66
"shared governance," 55. See also public
    engagement
Shell, 46
Simonsen, William, 253n. 34
Simpson, O. J., 39
Sirianni, Carmen, 39–40
Skocpol, Theda, 41
social activism, 58, 76, 78, 115
social capital, 41, 46, 51, 99, 115, 182
social change
    art and, 143–44, 251n.47
    capacity for, 223
    capitalism and, 230
    by clients, 7, 47, 133
    process of engagement and, 229
    selling of, in deliberations, 230
social control, 23, 155, 164, 177, 220
social entrepreneurship, 58
"social intelligence," 137
social justice, 26, 82–88, 158, 163, 184,
    227
social media, 180
social movements, 145, 157, 219,
    245n.55, 245n.59
social profit, 149, 163, 171, 221, 225–26
software, 179–181
Somers, Peggy, 51
sponsors
    alignment with interests of, 7,
        181–82, 226
    categories of, 48
    clients and, 49
    compassion and empathy for, 136
    culture of, 249n. 39
    D&D Practitioners Survey on,
        48–49, 135

definition of, 57
demographic data collection for, 181
empathy for, 218
goals of, 155, 171
Jacobs, Cook, and Delli Carpini
    study of, 47–49, 239, 247n.100
misconceptions of, 127
neutrality of, 204
position and role of, 149, 221
priorities of, preference for, 185
research on, 53
suspicion of, 204
Stark, David, 141
storytelling, 146–47, 230
Strengthening Our Nation's
    Democracy conferences, 35
Study Circles model, 31–32
Study Circles Resource Center,
    159–160
subsidy, 57
Surdna Foundation, 12
Swyngedouw, Erik, 50

taxes
    deliberations on, 255–56n. 17
    increasing, 38, 153, 168, 253n.34
    Michigan "Hard Times, Hard
        Choices" poll on, 168
    payment of, 175
    progressive movement and, 253n. 34
    Tight Times, Tough Choices report
        on, 168
Tea Party, 211–12
team building exercises, 207, 217–18,
    253n.17
television, 49
Theiss-Morse, Elizabeth, 241n. 6,
    242n.18, 255n.10
theoretical saturation, 150
think tanks, 247n. 91
3M, 52
Thrift, Nigel, 250n. 9
Tight Times, Tough Choices process,
    167–68, 203, 205–6, 210–11

Time Magazine, 152
Tolle, Eckhart, 182
Tomorrow's Europe poll, 50
topics
    choice of, 226–27
    D&D Practitioners Survey on top
        framing of, 171, 175
    gender and, 88
Toronto, 116
Torres, Lars Hasselblad, 141
Total Quality Management (TQM),
    161
Tough Choices in Health Care, 170
town meetings, 227
training
    D&D Practitioners Survey on, 156
    demand for, 59
    in dispute resolution, 44
    on facilitation strategies, 160
    formative programs for, 245n. 52
    providers of, 156
    revenue for, 245n. 50
transformations
    through art, 143–44, 154
    collective vs. individual, 7, 88
    framing of, 171
    1960s era activism and, 77, 94
    of practitioners, 75, 106–9
    process of engagement and, 229
    as quality indicator, 171
Travis, Trysh, 56, 73, 230, 248n.5
Truman Show, 207
21st Century Summits, 137
21st Century Town Meeting, 20, 38–39,
    59, 141–42, 148, 191
Twilight Zone, 207

UAMPA, 249–250n. 8
Unified New Orleans Plan (UNOP),
    11, 18–19, 141
Unilever, 46
United Kingdom (UK)
    Conservative Party online citizen
        participation platform, 53

Democratic Society activities in, 171
    protest mediation in, 216
    rioting in, 212, 216–17
United Nations Development
        Programme, 252n. 14
United Nations (UN), 52
United States. *See also* individual states
        *and cities*
    Bureau of Reclamation, 244n. 31
    Department of Culture for, 196
    HUD, 15
    Office of Public Engagement, 54
    Office of Social Innovation and
        Civic Participation, 54
Unocal, 138
"un-politics," 244n. 42
urban planning, 167
utilities, 49

"vending machine" model, 162
Viewpoint Learning, 170
Voices and Choices, 141
volunteers, 2–3, 18, 57
voter registration data, 180

W. K. Kellogg Foundation, 12
Walker, Edward, 53
We the People, 141
Weber, Max, 228
Wetzel, Christopher, 154
whites
    at Community Congresses, 13–15
    at conferences, 85
    in Our Budget deliberations, 249n.
        33
    participation by, 15, 21
    in practitioner corps, 85, 87–88
    recruiting, 88, 181
Whole Foods, 129, 229

"wiki," 113
Winfrey, Oprah, 182, 248n.5, 254n.62
women
    participation by, 15, 21, 249n.30
    in practitioner corps, 85–88, 249n.30
    in social justice conference sessions,
        85
    topic choice and participation of, 88
women's movement, 143
workforce engagement activities, 217
workplace participation, 36, 44, 102,
        249n.5
World Bank, 52
World Café, 147–48
World Wide Web
    Conservative Party citizen
        participation platform on, 53
    D&D Practitioners Survey on, 179,
        240, 245n.51
    Deliberative Democracy
        Consortium site, 247n. 98
    in democratization myths, 245n. 58
    "digital utopian" narratives on, 47
    microlending sites, 228
    NPAC site, 255n. 4
    open government feedback sites on,
        54–55
    political dialogue on, 33, 41
    surveillance capabilities of, 180
    Winfrey's webinar on consciousness,
        182, 254n.62

Yao, Margaret, 137

Zacharzewski, Anthony, 171–73, 175,
        176
Zen, 107, 118, 201, 229–230. *See also*
        Buddhism
Zukin, Cliff, 46